Improving Learning in a Professional Context

Improving Learning in a Professional Context provides vital new evidence on exactly how teachers learn to be teachers, evidence that is likely to affect and influence the profession for many years to come. Demonstrating that learning in schools is more than simple 'cognitive' knowledge of the curriculum and teaching skills, this book suggests that we need to pay more attention to the emotional, relational, ethical, material, structural and temporal dimensions of the teaching experience. Based on empirical research, including interviews with new teachers, by teachers themselves, on a scale rarely seen before, the book reveals the complexity of learning in a professional context and gives some basic truths about what really matters in teaching.

This book offers a fundamental critique of policy but also the prospect of constructive change for the better as the authors present accounts of what the 'real' experience of beginning teaching may be like, as well as lines for future research. Key questions are answered, such as:

- Do we really understand what beginners go through in the workplace?
- What is the experience of new teachers as they join one of the largest workforces in the developed world?
- What do teachers learn in the school, one of our universal institutions?

Becoming a teacher is a transformative search by individuals for their teaching identities and, with this book, teachers and teacher educators can at last begin to understand this complex developmental process.

Jim McNally is Professor of Teacher Education at the University of Strathclyde, Glasgow.

Allan Blake is Research Fellow in Education at the University of Strathclyde, Glasgow.

Improving Learning series

The Improving Learning series supports evidence-informed professional practice and policymaking in education. Each book showcases findings from the Teaching and Learning Research Programme (TLRP) – one of the world's largest coordinated educational research initiatives. For those with a commitment to the improvement of outcomes for learners, these books are essential reading.

Improving Learning TLRP

Series Editor: Andrew Pollard, Director of the ESRC Teaching and Learning Programme

Improving Learning through Consulting Pupils
Jean Rudduck and Donald McIntyre

Improving Learning, Skills and Inclusion
The impact of policy on post-compulsory education
Frank Coffield, Sheila Edward, Ian Finlay, Ann Hodgson, Ken Spours and Richard Steer

Improving Classroom Learning with ICT
Rosamund Sutherland

Improving Learning in College
Rethinking literacies across the curriculum
Roz Ivanic, Richard Edwards, David Barton, Marilyn Martin-Jones, Zoe Fowler, Buddug Hughes, Greg Mannion, Kate Miller, Candice Satchwell and June Smith

Improving Learning in Later Life
Alexandra Withnall

Improving Mathematics at Work
The need for techno-mathematical literacies (forthcoming)
Celia Hoyles, Richard Noss, Phillip Kent and Arthur Bakker

Improving Research through User Engagement (forthcoming)
Mark Rickinson, Anne Edwards and Judy Sebba

Improving What is Learned at University
An exploration of the social and organisational diversity of university education (forthcoming)
John Brennan

Improving Inter-professional Collaborations
Multi-agency working for children's well-being
Anne Edwards, Harry Daniels, Tony Gallagher, Jane Leadbetter and Paul Warmington

Improving Learning in a Professional Context

A research perspective on the
new teacher in school

Edited by Jim McNally and
Allan Blake

Routledge
Taylor & Francis Group

LONDON AND NEW YORK

First published 2010
by Routledge
2 Park Square, Milton Park, Abingdon, Oxon OX14 4RN

Simultaneously published in the USA and Canada
by Routledge
270 Madison Avenue, New York, NY 10016

*Routledge is an imprint of the Taylor & Francis Group, an informa
business*

© 2010 Jim McNally and Allan Blake

Typeset in Charter and ITC Stone Sans
by Pindar NZ, Auckland, New Zealand
Printed and bound in Great Britain by
TJ International Ltd, Padstow, Cornwall

British Library Cataloguing in Publication Data
A catalogue record for this book is available from the British
Library

Library of Congress Cataloging-in-Publication Data
Improving learning in a professional context: a research
perspective on the new teacher in school / [edited by] Jim
McNally and Allan Blake.
    p. cm. — (Improving learning)
    1. First year teachers—In-service training—Great Britain. 2.
First year teachers—Professional relationships—Great Britain. 3.
Teachers, Probationary—Great Britain. I. McNally, Jim. II. Blake,
Allan.
    LB2844.1.N4I53 2010
    370.71'155—dc22   2009017009

ISBN 10: 0-415-49340-4 (pbk)
ISBN 10: 0-415-49339-0 (hbk)
ISBN 10: 0-203-86702-5 (ebk)

ISBN 13: 978-0-415-49340-6 (pbk)
ISBN 13: 978-0-415-49339-0 (hbk)
ISBN 13: 978-0-203-86702-0 (ebk)

Contents

Tables

Contributors

Allan Blake is a research fellow in the Department of Curricular Studies, University of Strathclyde. His interests include modernist writing, professional learning and the study of educational research methods in general.

Nick Boreham is Professor of Education and Employment at the Stirling Institute of Education, University of Stirling. His research interests include the knowledge and cognitive skills needed in complex, dynamic working environments, curriculum development in post-compulsory education and learning in the workplace.

Peter Cope has worked in secondary schools in England and Scotland as a teacher of science subjects and of computing. As a professor of education at the Stirling Institute of Education, University of Stirling, his research interests include professional education, and the ways in which student teachers and student nurses become inducted into the community of professional practice.

Brian Corbin was a research fellow on the EPL project. His principal research interests include professional development, teacher professionalism and identity, and the relationship between subject or disciplinary content and pedagogy.

David Dodds, a teacher-researcher on the EPL project, is a principal teacher of learning support. He has been involved in supporting the integration of pupils with special educational needs into mainstream schools. He was a contributing author to *Dyslexia: Successful Inclusion in the Secondary School*, by the British Dyslexia Association.

Lesley Easton, a teacher-researcher on the EPL project, has taught music and media studies for more than ten years. A mentor for student and probationer teachers, she works closely with students and new professionals, providing support and advice in both formal and informal contexts.

Peter Gray was a research fellow on the EPL project. His research interests include the relationship of space(s) and learning, learning at and through work, including organizational learning and the development of teacher education research networks.

Jim McNally is Professor of Teacher Education and head of the Department of Curricular Studies at the University of Strathclyde. He is a former assistant rector, principal teacher of physics and national development officer for teacher induction. He has published extensively in the fields of beginning teaching, mentoring and investigative science teaching.

Colin Smith, a teacher-researcher on the EPL project, recently retired from teaching biology. He was active in his school's development process, leading initiatives in learning and teaching and guiding professional development. He has had academic and professional articles published.

Ian Stronach is Professor of Education at Liverpool John Moores University. His interests span a range of qualitative approaches to educational research: teacher research, action research, illuminative evaluation, deconstruction of the same, research methodology and theory from a poststructuralist/postmodernist perspective.

Phil Swierczek, a teacher-researcher on the EPL project, recently retired from teaching home economics. Her previous research experience includes the study of the career paths of women in senior management posts in schools in central Scotland.

Lesley Walker, a teacher-researcher on the EPL project, is a teacher of English. She has been involved in the development of whole school support systems for probationer teachers and students, and worked as a school mentor for probationers.

Series Editor's Preface

This book grew out of a four-year research project on the learning of new teachers. In 2004, the writers within assembled under the aegis of the Early Professional Learning project to undertake empirical research into the experiences of new – or more accurately, newly qualified – teachers in school. The motivation for the research arose from a concern about the fragmented experiences of beginning teachers in Scotland and England (as expressed in academic publications and official reports), though we later found that teacher induction was of wider global interest than we had first supposed. We felt that learning in a professional context – teachers in schools, in this case – required a broader and more robust research base. Did we have enough understanding of what beginners go through in the workplace? What, for example, is the experience of new teachers as they join one of the largest workforces in the developed world? What do they learn in school, one of our universal institutions? In responding to such questions, we were supported by the Economic and Social Research Council. As part of their Teaching and Learning Research Programme, we commenced a multi-method study of professional learning based first of all on the ethnographic case study of 25 new teachers in six secondary schools in Scotland, with later phases of investigation, model-building and testing taking place in primary and secondary schools in Scotland and England. Between 2004 and 2008, the project researched the experiences of 154 new teachers in 45 schools in Britain and, based on in-depth interviews with these participants, this book now reveals the complexity of learning in a professional context. It portrays the holistic nature of engagement beyond the description of a formal standard and unearths instead a transformative search by individuals for their teaching identities.

The main part of our evidence is story-based. But these stories are not simply one-off interviews with visiting researchers; they were captured by teachers as researchers, initially in their own schools, and then in other schools. The 25 new teachers with whom the project began were interviewed approximately each month; the progress of 12 of these teachers continued to be tracked over the course of two further years. Subsequent participants were interviewed on typically three occasions over the course of their first year of teaching. Our multidimensional model of beginning teaching is grounded in these stories, upon which we draw extensively throughout the book. Quotations are largely verbatim, with minimal editing only to give continuity. We also developed five purpose-specific indicators of new-teacher development. The development of one of these, the indicator of job satisfaction, is described in some detail. The others were developed along similar principles but space does not allow us to describe them as fully. Indicator statistics are used in a number of chapters where it is felt they add a layer of understanding that complements the more qualitative account. Most of the statistics refer to secondary teachers in Scotland, as these were the first group to be studied, but numerical data was also gathered from secondary teachers in England and primary teachers in Scotland.

The emotional and relational dimensions of new teachers' learning are described and discussed in separate dedicated chapters since these were components of the experiences that featured most strongly in interviews. The material dimension is also discussed separately because it seems to matter greatly in frustrating or supporting the experience of becoming a teacher, in specific, concrete ways that are more amenable to identification and rectification. Our dimensional model is rather like separating a projectile trajectory into its x, y, z and t components, breaking down a phenomenon into constituent parts for the purpose of analysis, while recognizing that the actual journey is a more complex whole than the sum of its parts. Thus we also make the case for a holistic concept of identity formation in the process of becoming a teacher, partly from grounded theorizing, partly from the theoretical perspectives of others. The model is not intended to be neat and tidy and we hope that even a leaf through some of the chapters, with their glimpses into new teachers' experiences, will demonstrate this. The dimensions flow into one another, overlap, compete and vary in their intensity from one individual to another, and from one point in time to another – but with the individual new teacher at the centre of it all.

If there was an emergent and unifying theme of the research and now of the book then it is perhaps the sense of an emerging self-as-teacher identity. Becoming a teacher is an intense experience in an ontological more than an epistemological sense – they know (just) enough about teaching, but not nearly enough about themselves. Our specific focus on the beginner has revealed the understated importance in existing theorization of those dimensions of learning other than the cognitive, and the flawed presumption that occupational standards might govern the learning experiences of beginners. Though we offer some practical recommendations in Chapter 12, the book is not a 'how to' book for new teachers, but rather a 'how it is'. We do not yet report on our preliminary exploration of learning in other professional contexts but already there are grounds for thinking that there may be common ground. For example, a recent doctoral thesis (Blaney 2006), supervised by one of the EPL project's co-investigators, Professor Nick Boreham, indicated that the learning of trainee general practitioners in medicine mirrors much of our project's findings. Broadly, the study confirmed that the probationary year challenged trainees' assumptions about their identity and, in particular, their role as a doctor. Their learning during the year was dynamic; primarily a self-directed voyage of discovery through building relationships with patients and colleagues, which at one point in the year comes into conflict with their external assessment according to the standards for full registration as a GP.

The book is eclectic not only through its grounded theorization but in its attempts to connect with a wide literature. The experience we report is complex and, for the book to be able to make sense of this, we have resisted reductionism and the academic tendency to simplify and organize. We have not homogenized the different interpretations in the book. We all worked together on the project so there is much use of 'we' even though each of us, five teachers and seven academics, more or less led on at least one chapter. We took the view that all were entitled to have their individual say – and the stylistic range of the book reflects that and possibly flirts on occasion with anarchy. Does this imply a lack of consistency? Perhaps so; but is the book any the less for that? We suggest not.

Chapter 3 describes the possibly unique role that teachers played as practitioner-researchers in the research. In relation to those of us on the project who inhabit academic life, it is probably fair to say that the teacher-researchers kept our feet on the ground while keeping us on our toes at the same time. So the book is also a research story of design evolution in which a full cast of players collaborate to find out some fundamental and worthwhile things about learning.

The research is based on stories, on the sustained narratives of new teachers, all with their own individual experience. It was therefore important to us that we did not lose sight of that. Mikhail Bakhtin's position is that the self can only be understood in the particular and the situated. Therefore we begin with the particular situation of one new teacher. Linda's story is drawn from the longitudinal phase of the project, and is based on 17 interviews over three years with a teacher-researcher who was also a colleague in the same school. The chapters in this book can probably be read in any order; behind them all is an array of stories. We recommend no particular order but we hope that you will read Linda's story first.

Reference

Blaney, D. (2006) 'The early professional learning of GP registrars', unpublished EdD thesis, University of Stirling.

Acknowledgements

The Economic and Social Research Council of the United Kingdom deserve recognition for the substantial financial support given to the project, part of their funding of the huge Teaching and Learning Research Programme. We were held accountable, of course, through a range of procedures but we have to acknowledge that we could simply not have engaged in such an extensive study, and reached whatever range and depth of understanding we did, without the support of the Council.

We owe a debt to all the teachers in all the schools. The colleagues of the new teachers who participated in the project cooperated in indicator data collection and helped us in various ways to manage the project. The new teachers who collaborated in our research, even while under enough pressure to make it as teachers them-selves, are a special group; the project was about them, for them and could not have worked without them. Though they were known as individuals to only the teacher-researchers, we got to know them in discussion through their pseudonyms – so thanks to Cruella, Butterkist, Bill Shakespeare *et al.* – and pass on our thanks to the children you teach. If our work helps you, then it ultimately helps them as well.

All the schools we visited gave us a warm welcome and an atten-tive ear. We gratefully acknowledge the support of the various heads and deputies who listened, questioned and made their schools available to us. We spent an hour or so on preliminary negotiations in every school, all at different times of the day, and were unfail-ingly impressed by this inadvertent sampling of happy, purposeful activity. It does make you wonder about the representative nature of some news headlines. We met with Education Officers from local councils individually and together. They asked hard questions that forced us to clarify some of our own thinking. We want to record our thanks for that and also for identifying schools and granting us access to them.

As editors, we have to thank our colleagues on the project. Through its four years we had to handle distance, pregnancies, promotion, retirals, emigration and illness. We regrouped somehow, carried on and here is the result. We know that the research team will permit us finally to single out one person. Our project administrator, Lynne Learmonth, was the hub of the project, assuming the additional roles of mentor, facilitator, confidante, poster designer and more, even pointing out new updates that we had missed. Her many stories behind the scenes may be the great unwritten chapter.

Jim McNally and Allan Blake

Abbreviations

CEPSATI	classroom environment, pupil satisfaction and achievement instrument
CPD	continuing professional development
EPL	early professional learning
EXJUDGE	expert judgement of teaching indicator
GTCS	General Teaching Council Scotland
HMI	Her Majesty's Inspectorate
INTERACT	interactivity indicator
INTSCHED	structured interview schedule
ITE	initial teacher education
JOBSAT	job satisfaction indicator
NQT	newly qualified teacher
NT	new teacher
PDI	pupil development indicator
PGCE	Postgraduate Certificate in Education
PGDE	Postgraduate Diploma in Education
PT	principal teacher
SFR	Standard for Full Registration
SMT	senior management team
TR	teacher-researcher

Chapter 1

Linda's story
A new teacher's tale

Lesley Walker

Foreword

There may be no better description of a common effect of academic publishing on the subjectivities of research participants than that afforded Leopold Bloom, the main character of James Joyce's *Ulysses*. In 'Ithaca', a section of the novel which parodies the nature of scientific inquiry through a series of blankly worded (and yet madly pedantic) questions and answers, Bloom is dissected thus: 'Reduce Bloom by cross multiplication of reverses of fortune, from which these supports protected him, and by elimination of all positive values to a negligible negative irrational unreal quantity' (Joyce 1992: 855). It might come as a surprise to some readers that we begin a research text with a quotation that threatens to bite the hand that (under)writes us. For the quantitative-analysis-gone-mad that was lampooned by Joyce in 1922 is of a kind prescribed to educational research as recently as 2000. Then Secretary of State for Education and Employment, David Blunkett suggested in a speech to the Economic and Social Research Council the need 'to be able to measure the size of the effect of A on B. This is genuine social science' (in Hammersley 2002: 83). Reverses of fortune apart, the fact that his tenure as a cabinet minister dissipated in less time than it took Joyce to complete his masterpiece, might in some small part be explained by his perception of 'genuine social science' as being derivative of the methodologies employed rather than the positive values achieved. Certainly, it was as a strategy to remain relevant to the experience of our audience for at least as long as it takes to read *Ulysses*, that the Early Professional Learning project pursued both qualitative and quantitative methods of inquiry. And in the chapters that follow, we attempt to demonstrate that a distinctive result of such methods is that statistics of specific curiosity can be cross-referenced with contextualizing insights from the individual narratives in the project's associated qualitative database. That is to say, we refute the so-called 'worthless[ness]' of 'correlations based on small samples from which it is impossible to draw generalisable conclusions' (ibid.: 84), and take instead the view of case researchers in seeking both what is commonplace and particular about a case, with the possibility of portraying something of the uncommon (Stake 2000), as opposed that is to the irrational unreal.

Our intention to portray something of the uncommon begins, then, with 'Linda's story: a new teacher's tale'. Fashioned from the transcriptions of interviews with Linda that commenced during her probationary year of teaching in the social studies department of a large secondary school in Scotland, this is a story which records some of the highs and lows of the events, influences and relationships of her beginning career in a manner that we hope instates Linda's agency in the research by making it 'unthinkable for a bystander to say, "So what?"' (Labov cited in Flyvbjerg 2001: 86). In the chapters ahead we revisit Linda's evidence to undertake our own cross multiplication of data in support of a research-based model of early professional learning; for the moment however, we present a narrative of new-teacher induction, told in the words of Linda, with occasional commentary by Lesley, the teacher-researcher to whom she spoke throughout the life of the project. As distinct from the expression of positivism with which we began, we see in this confluence of practice and research the possibility of a dialogic moment of freedom in which the monologic certainty (Bakhtin 1996) of the researcher might be overtaken by scepticism 'about erasing phenomenological detail in favour of conceptual closure' (Flyvbjerg 2001: 85).

Linda's story

On the way down I had two boys approach me saying they wouldn't be in Philosophies on Thursday because of football practice and we had a bit of a conversation and that didn't really happen on student placement because they would go to their RE teacher even though I was taking their class. That's definitely been a huge thing.

Linda recounted this in October 2004, just into the second term of her probationary year, and its importance to her is clear. It was a 'huge thing'. It marked, for her, an acceptance by the pupils that she was not just a teacher but also *their* teacher – a feeling she had never experienced on student placements. As a religious education specialist, teaching pupils one period a week, she had found it hard to get to know them individually. Learning names had been a challenge, let alone forming relationships. So a moment which outsiders to the profession, or even established teachers, might see as normal or routine took on an added significance because it literally made her feel part of the school community. It marked a significant change in how she was perceived by the pupils. She belonged at the school. She had a professional identity as a teacher in the school.

In August 2004 three probationers joined the staff of Forth Academy, a large Scottish comprehensive school with over a thousand pupils. Linda in social studies, Ann in science and biology and Rachael in English had never met before, but, throughout the year, their relationship and friendship grew. Although the school's mentoring programme was in place and appreciated by this group, what emerged from their interview data was the importance of the probationers to each other. They formed a team giving informal support to each other and to other probationers who had joined the staff. Ann and Rachael worked in large departments, which gave them an immediate network of colleagues in the school. Linda's experience in a two-teacher department, before the introduction of the faculty system, was different. Her story is now told in the first person, using her own words as recorded in the transcriptions of the 17 interviews she gave during her first three years. Commentaries on Ann and Rachael are included to illustrate similarities or differences in experiences.

School life

I joined the staff at Forth Academy in August 2004 to start my probationary year. Over the summer I had been thinking a lot about my classes. 'What if they are really bad?' and 'What if I can't control them?' summed up my feelings. Although I came into the school a few times over the summer, I would have welcomed an induction week or something at the change of timetable in June, so I could go in and check classes and find my way round the school, because that's one of the daunting things. I would like to have been able to ask someone questions when I came in over the summer. It would have been nice to arrive in August and know things.

Rachael felt the same. She met her principal teacher (PT) in June, but, on reflection, would have liked to have shadowed a class for the day so she could get her bearings in the school. Ann admitted she had half expected starting at Forth to be like a student placement but the realization that the classes she taught were hers struck her immediately and after the first day, which was like being 'on a roller coaster', she did not feel like returning. She did, however, and at the end of the year, her head teacher described her as 'a teacher for the 21st century'. Linda explained the importance of having a room of one's own in establishing her place in the school.

Having my own classroom was a major advantage for me. I think having my own room makes a huge difference and I particularly appreciated this when other probationers in the school did not have this. I felt I could move and arrange the desks, put things in the walls and establish myself in this way without having to ask anyone's permission.

Ann also had her own room, which she realized she had taken for granted. All her resources were at hand and she knew where the books and jotters were. She had also put her name on the door and felt this was a way to establish her identity as a teacher in the school as a whole. She felt many pupils, including those she did not teach, knew who she was because they saw her name on display. Rachael had to move between classrooms, however, and because of the extra time thus required to organize materials for lessons, she did not go to the staffroom.

At the change of timetable in June 2007 all of Rachael's classes were scheduled in one room. And although other staff did use the room, Rachael felt she could now establish herself in her workplace. Within weeks the room changed physically; but more noticeable was the change in Rachael herself. She was happier, more relaxed and felt more established in the school. This change also affected her teaching. She admits she is now more adventurous in her lesson content because if something does not work she has all her other resources to hand and can make a quick change.

But as well as having a classroom of one's own, the staffroom too can influence new teachers' development. Linda explains:

> I was concerned about how easy it would be for me to meet other staff, as there were only two people in my department. Fortunately, I soon started going out for lunch with Ann and other teachers in her department. This was useful because it was almost a sounding-off time where you don't spend the whole time talking about kids and lessons, but it comes up and you realize other people have problems, too. Although I found meetings like this were reassuring I did worry about going to the staffroom. If you're not used to going you don't have a group to go and sit with everyday and that does make it a little bit more difficult. Even by November I still felt unsure about going to the staffroom. In fact I was spending most intervals and part of my lunchtime in my room talking to my PT.
>
> I didn't feel isolated from the rest of the staff though, because one day when I was going into the staffroom everyone was leaving for registration, so I was saying 'Hello, Hello, Hello' as they passed. So I felt as if I did know people. I was meeting people in all sorts of places: at the photocopier, going out for lunch and by chance in the corridors. I certainly felt the need to do this as it made me feel more confident. I was building up relationships with other teachers on a more personal level, so I felt more comfortable about going into classrooms to speak to teachers. In fact, by November I felt I knew a lot of people by face and I could stand and have a conversation with them – but ask me their name and I wouldn't be able to tell you.
>
> Something that helped me considerably was the fact that there were two other probationers in the school and we got on well together. I liked knowing that others were in the same boat as me. For example, if they were busy filling some form in for probationers and I wasn't, then it reminded me that I should do that too.

Because Ann and Rachael travelled to work together, their friendship and support for each other grew during the year. As Rachael put it, 'Ann is my lifeline'; but, as Linda said, 'I know Rachael and Ann travel together ... but I don't feel I know them so well'. Linda would have liked a specific time allocated in the week when the probationers met to 'just talk'. Neither Ann nor Rachael voiced this need, but then their car journeys provided them with exactly this opportunity. This informal support is something that can easily be underestimated. Rachael's interviews in November 2004 revealed the practical help she and Ann gave each other during the drive to and from school. They bounced ideas off each other, let off steam at the end of the day, discussed classes they both taught and gained reassurance from doing this; they cheered each other up and provided the emotional support which planned mentoring cannot always address.

The following year another probationer joined this car pool. She found the experience of starting teaching 'intimidating' and, though she acknowledged that the school support was good, she found that travelling with two teachers who had just been through the probationary year was 'brilliant'. She knew right away that she was travelling with 'exactly the right people to talk to', because she could ask the 'silly' questions in the car. Again the importance of informal support is highlighted.

> As well as settling in to school life, I was learning a lot about behaviour management. The classes were quite difficult when I started and it was a struggle. My PT told me that some of the classes hadn't had a qualified RE teacher for some time. I'd been getting quite confrontational with some classes and I realized it wasn't working. Then we got a talk at the local authority probationer meeting about not being so confrontational and showing the pupils that they had a responsibility. I noticed it made a difference in quite a few classes because they were waiting for me to blow up and get really mad at them, whereas now I ask them to just go and stand outside and I have a few quiet words with them. It's amazing how different they are and I think 'Wow!'

Ann and Rachael also valued the local authority support on behaviour management which took place early in the school year, in which different scenarios were demonstrated. They tried some of the suggestions, and found 'they worked'. During an interview in September 2006, a probationer in the primary sector of the same authority noted that the CPD on behaviour management had been 'the most useful lecture that I have had on behaviour management through the whole postgrad training'. These types of breakthrough moments in which a probationer feels that something has worked well, or in which progress can suddenly be seen, have a strong impact on their feeling of achieving success. These probationers also appear to be acknowledging the importance of experiencing the right CPD at the right time in the probationary year.

I was constantly trying to find ways to interest reluctant pupils. I soon realized that my degree in Christianity and indigenous religions was not going to be used and I was continually working to find different ways to teach the subject. I also kept in touch with people on my PGCE course and regularly swapped ideas and information with them. I was reluctant to share my Forth Academy email address with them though because I didn't want to start using it for a year and then find I had to change it all. I did find that some of the resources in the department were old and dated, and even I was bored watching one of the documentary videos. So I suggested, and used, some more up-to-date films and the pupils were definitely more responsive. I also used an episode of *The Simpsons* to illustrate religious authority and I used the Critical Skills approach with several classes.

All this led to long hours of preparation to the point where I felt my work–life balance had tipped the wrong way. Even in March I felt as if I was working flat out just as I had done on a student placement. I was starting to get grumpy and not just with the pupils but with my own family and friends as well. I think it was because I wasn't having the chance to say 'I'm going to the cinema tonight and I'm not thinking about school'. I was also finding it difficult to get out of teacher mode, to the point where both my Mum and my boyfriend were commenting on the tone of voice I used when speaking to them!

Observations about outdated and old materials occurred in several interviews during the course of the project. In each case the probationer was more than willing to develop new resources or approaches and offer them to the department. When a class was working on a project in biology, Ann asked them to produce a PowerPoint presentation as the end product rather than a poster or report. This was a highlight for her because not only was the class more motivated, but the idea was incorporated into the courses for all classes. Ann felt 'really chuffed' because her PT thought it was a good idea: another breakthrough moment.

Professional observations

Linda clarified for herself what professionalism meant, and in a way that was unplanned yet effective.

> Someone else who influenced me in a different way was the teacher I had taken over from. Although I never met her I found out directly from the pupils some of the personal anecdotes and experiences she had apparently told the classes. She was speaking about things I wouldn't speak to my friends about and the pupils were hoping I would talk about any similar experiences of my own. This helped me to clarify in my head exactly what professionalism is, and I formed a code in my mind about what and what not to talk to classes about, and where to draw the dividing line in conversations.

Formal CPD discussions can be planned to cover this aspect of the Standard for Full Registration, yet here Linda learned from someone who, in her mind, had pushed the boundaries of professionalism too far. What Linda learned very effectively, from someone she had never met, were the consequences of inappropriate professional behaviour.

Other probationers also talked of hearing stories, from the past or sometimes from other schools, concerning a teacher, an incident or a pupil, and acknowledged that they too had learned something (either positive or negative) that helped them to develop as a teacher. Although the Scottish Induction Scheme includes formal and direct aspects of professional development (such as mentoring), probationers are also learning to become teachers from the school as a whole. Sometimes this takes the form of stories about teachers who have long since left the school, but whose histories are recounted and passed on. These echoes of the past are not just nostalgic remembrances, for they can be influential in the present.

> A more positive influence was my mentoring time, which I appreciated because it was a place when useful conversations took place because I was on my own and people weren't interrupting all the time, and I could sit down for a period and just talk.

Linda's need to talk is interesting and something that the other probationers did not mention to the same extent. Does this simply reveal the different needs of individuals or emphasize the requirements of someone working in a small department where fewer informal interactions occur in a day? In some schools two probationers have been allocated to the same department and this can generally be beneficial and supportive, especially at the start of the probationary year. For Linda, however, the desire to express something of herself informed her attitude towards teaching observations, as well as her completion of the Standard for Full Registration.

> I think being observed is useful because you are getting more feedback on yourself and you are more aware of what you are doing right or wrong. I was getting ideas on what to try and it built my confidence because I was being told things I was doing well and I could incorporate new ideas into my lessons. I also liked observing some of the pupils I taught in other lessons even if it just showed me some pupils were the same in other classes.
>
> My observations took place every three weeks and I received written and oral feedback. These were recorded in my interim and final profiles, which I updated during the terms and completed by December and May respectively. I did not find the form difficult or time-consuming to complete, but I half expected to get a box for my own personal statement, my own evaluation of how I was doing. I expected to have to include whether I thought I was meeting the requirements, whereas there isn't anything like that. It's a case of filling in the dates and that's it and I don't think I got anything out of filling in the form. I didn't really think of the Standard for Full Registration on an everyday basis very much. I know the mentor used it when she was planning meetings but I didn't need to look at it to complete my profiles. I sometimes felt as if I had to cover certain topics, for example, child protection, so that I could get that date in the box rather than the fact that I really needed to do child protection. This is one of the main changes I would make to the probationary year, because I didn't feel I got anything out of completing the profiles. I wouldn't want to add to the workload but I would have found it more satisfying to include something which showed my progress, perhaps in the form of a personal statement.

What mattered to Ann were the comments on her observed lessons and the targets set for the second part of the year. Rachael also found the Standard for Full Registration 'heavy going', and she ended up 'tuning out if it'. She would have liked to tell the story of how she progressed because for her it didn't really reflect 'Rachael the teacher'. Both probationers knew that other staff were consulting the Standard but it was not a priority for them.

Moving on up

> After Christmas I began to think more about the future and getting a job. I was lucky because there was a job coming up at Brady High and maybe one at Forth Academy, but people didn't really know when they could apply. I just think there are too many different stories and too many different ways of doing things for probationers in different local authorities. I think if they're going to put jobs out late in the year for after the summer, then to me, all local authorities should be trying to put them out at the same time.

Linda left Forth after her probationary year and took up a full-time permanent post at Brady High, the school she attended as a pupil. Her story continues:

> I was pleased to move school because it was a completely fresh start and I thought staff wouldn't think of me as someone who had just been a probationer. When the new staff were introduced there was a bit of a muddle so I think some staff missed my name and I soon realized that some staff were thinking of me as the pupil they had known. Some even still thought I was a probationer. Although I was fully qualified it was like finding my feet again, but I was re-learning in some ways and learning from my own mistakes from last year. I had to establish myself with classes and I kept thinking back to last year and asking myself what I could do to make things smoother.
>
> What has really helped me was that the course in the department was more prescribed. I may work in school to 6pm but I'm going home without my big box. I also feel more confident. I've lost that new feeling and it's as if I've moved one rung up the ladder. I have had really good support from my PT and curricular head. In fact, only the other week they asked me if they were giving me enough support. Even though this is year

two I still feel as though I need help, especially with behaviour management. Some of the girls in my Standard Grade class have a difficult attitude and I don't know if it's because they feel threatened by me because I'm a young teacher. A principal teacher on one of my student placements said that could happen.

By April 2007 Linda's PT had been promoted and, because she was the only RE specialist, she had full responsibility for all the certificate classes in the school.

I've also been given a fair amount of responsibility because my PT has been out of school for some work he is doing on Raising Achievement and I have to make sure things run smoothly in his classroom. I think he was aware that one day I am going to get the PT's job and he has to make sure that I am ready and capable of being left with the department, so he started throwing more responsibilities to me, to the point that just before he left I was doing the ordering – I was having to manage the budget.

Part of that responsibility is also apparent in Linda's involvement in such extra-curricular activities as the Duke of Edinburgh Award. Linda's tone of voice revealed the pleasure and surprise she felt at taking part in the expedition. It was a positive experience which gave her the opportunity to realise that she could achieve and do new things too.

I would say my relationships with other staff are better than at Forth, probably because I know I'm permanent. I feel as if I'm consulted more and I use the staffroom here more than ever I did at Forth. There is another young teacher in the same curricular group as me and I feel comfortable going in and sitting with her. Towards the end of the year I began to feel really settled – not like the same time last year, when I knew I was only there for a year. It was nice to know I had job security and I didn't have to battle with applications and interviews. I've actually just last week come back from a Duke of Edinburgh hike and it was good seeing the kids out of school as well. They saw a different side to me, especially coming out of a tent first thing in the morning.

It has given me a lot more opportunities; it is making me think, 'Where am I going to go from here?' A guidance course came up, so I am interested in maybe doing that. All this extra responsibility is giving me the opportunity to become a PT of RE; if I wanted, I could probably use all this experience and do the guidance course. And if I decide not to go down that route, I can go down the chartered teacher route. So my options are still all open. It is a good thing even though it is more difficult just now. I wouldn't say stressful, I suppose stressful is the wrong word because I would say that I am just busier.

References

Bakhtin, M. (1996) 'Discourse in the novel' in P. Rice and P. Waugh (eds) *Modern Literary Theory* (3rd edn), London: Arnold.

Flyvbjerg, B. (2001) *Making Social Science Matter,* Cambridge: Cambridge University Press.

Hammersley, M. (2002) *Educational Research, Policymaking and Practice,* London: Paul Chapman Publishing.

Joyce, J. (1992) *Ulysses,* London: Penguin.

Stake, R. E. (2000) 'Case studies' in N. K. Denzin and Y. S. Lincoln (eds) *Handbook of Qualitative Research* (2nd edn), London: Sage.

Chapter 2

The early professional learning of teachers

A model beginning

Jim McNally, Allan Blake, Nick Boreham, Peter Cope, Brian Corbin, Peter Gray and Ian Stronach

Research, policy and practice in teacher induction

Professional standards in teaching do not have an explicit theoretical or research-informed foundation. Their typical competence-based framework has been the object of much criticism in the academic literature (Stronach *et al.* 1994, 2002; Ball 2003) precisely because they are not based on beginners' experiences of learning to teach but do tend to be held up as the benchmark and reference documentation for that process. The statutory system of competences is at odds with an extensive literature that identifies teachers' knowledge as being personal, context-rich and elusive (Russell and Bullock 1999), involving processes of identity formation, emotionality (Hargreaves 1998) and intrinsic purpose. The Early Professional Learning (EPL) project was conceived therefore to explore the extent to which a grounded theory of early teacher learning could enhance the competence-based model for new teachers and contribute to current theoretical and practical formulations of that process.

The models implied in the standards documents in Scotland and England, though not identical, are similar, both in their support arrangements as well as in their content and format of specifications as standards. In England there is the Career Entry and Development Profile (CEDP) for 'newly qualified teachers' (NQTs) and in Scotland the Standard for Full Registration (SFR) for 'probationers'. Their aims are similar, namely that new teachers and those supporting and assessing them can refer to standardized statements of what is being looked for to achieve full professional status to teach in state schools. These were elaborated as 96 'expected features' (competences) in Scotland (GTCS 2002) and as the 'requirements' of 44 standards in England (TTA 2002). Both have three major categories: knowledge and understanding, teaching skills and abilities, values and commitments. These stress the cognitive and the need for judgement and neither refers explicitly to the affective, the uncertain or the biographical in new-teacher development. Both are offered as guidance, requiring judgement, self-evaluation and reflectivity in use. Both also refer to the temporal status of induction, as at a 'threshold' (GTCS 2002) or involving 'transition points' (TTA 2002) between initial qualification and the 'lifelong learning' of continuing professional development. However, crossing the 'threshold' has a limited shelf life of a year (though some get 'deferred' for an extra school term). Though the SFR's discursive mix bears the marks of research and practitioner consultation (McNally 2001), in our data it is a competence register that imposes rather than reflects its impact on new teachers.

We found that the main engagement with the SFR by new teachers was in relation to their need to complete their interim profile. There was, additionally, a small but significant connection with the SFR when many new teachers began to adjust their teaching to differences between children and between the classes they taught, and which occurred a few months into their first year of teaching. But the all-encompassing process in learning to teach was about becoming a teacher: that is, gaining an identity through a number of discernable dimensions of experience – emotional, relational, material, temporal, structural, cognitive, and ethical – a process for which the SFR provided no guidance or structure; as one new teacher put it, the 'idea that we can give everything an [interim profile] code ... it's completely meaningless'.

The policy background for our research developed initially from a concern about new teachers in Scotland. A two-year project to devise a framework for teacher induction was jointly funded in 1999 by the Scottish Government (Executive at that time) and the GTC Scotland. The project report and the resulting teacher-induction scheme (McNally 2001) – drawing partly on a study by Draper et al. (1997) – identified the serious fragmentation of the induction period for many beginners and recommended stability of placement and continuity of contact for all new teachers in employment. The seriousness of the concern was subsequently emphasized in the report of the committee of inquiry into professional conditions of service for teachers (McCrone Report 2000), in which the situation was described as nothing short of scandalous. The landmark induction scheme that resulted now offers to new teachers/probationers a guaranteed one-year training post; a maximum class commitment of 0.7 full-time equivalent; dedicated time set aside for professional development; access to an experienced teacher as a nominated probationer supporter; a consistently high-quality probation experience; a good salary which compares well with other professions. Aspects of professional development include meetings with a designated supporter and observation of teaching. The post new teachers occupy during the induction year may be supernumerary or they may be filling a vacancy, but in either case, after successful completion of the induction year, they may apply for a permanent post but are not guaranteed one.

A similar package of measures, on similar grounds, had already been introduced in England in 1999 (though, here, inductees must apply for a vacancy). Initial studies of these NQTs suggested, however, that the EPL project's concerns about the disposition of the competence model were not unfounded. Some focused on the induction format itself, as likely to encourage an 'instrumental' model of teaching, unresponsive to the 'individual professional needs' of NQTs (Heaney 2001: 253). Others noted its dependence on the right school context, such as an 'institutional ethos' conducive to supportive dialogue (Jones 2002: 523), especially given that personal stories and coping strategies were seen as crucial to a reflective use of the induction model (Harrison 2002). This in turn depended on the 'most highly valued induction activity' of informal discussion (Williams 2003: 212). There were also suggestions that the wider socio-economic and resource challenges faced by schools were the problem, and that too much still depended on 'being in a "good school" or "bad school"' (Jones et al. 2002: 507). Some five years after its inception, a major systematic review of research on its impact in England found little evidence for 'a definitive model of induction' and confirmed the importance of 'local circumstances' and 'flexibility, sensitivity to context and imagination' (Totterdell et al. 2004: 38). Overall, although better resourcing and a formally raised profile were widely welcomed, induction seemed troublingly caught between the 'outer' of over-prescription and imposition and the 'inner' engagement and vagaries of collegial and local practices.

In the EPL project, we have conceptualized such conflicting experience as an uneasy and often unacknowledged amalgam of 'induction' and 'initiation'. In Chapter 13 of the present volume, Ian Stronach identifies the gap between these as constituting the unpredictable, unstable space of informal learning where teachers have to 'invent' themselves, and where the emotional nature of the immersion is most immediately and sometimes painfully felt. Such a necessarily individual, we might even say autochthonous, place of learning is obscured by some of the past and current literature on 'communities of practice', collegial support, and nostra for 'effective teaching' routines. These tend to downplay the 'becoming' of the teacher, reducing the role to ethos, technique, competence or skill. These are all important enough, but peripheral to what we claim to be the idiosyncratic and individual nature of the beginning teachers' experience.

A model of early professional learning

Given the very low failure rate (1–2 per cent) of new teachers to 'pass' their induction (GTCS 2006; Totterdell *et al.* 2002), as well as the EPL's own quantitative finding in Chapter 8 that some 82 per cent are satisfied with their induction, the temptation might be to leave well enough alone rather than offer another model of induction. Yet earlier research had indicated that a more grounded understanding would benefit the practitioners involved (McNally and Oberski 2003; Rippon and Martin 2003; Totterdell *et al.* 2002). In addition, the initial phase of our research (2004/05) had indicated distinctive features of professional learning during induction, both in the project's qualitative and quantitative data.

The model that we propose was based initially on the narratives of new teachers, mainly in their induction year as 25 probationers in Scotland. Some comparative data from 22 NQTs in England confirmed the relevance of the model's dimensions. These teachers were being formally guided and assessed by existing models as embodied in the specifications of the SFR (Scotland) or CEDP (England). The qualitative data collection, though based on interviews in both countries, differed in that in Scotland six teacher-researchers were involved in talking with probationers in their own schools. Because they were 'insiders', these interviews were more frequent (typically 12 during the first year of the project) and more punctual in relation to probationer experiences. They were also able to draw on intimate knowledge of their own schools. These interviews provided the basis for a more grounded narrative approach, as the new teachers sought to construct their professional identities over their crucial first year.

The formation of identity was an aspect of teacher experience that was prominent in our extensive and in-depth ethnographic interviews, which gave rise to longitudinal narratives in a field otherwise typified by synchronic analyses. Our earlier research had identified the need for a more progressive focusing on EPL, including the need for a sharper instrument that might better elicit the subtler layers of the beginning experience, as indicated by Eraut (2004) in his discussion of implicit learning and tacit knowledge. It was in order to realize these intentions that we employed teachers as researchers in Scottish schools, and it was precisely their insider knowledge that elicited data which struck us as 'hot' (immediate, spontaneous) in contrast to more conventional, 'cold' ethnographic interviewing where respondents recall their experiences in more reflective and arguably rationalized ways. The work and experience of the teacher-researchers represents a considerable resource in the conceptualization of practitioner research in a project of this scale, and this is a brief to which two of their own (our own), Colin Smith and Lesley Easton, turn in Chapter 3.

The interviews by the teacher-researchers were responsively con-structed around what new teachers thought significant in their early experiences. There were areas in common of course, as all engaged with pupils, new schools, procedures and colleagues, as well as the formal induction documents, profiling and the SFR. The majority of the 800 pages of transcripts were therefore of Scottish data, on the basis of which the teacher-researchers participated in identifying what turned out to be a model with seven key dimensions. Although the main focus was on the Scottish context, the comparative English data suggested that the experiences and processes involved were closely related in both countries.

The dimensions of the EPL model are more holistically indicated, and rather than learning focused solely on expected features (competences) for assessment, they emphasize the connections between new teachers and the contexts of their learning. They are as follows:

- emotional: the range and intensity of feeling from anxiety and despair to delight and fulfilment that permeate the new teach-ers' descriptions of their learning experiences;
- relational: the social interactions with others, essentially pupils

and teachers, as well as 'internal dialogues' with notions of self as becoming a professional;

- material: concrete manifestations of structure as resources, rooms, etc. as they apply to teachers as embodied and spatially located subjects;
- temporal: recognizing the changes and trajectories over the induction year, including subjective aspects such as memories and aspirations;
- structural: organizational aspects of the school and the wider educational system, including the formal induction processes, the idea of education in society and relevant wider social factors and changes;
- cognitive: knowledge, understandings and thinking processes in professional practices, especially on pedagogy and curriculum;
- ethical: the commitments, purposes and values expressed by new teachers.

Though there are importantly different emphases, the formal competence models do have similarities with that of the EPL project: the cognitive, ethical, temporal and relational dimensions are immediately obvious. Also, there is a common reliance on support arrangements, such as induction tutor/coordinator, reduced timetable, CPD, observations and so on. However, given that its dimensions were informed by new teacher accounts, the EPL project assumption was that new teachers ought to be able to recognize themselves more readily, thus increasing the likelihood of their engagement with the model.

Although the discourses of experience and the formal SFR are very different, and conceptual connection is not immediately apparent in the data, we have suggested that particular aspects of competence may emerge later in the first year. An example is the emergence of a capacity to 'differentiate' as new teachers' relationships with pupils form and grow into a fuller sense of the pupils as individuals (McNally *et al.* 2008). Thus, further exploration of potential conceptual links may help build a clearer evidence base for interpreting the SFR with greater sophistication in the realms of policy and practice. An important counterpoint to this thematic analysis, however, is that the identification of these dimensions should not obscure the integrity of each new teacher's personal narrative and the sense of individual identity formation obtained in reading the transcripts. In writing this book, we have returned throughout to the language and expression of the new teachers themselves (in pseudonymity, albeit), even taking the uncommon step, in Chapter 1, of beginning a scholarly text with Lesley Walker's story of one new teacher.

However, even deriving a model from new teacher accounts necessarily creates a gap between source and analytic artifact. For a start, the EPL's dimensions are not named by terms used by new teachers themselves, and even to identify dimensions inevitably decontextualizes, separates and freezes what in their accounts is more situated, interconnected and mobile. It is clear that such a gap cannot be closed up altogether, and that any 'enhancing' is more a matter of encouraging other kinds of engagement, an argument that Brian Corbin illustrates in Chapter 4, in relation to the emotional dimension.

Regarding our expression of the model itself, although we did construct some graphic representations of the interrelationships between its dimensions, we retained serious reservations about whether these could have reflected the complexity of the insights we gained from reviewing the ethnographic data and the kind of model we wanted to develop. Like many representations on the page, they can mislead and distort through apparent over-simplification; we focused instead on producing a theory that could reveal some of the complexity of EPL. The simple model outlined above has proved useful for conceptualizing the important finding that the emotional and relational dimensions are much more prevalent in the first few months of induction, with the cognitive dimension emerging later in the year. The dimensions change in intensity over time and in relation to context, and this multidimensionality of professional learning is key to understanding identity formation in the beginner: a fundamental process, writes Jim McNally, in Chapter 5, that incorporates relationality, emotionality and a sense of a changing self.

The research design

In the original research design, the EPL model that was developed from the ethnographic phase (2004/05) was intended to form the basis of an intervention in teacher induction which we would evaluate in a controlled field trial in the second stage of the project (2005/06). This was provisionally conceived as a naturalistic experiment with matched pairs of schools forming experimental and control groups – although in our proposal we did raise caveats about the feasibility of achieving this, and these caveats were accepted by the TLRP directorate when they commissioned the project. In the event, we found that the naturalistic setting of the proposed experiment made it difficult to achieve the degree of control required for comparisons between control and experimental groups. The main factors were the need to work within local authority control of access to schools, the national system of allocation of new teachers to schools and the ethical requirement to respect the sensitivities of new teachers about being allocated to experimental and control groups. Thus, most of the local authorities that agreed to participate insisted on nominating schools for the experimental or control group (e.g. if in their view a school needed to improve its induction, it would be allocated to the experimental group). Also, to allocate new teachers to experimental groups would be to use them as objects, not to collaborate with them as equal partners. A further factor was that we became aware that teachers in one school in a given authority were likely to share information about our intervention with colleagues in other schools in the same authority. This inevitable 'contamination' of the control group by the experimental group further weakened any claims we could mount in defence of conventional experimental testing.

Having also recognized that potential interventions in test schools might have fallen beyond the power of the project to modulate (and these could hypothetically have included full-scale modifications to the induction procedure by the then Scottish Executive Education Department or GTC Scotland, changes to ITE, or increases in salary or other conditions of service), we made the decision to adapt the design so that it was correlational rather than experimental. Using the sample of schools that provided the second tranche of data, we therefore sought to measure variations in the extent to which the criteria of the EPL model were being met.

Although we had to sacrifice the idea of a controlled experiment, we did succeed in the by-no-means simple task of recruiting 82 new teachers from 13 schools across a broad geographical sweep of Scotland. These new teachers were tracked through the induction year with repeated administrations of five quantitative indicators of development. They were also interviewed by the project's teacher-researchers about their experiences, and observations of the schools' environments were likewise compiled. This has established a unique data set in which each of the 82 teachers' learning trajectories through the induction year is recorded quantitatively, while, at the same time, natural variations occurring in the external events impacting on them, arising from differences in the way they were supported/managed by their departments, schools and local authorities, have been recorded by the teacher-researchers in their visits to participating schools.

The EPL project was methodologically innovative, therefore, in two pioneering ways: first, the use of practitioners in a central research role as insider-researchers, leading to the project's unique ability to develop distinctive, close-grained, longitudinal narratives of teacher development (as exemplified by David Dodds in Chapter 11); and second, the building in of a complementary quantitative research instrument in which a set of five unique, purpose-specific indicators of new teachers' development was designed and implemented through user engagement, and used in triangulation of the qualitative model.

Five important outcomes were identified from the analysis of interview data in phase one, for which the project's quantitative instrument of new-teacher development was designed. These were job satisfaction (JOBSAT), children's views on their learning environment (CEPSATI), interaction with others (INTERACT), teaching ability as judged by an external expert (EXJUDGE) and the development of pupils in classes taught as judged by colleagues (PDI).[1] While these areas were broadly based on previous research and professional experience, each indicator was primarily designed for its specific learning context in a series of workshops with the teacher-researchers, taking into account the emergent narrative evidence and practicability in the school setting. The resulting instruments were piloted by the teacher-researchers in their own schools and thus further honed for their specific purpose. The five-indicator instrument was administered by the teacher-researchers in Scotland and by a project research fellow in England as a measure of learning outcomes in the second tranche of data collection (2005/06). In addition to the correlational analyses, the indicators' descriptive statistics were themselves educationally significant; INTERACT, for example, revealed that mentoring in practice was a much broader experience than learning from an officially appointed supporter, and there was even evidence to show that some participating teachers used class results from CEPSATI to effect self-evaluation, in some cases changing their practice according to pupil responses. It is to the development and analysis of these instruments that Nick Boreham, Peter Gray and Allan Blake turn in Chapters 8, 9 and 10 respectively.

It was important that the EPL project be able to demonstrate that its research-based model could be embedded in practice in such a way as to enhance professional learning and performance, and thus contribute to policy on early professional development. The present volume forms part of that programme for enhancement, naturally; we are realistic, however, in thinking that (family and friends, and colleagues in our own departments apart) not everyone will be motivated to read from start to finish. But it was for the more immediate purpose of making operational the EPL model during the life of the project itself, that a structured interview schedule (INTSCHED) was developed. The variables identified in this instrument were interpreted as a basis for a practice-setting discourse aimed at helping new teachers avoid unnecessary difficulties and understand the particular ways a school does things. For example, in asking 'How much do you use the Standard for Full Registration?', INTSCHED expressed a component of the model's structural dimension; likewise, 'How would you describe the availability of teaching materials and other resources in your school?' interpolated the material dimension; 'How would you rate your working relationships with colleagues in your department?', the relational; and 'To what extent did your Initial Teacher Education prepare you for teaching?', the cognitive (and so on).

In the project's correlational design, the dimensions of the model were thus operationalized as independent or predictor variables in relation to a series of learning outcomes as measured by the project's five quantitative indicators. By correlating new teachers' responses to INTSCHED with those from JOBAST, for example, we were able to determine that variations in new teachers' working relationships with colleagues in their departments (relational dimension), variations in pupil behaviour in their schools (structural) and variations in the availability of teaching materials and other resources in their schools (material) were each statistically related to variation in new teachers' overall levels of job satisfaction. These results suggested that as much as 41 per cent of the variation in the new teachers' overall job satisfaction was attributable to their working relationships with colleagues in the same department ($\rho = 0.642$, $p<0.01$, $N = 29$); insofar as these relationships improved or deteriorated, there could occur an equivalent response in the level of overall satisfaction with the job. Regression analysis confirmed causality, showing that for every increment in new teachers' working relationships with colleagues in the same department, there was a predicted rise of 0.438 (p<0.001) in overall job satisfaction. We do not go as far as to suggest that schools can legislate so that new teachers experience positive working relationships with colleagues. The practical implications for schools in helping new teachers to feel welcome and establish their identities, says Colin Smith in Chapter 12, are not a set of prescriptions but a set of questions for each school to apply to its own context. The questions to which he refers are among those first asked by INTSCHED.

The revised correlational design revealed that there were educationally significant variations between schools in the extent to which they conformed to the EPL model as measured by INTSCHED. The Scottish induction year has many benefits but there are important variations in its implementation across different authorities, schools and departments, which we hypothesize are relevant to the quality of learning outcomes. In Chapter 6, for example, Phil Swierczek observes a correlation between the efficacy of schools in providing new teachers with basic material resources and how new teachers regarded their own performance at the end of the induction year. Overall, the emerging statistical correlations have tended to confirm the EPL model; that is, conformity to the model tends to produce better learning outcomes for new teachers.

Conclusion

There is nothing in this volume that denies the need to have some formal structure and support in place for new teachers. Responsible policy could not simply place new teachers in schools and let them get on with it, and it is to the credit of government that substantial resources have been allocated for the purpose of formal induction. But a difficulty arises when formality is over-emphasized, when a support system is put in place for which there is no underlying theoretical or practical evidence. For example, the induction scheme recommends that for observation of teaching, the supporter and probationer teacher should agree beforehand on the element of the SFR being observed. However, our data suggests that new teachers do not use the SFR in talking about their teaching – it is too general in its expression (inevitably so) and cannot capture the essence of classroom teaching for beginners. The SFR has a different purpose.

It is a statement of public accountability, not a useful reference for making sense of everyday teaching.

Our evidence is that learning to teach is a process of 'becoming', rather than one of incremental learning. It is about who you are as much as what you know and should perhaps be understood first as an ontological rather than epistemological process. The voices we heard spoke in an emotional language about relationships. There was little to identify that was specific or precise about what was being 'learned' during or from these early experiences. This surely points to the need for a broader conceptual foundation for early professional learning and an associated standard in which the nature of professional identity is defined beyond the impersonal and decontextualized expression of policy.

What would the acceptance of our arguments mean for the induction of teachers? The ideas in this book, which we claim is well grounded, cannot be rendered superfluous because they are not easy to prescribe through theory or simplistic policy. As we have suggested previously (McNally *et al.* 2008), formal statements of competence should surely acknowledge that teaching cannot simply be assimilated as a craft or set of technical skills, or even as parts of professional knowledge (e.g. a maths curriculum or approaches to difference). The standards and collections of competence require-ments lay out laudable, vaguely articulated aspirations that may help illuminate but cannot of themselves hold the key to success-ful teaching or acceptance as a teacher. A standards-centred or competence-based discourse may have a place in the rhetoric of product rather than process; a hopeful outcome is that the concepts in this book may be seen as complementary to the meta-language of policy, which would be to recognize Halliday's (2004) prescrip-tion for rich descriptions of becoming competent and the contexts in which it happens. In Chapter 13, we suggest that teachers in training lack access to accounts of what the 'real' experience may be like, and that such anticipatory accounts would help reduce the unknown aspects of beginning teaching. It is our hope that the accounts of new teachers in this book will contribute to a more real-istic understanding of that process. The stories speak for themselves of course, but in translating them for a volume such as this, the main theme could be described in terms of a warm, welcoming culture with a clear sense of purpose in the midst of a friendly, supportive chaos of unpredictable interactions; a premise that might yet serve as a model for beginning a book about the same.

References

Ball, S. J. (2003) 'The teacher's soul and the terrors of performativity', *Journal of Educational Policy*, 18:215–18.

Draper, J., Fraser, H. and Taylor, W. (1997) 'Teachers at work: early experiences of professional development', *Professional Development in Education*, 23:283–95.

Eraut, M. (2004) 'Informal learning in the workplace', *Studies in Continuing Education*, 26:247–73.

GTCS (2002) *The Standard for Full Registration*, Edinburgh: GTC Scotland.

GTCS (2006) *Teacher Induction Scheme Statistics*, Edinburgh: GTC Scotland.

Halliday, J. (2004) 'Competence in the workplace: rhetorical robbery and curriculum policy', *Educational Philosophy and Theory*, 36:579–90.

Hargreaves, A. (1998) 'The emotional politics of teacher development', keynote Address to AERA, San Diego.

Harrison, J. K. (2002) 'The induction of newly qualified teachers in secondary schools', *Journal of In-Service Education*, 28:255–75.

Heaney, S. (2001) 'Experience of induction in one education authority', *Mentoring and Tutoring*, 9:241–54.

Jones, C., Bubb, S., Totterdell, M. and Heilbronn, R. (2002) 'Reassessing variability of induction for newly qualified teachers: statutory policy and schools' provision', *Journal of In-Service Education*, 23:495–508.

Jones, M. (2002) 'Qualified to become good teachers: a case study of ten newly qualified teachers during their year of induction', *Journal of In-Service Education*, 28:509–26.

McCrone Report (2000) *A Teaching Profession for the 21st Century: The Report of the Committee of Inquiry into Professional Conditions of Service for Teachers*, Edinburgh: SEED.

McNally, J. (2001) *The Induction of New Teachers in Scotland: A Report for the General Teaching Council for Scotland and the Scottish Executive Department*, Edinburgh: GTC Scotland.

McNally, J. and Oberski, I. (2003) 'Right at the start: an agenda for research and development in teacher induction', *Teacher Development*, 7:59–73.

McNally, J., Blake, A., Corbin, B. and Gray, P. (2008) 'Finding an identity and meeting a standard: connecting the conflicting in teacher induction', *Journal of Educational Policy*, 23:287–98.

Rippon, J. and Martin, M. (2003) 'Supporting induction: relationships count', *Mentoring and Tutoring*, 11:211–16.

Russell, T. and Bullock, S. (1999) 'Discovering our professional knowledge as teachers: critical dialogues about learning from experience' in J. Loughran (ed.) *Researching Teaching: Methodologies and Practices for Understanding Pedagogy*, London: Falmer Press.

Stronach, I., Cope, P., Inglis, B. and McNally, J. (1994) 'The SOED "competence" guidelines for initial teacher training: issues of control, performance and relevance', *Scottish Educational Review*, 26:118–33.

Stronach, I., Corbin, B., McNamara, O., Stark, S. and Warne, T. (2002) 'Towards an uncertain politics of professionalism: teacher and nurse identities in flux', *Journal of Educational Policy*, 17:109–38.

Totterdell, M., Heilbronn, R., Bubb, S. and Jones, C. (2002) *Evaluation of the Effectiveness of the Statutory Arrangements for the Induction of New Teachers*, Norwich: DfES.

Totterdell, M., Woodroffe, L., Bubb, S. and Hanrahan, K. (2004) 'The impact of NQT induction programmes on the enhancement of teacher expertise, professional development, job satisfaction or retention rates: a systematic review of research on induction', in *Research Evidence in Education Library*, London: Institute of Education.

TTA (2002) *Qualifying to Teach (Professional Standards for Qualified Teacher Status and Requirements for Initial Teacher Training)*, London: DfES.

Williams, A. (2003) 'Informal learning in the workplace: a case study of new teachers', *Educational Studies*, 29:207–19.

Note

1 The indicators are available for download at the project website: http://www.strath.ac.uk/curricularstudies/eplproject/

Chapter 3

A new concept of teacher-researcher?

Colin Smith and Lesley Easton

Introduction

The Early Professional Learning project is concerned with the questions of how new teachers learn and the effects of the competences expressed in the Scottish Standard for Full Registration upon this learning. The project's design involved the recruitment of secondary school teachers to form a group of teacher-researchers (TRs) who were initially to undertake ethnographic research in their own schools. A group of six experienced teachers was recruited part-time to this role. This number was regarded as giving the group 'critical mass' and an ability to cover the range of tasks required by the project (Gray *et al.* 2005).

The first phase of the ethnographic research was conducted in part by interviewing the new teachers (NTs) in their own schools and partly by observing first-hand the conditions in which their learning occurred (McNally *et al.* 2004). The rationale of this relatively new research approach rested upon previous experience of the academic team and their reading of the literature which suggested that conventional interviews by external researchers have difficulty getting at processes that tend to be tacit rather than readily explained (Eraut 2000). Being embedded in the workplace, it was reasoned that the teacher-researchers would have naturalistic opportunities to gather a richer set of evidence concerning the activities and social transactions of the new teachers in their schools (ibid.). The second phase involved the teacher-researchers in interviewing new teachers in other secondary schools and the third phase in primary schools. Each phase involved meetings in which the academic researchers and teacher-researchers reported to each other on progress, devised or modified research processes and instruments, or debated interpretation of the data. The teacher-researchers, when necessary, would meet to discuss issues or prepare for dissemination events.

This chapter explores the possibility that the form of engagement of this group of teacher-researchers cuts across what appear to be the existing norms of teacher involvement in research in a way that suggests a new concept of teacher-researcher is emerging. It is not claimed that any one of the features of the roles of the teacher-researchers in the EPL project is necessarily unique. It is the way they combine that may indicate a new concept of teacher-researcher.

Teachers and academic research relationships

Although teachers may often be suspicious of research, at best believing it should be left to professional researchers (Garner 2000), many have been involved for some time in collecting data on their own practice. As Johnson (1975) notes, whatever their views about it, teachers have always been involved in educational research, at least through completing or administering tests and questionnaires. Dick (2006) notes that education has been the busiest sector in action research publication, presumably because there is an audience among practitioners. This research, sometimes also called 'practitioner research', generally has the purpose of improving one's practice and of sharing the resulting knowledge and understanding of it with others (Capobianco and Feldman 2006; Whitehead 1989, 2000). However, administering tests and questionnaires, or engaging in some form of action research into one's own practice, does not necessarily involve any direct meetings or relationships between teachers and researchers. In fact, any contributions from action research to general theories tend to be limited (Dick 2006) and are not necessarily valued by education's academic community (Bartlett and Burton 2006).

One reason for this appears to be concern about the quality of the research and of the data collected (Bartlett and Burton 2006; Capobianco and Feldman 2006). Capobianco and Feldman (2006) argue that quality of action research lies in its ability to improve practice. If it can do this well, it is high-quality research. However, they make the following comment.

An impact on practice is the first marker of quality in action research, but the value of this impact is, of course, grounded in the knowledge and understanding the research generates. The nature of the impact is important: it is possible to change for the worse, if the knowledge is not trustworthy.

(Somekh, in Capobianco and Feldman 2006: 499)

So, it can be argued, despite reservations from academics on the quality of data or theory, if action research impacts positively on practice through generating some form of trustworthy knowledge it is worthwhile. Indeed, it may be possible to theorize a general relationship between explanatory theories of academic research and the theories of practitioners (Smith 2002) that could be mutually beneficial. Also, Leat (2007) reviews research involving teachers in this type of 'tinkering' with practice and finds it worthwhile for various reasons, including improved job satisfaction. We shall see later that the same features can apply also to projects that do specifically aim for collaboration between academics and teachers.

From at least 1975 there has been a pressure for research that purposefully involves collaborative analysis between teachers and academics and joint reporting of findings (Johnson 1975). The model of research envisioned seems to be a researcher or group of researchers working in a single school or group of schools with appropriate members of staff. It might also be hoped that this research would more easily meet the quality criteria of academic publishing. However, even with academic involvement, the nature of the research itself, even when it provides insights that are valued by all the team members, does not always appear easily to fit these criteria, particularly that of theoretical rigour (Clark *et al.* 1996).

Various forms of this type of research can be found in the years that follow 1975. For example, the teachers may research individually, but meet as a group with the academic researchers (Capobianco and Feldman 2006). Sometimes a common theoretical framework may be supplied by the academics, for example, approaches to learning disabilities (Klinger *et al.* 2001) or mastery learning (Postlethwaite and Haggarty 1998), and applied across the classes of the staff involved. In other examples, teachers individually identify issues they wish to research and work singly and closely with an academic mentor whose role is to offer a different perspective, giving rise to challenging questions concerning teacher research and development of practice (Angelides *et al.* 2005). One impetus for teacher participation is often participation in an academic course, such as a master's programme (Angelides *et al.* 2005; Capobianco and Feldman 2006). For some, research (finding out) is a motivation in itself (Watkins 2006). Perhaps related to this, another stimulus to engagement is participation in major projects such as Professional Development Schools (Clark 1999), the Teaching for Understanding Project (Wiske 1998) or, indeed, the EPL project.

Clark *et al.* (1996) identify three models of collaboration between teachers and academics that can perhaps be thought of as a continuum (Bergman and Feiring 1997) (Table 3.1). In Bergman and Feiring's characterization, one end of the continuum is anchored by the *researcher-driven* model. Here, a university academic acts as lead researcher and takes responsibility for all aspects of the research other than the collecting of data, this being the responsibility of the teachers. At the other end of the continuum is the *participant-driven* model. In this model, an academic acts as a facilitator of the research but all aspects of the research process are shared. Somewhere in between these is the *co-investigational* model. In this model, a university-based lead researcher initiates the project and secures funding and may be joined by other university-based researchers and administrators. Teachers also act as field-researchers. All members of the team are involved in negotiating methodology, evaluation and publication. Work is divided according to interest and expertise into manageable units. Again, however, these models appear to be envisaged as applying to research into the teachers' own practices.

The EPL project probably sits closest to the co-investigational model. The research questions were determined by the project directors prior to the recruitment of the teacher-researchers. Also, the methodology was broadly planned in advance. However, once the teacher-researchers were 'on board', they began to influence the finer details of the methodology and data interpretation, despite some initial feelings of insecurity and isolation from each other (Smith *et al.* 2005; Walker 2007). These feelings arose despite the camaraderie between academics and researchers. In retrospect, they possibly arose because the academics, perhaps inevitably in the earlier stages of the project, were very much directing the meetings. They had an agenda to get through to 'kick start' the project. The teacher-researchers' views on the interpretation of the data and the

Table 3.1 Models of collaboration between teachers and academics

Model of collaboration	Academic participants' contributions	Teacher participants' contributions
Researcher-driven model (one anchor in the continuum)	Supply the lead researcher who has all responsibility for all aspects of the investigation: Initiating the research question Obtains and manages funding Determines methodology Oversees evaluation Publishes results	Convey information to the lead researcher and gather data
Participant-driven model (the other anchor in the continuum)	Provide a facilitator and some of the field researchers and/or administrators All participants work together to: Determine the direction of the research Establish the research question Determine methodology and evaluation strategies Publish results by consensus	Be some of the field researchers

(continued)

Model of collaboration	Academic participants' contributions	Teacher participants' contributions
Co-investigational model (somewhere in the middle of the continuum)	Provide a lead investigator who initiates the research question and secures funding Provide field researchers and/or administrators who contribute their own expertise to the project All members of the team negotiate: Methodology Evaluation Publication Division of workload into manageable units depending upon their skills and interests	Be some of the field researchers contributing their own expertise to the project

Note: Based on Bergman and Feiring (1997) and Clark et al. (1996).

final design of the research instruments were actively looked for, but it was not until they were able to meet as a group without the academics that the teacher-researchers really felt part of a team. A number of lessons have been learned from this phase of the project that could be used to avoid this in the future (Smith *et al.* 2005). However, the project did become fully cooperative with roles being assigned according to whoever had the expertise and/or time to manage them. For example, teacher-researchers generally have a limited experience of publications so it is sensible that academics should lead the compilation of the project book; similarly, for the statistical analysis of the data. However, as the project evolved, the teacher-researchers assumed much of the responsibility for dissemination to members of the profession (Smith 2006, 2007; Swierczek 2008; Swierczek and Smith 2006). They are now also conscious of their role in refining methodology and interpreting the data and are often proactive, rather than reactive, in making suggestions (Walker 2007). A point has also been reached where it is clear that the academics have learned from the teachers, as well as the other way round. It is in these factors that a new concept of teacher-researcher may be found.

EPL project as an environment for the evolution of a new concept of teacher-researcher

Personal investment in research outcomes

Although many of the projects discussed above, and more, have involved teachers from different subject backgrounds and schools, participation is generally open in the sense that 'if you volunteer, you are in'. There also tends to be common threads, such as working for the same authority. Also, although they are from different subjects, their subject experience is often relevant in the sense that it is intended to be either improved in some way by the project – directly or through changes brought about in school conditions and/or policies. In contrast, the teacher-researchers for the EPL project went through what they experienced as a fairly intensive competitive selection process. They began to emerge as the favourites when the academics could see them working as a team (McNally *et al.* 2004). Other criteria that were important in the selection process were evidence that the teachers were well respected in the school, that they showed insight beyond policy statements into the new teachers' experience, that they were genuinely interested in the project and not actively seeking to use it as a route to promotion (ibid.). Thus, in contrast to most projects involving teacher-researchers who are seeking in some way to improve their own practice, the teacher-researchers were, to a greater degree than usual, free from a direct personal investment in the outcomes. With one exception, none of the teacher-researchers had any formal responsibility for the induction of new teachers into their schools or for their learning within it. However, the exception had no responsibility for new-teacher assessment. Although it can be said that she was interested in how project findings could help her in her mentoring role, like the others she was not committed to any particular model of early professional learning. The teacher-researchers in the EPL project could be described, therefore, as combining relative disinterest or impartiality with being insiders. Any improvement in practice was not of direct benefit to them, though obviously it would benefit the profession as a whole. Indeed, even the academic members of the research team have some interest as members of the public in improvements to the teaching profession. If, however, they can be described as disinterested outsiders when conducting research in schools, the teacher-researchers in this project are probably as close as it is possible to get to being disinterested insiders.

Collecting data neutrally

This role as disinterested insiders was important in the data collection. As noted earlier, teacher-researchers generally have data-gathering roles, but since they usually have a direct stake in implementing implications in their practice, the quality of the data, as noted above, may be measured against this rather than academic standards. In this case, the focus was not on the teacher-researchers' own, or their school's practice, but on a topic (the experiences of new teachers) across schools and authorities. So, although the teacher-researchers initially collected data in their own schools, the focus of analysis was not particular to them. This again probably helps to reduce any bias that might be expected in data gathered by practitioners.

However, the data in the EPL project could also be argued to serve both the purposes of academic rigour and improvement of practice. A number of research instruments were devised that can be interpreted qualitatively and quantitatively. Nevertheless, the quality of the data collected depended as much on the teacher-researchers as the academics. As established practitioners, the teachers had up-to-date knowledge of the working environment the academics wished to explore. The advantage of this for the academics was that their questions about such things as the mechanics of implementation could be answered, relevant advice given, suggestions made and issues anticipated.

When research instruments were devised the teacher-researchers took the prototypes back to their own classroom and, putting themselves in the position of the probationers, piloted the materials. As well as helping refine these for the research project, this also gave these experienced teachers some formative assessment on themselves. In addition, many of the new teachers commented on the usefulness of viewing some of their own data in improving their practice – particularly that from an instrument designed to measure the classroom environment.

Conducting interviews has been a key feature of the teacher-researcher role in this project. The quality of the data collected seems to reflect the fact that it may be easier for new teachers to talk more openly or freely to a fellow teacher knowing there is a common understanding of the job. It was probably easier for teacher-researchers to understand their response and develop the next question. They spoke the professional language the probationers were learning. As one of the academic researchers commented:

> I think the TRs' work showed us that it is possible for 'insiders' to get a view on what's happening (e.g. via new teacher responses) that no others in the school could (this involved winning trust – that the different and difficult demands of teaching and research can be handled by the right people).

One possible indicator that the data collected was objective was the fact that the teacher-researchers could be surprised by what they found in their own schools – there was an element of surprise, even for the insiders (Walker 2007). So, in summary, the EPL project, through its teacher-researchers, seems to have managed to gather data it would not otherwise have accessed – data that is more likely to meet the academic criterion for as much objectivity as possible, yet is simultaneously of use to practitioners.

Influencing the research process

As the project developed, the two groups, academics and teachers, formed a team and learned about each other's worlds. The benefit of the teacher-researchers to the project, as disinterested insiders, has been their ability to be open and honest and so provide a unique insight into the world that the researchers wanted to explore. However, there are other aspects to the partnership that formed between academics and teachers. The teacher-researchers have had an experience open only to a few: namely, participating in a major research project as researchers, not subjects. They have learned new skills and have gained knowledge of the research process, as well as coming to better appreciate its importance (Smith *et al.* 2005; Swierczek and Smith 2006; Walker 2007). The technical contribution to the research process, data analysis and its placement within the literature remains the major responsibility of the academics. However, as their skills and knowledge developed, the teacher-researchers became more confident in their own contribution to ensuring the quality of the research process and instruments, as well as of interpretation of the data. One indicator of the trust and respect developed is the willingness of the academics to submit their writing for comment, not only to each other but also to the teacher-researchers. One outcome for the academics was therefore a greater awareness of how they might otherwise have 'talked past' some of their intended practitioner audience through the (excessive) use of technical terminology. They have also benefited from comment on their data analysis:

> I got some very useful feedback on my analysis of probationer cases, e.g. L was able to add to how I saw April by sending me further material and comment on what I had said based on the transcripts alone.

Finally, through the partnership, the teacher-researchers have been empowered to disseminate in their own way (Smith 2006, 2007; Swierczek and Smith 2006; Walker 2007) and even theorize their own role. In summary, the project has fully settled into the co-investigational model outlined in Table 3.1.

Identity formation

Perhaps paradoxically, the fact that the academic and teacher members of the research team gelled into a co-investigational team did not prevent the teacher-researchers from developing their own identity as a coherent team. Perhaps inevitably and due to the fact that they initiated the project and could readily meet and communicate, the academic team has always maintained an identity of its own. As noted earlier, this did cause some tension in the earlier phase of the project as the teacher-researchers felt isolated from each other, despite regular meetings of the whole team. This was only resolved when it was suggested by the teacher-researchers that they should meet together without the academics, an idea that was immediately accepted and encouraged by the academics (Smith *et al.* 2005; Walker 2007). As a result, when it came to presenting the project from their perspective to academic conferences or presenting its implications to practitioners, local authorities and policy-makers, the teacher-researchers were able to develop into a distinct team of and in themselves. Naturally, the academics were heavily involved in dissemination in the usual ways. Thus, the academic and teacher members complemented each other in dissemination.

Conclusion

The EPL project is unusual in how it uses teacher-researchers. This derives from its aim to provide a model of early professional learning that is robust across all schools and perhaps even beyond, into other professions. The teacher-researchers are not involved in researching their own practice, yet are school insiders in the sense that they see the schools through teachers' eyes and share some of the perspective and language that new teachers are developing. However, they have no direct stake in the outcomes of the research, other than those shared by the profession as a whole, and indeed the wider public of which the academic team are also members. As such, they can be described as disinterested insiders. This idea of teacher-researchers as disinterested insiders seems relatively unique in educational research and allows other features of what is, perhaps, an emerging new concept of teacher-researcher to develop. These include a relative neutrality or objectivity compared to other teacher-researchers in collecting the data, both in their own and other schools. The collection of data beyond their own schools seems also to be a wider role for teacher-researchers than normal. Being disinterested insiders also enabled the teacher-researchers to play an open and honest role in both collecting the data and in its interpretation so that they became fully integrated members of a co-investigational team. However, the data collected seemed, in some cases at least, to be not only of sufficient quality to satisfy academic demands, but also to be of use to practice – something educational research is often accused of not managing (Watkins 2006). This may be a feature not only of the research intention, but also of the input from teacher-researchers into the design of the research instruments. The final part of the emerging concept is of teacher-researchers who are able to be both partners with the academics in the research process and data interpretation, where both use their expertise and experience but also keep a separate and coherent identity in the dissemination process. One test of the validity of the above concept of the teacher-researcher would be the joint publication of findings by teacher-researchers and academics.

References

Angelides, P., Evangelou, M. and Leigh, J. (2005) 'Implementing a collaborative model of action research for teacher development', *Educational Action Research*, 13(2):275–90.

Bartlett, S. and Burton, D. (2006) 'Practitioner research or descriptions of classroom practice? A discussion of teachers investigating their classrooms', *Educational Action Research*, 14:395–405.

Bergman, L. M. and Feiring, N. C. (1997) 'Bridging the gap between the university researcher and the classroom teacher', *Art Education*, 50:51–6.

Capobianco, B. M. and Feldman, A. (2006) 'Promoting quality for teacher action research: lessons learned from science teachers' action research', *Educational Action Research*, 14:497–512.

Clark, C., Moss, P. A., Goering, S., Herter, R. J., Lamar, B., Leonard, D., Robbins, S., Russell, M., Templin, M. and Wascha, K. (1996) 'Collaboration as dialogue: teachers and researchers engaged in conversation and professional development', *American Educational Research Journal*, 33:193–231.

Clark, R. W. (1999) 'School-university partnerships and professional development schools', *Peabody Journal of Education*, 74:164–77.

Dick, B. (2006) 'Action research literature 2004–2006: themes and trends', *Action Research*, 4:439–58.

Eraut, M. (2000) 'Non-formal learning, implicit knowledge and tacit knowledge in professional work' in F. Coffield (ed.) *The Necessity of Informal Learning*, ESRC report, Bristol: Policy Press.

Garner, P. (2000) 'Teachers as researchers: an uneasy relationship?', paper presented at the European Conference on Educational Research, Edinburgh.

Gray, P., Boreham, N., Cope, P., Corbin, B., McNally, J., Stronach, I. (and Dodds, D., Easton, L., Smith, C., Swierczek, P., Walker, L.) (2005) 'User engagement and research design in the EPL project', paper presented at the Annual TLRP Conference, Warwick.

Johnson, D. (1975) 'Enlisting the participation of teachers in research: proceedings of the 1975 BERA conference', *Research Intelligence*, 1:38–41.

Klinger, J. K., Arguelles, M. E., Hughes, M. J. and Vaughn, S. (2001) 'Examining the schoolwide "spread" of research-based practices', *Learning Disabilities Quarterly*, 24:221–34.

Leat, D. (2007) *Partnerships and Participation in Teacher Research*, Cranfield University: Network Learning Communities, National College for School Leadership. Available online at http://www.ncsl.org/ (accessed 22 February 2007).

McNally, J. (2006) 'A loose thread of research in a seamless garment of professional development', paper presented to the TLRP Programme: Changing Teacher Roles, Identities and Professionalism (C-Trip), King's College, London.

McNally, J., Boreham, N., Cope, P., Gray, P., Stronach, I. and Corbin, B. (2004) 'First steps and second thoughts on method: beginning to research the learning of new teachers', paper presented at the TLRP Annual Conference, Cardiff.

Postlethwaite, K. and Haggarty. L. (1998) 'Towards effective and transferable learning in secondary school: the development of an approach based on mastery learning', *British Educational Research Journal*, 24:333–53.

Smith, C. A. (2002) 'Supporting teacher and school development: learning and teaching policies, shared living theories and teacher-researcher partnerships', *Teacher Development*, 6:157–79.

Smith C. A (2006) 'Welcoming and integrating new teachers into our schools: 1) School buildings and school systems', *Secondary Headship*, 49:6–7.

Smith C. A (2007) 'Welcoming and integrating new teachers into our schools: 2) Social relations and delivery of lessons', *Secondary Headship*, 50:8–9.

Smith, C. A., Curwen, K., Dodds, D., Easton, L., Gray, P., Swierczek, P. and Walker, L. (2005) 'Teacher-researchers in a major research project: some reflections and lessons learned', paper presented at the Scottish Educational Research Association Conference, Perth.

Swierczek, P. (2008) 'Teaching: a welcoming profession?', paper presented at the ISTE Conference, University of Stirling, Scotland.

Swierczek, P. and Smith, C. A. (2006) 'Research as a learning experience', paper presented at the EPL Project Dissemination Day, University of Stirling, Scotland.

Walker, L. (2007) 'Working with researchers: the practitioner's perspective', *TLRP Technology-Enhanced Learning (TEL) Programme, Invited Seminar on Developing Research Capacity*, Dynamic Earth, Edinburgh.

Watkins, A. (2006). 'So what exactly do teacher-researchers think about doing research?', *Support for Learning*, 21:12–18.

Whitehead, J. (1989) 'Creating a living educational theory from questions of the kind, "How do I improve my practice?"', *Cambridge Journal of Education*, 19:41–52.

Whitehead, J. (2000) 'How do I improve my practice? Creating and legitimating an epistemology of practice', *Reflective Practice*, 1:91–104.

Wiske, M. S. (ed.) (1998), *Teaching for Understanding. Linking Research with Practice*, San Francisco: Jossey-Bass.

Chapter 4

Feeling professional

New teachers and induction

Brian Corbin

Introduction

This chapter argues that the prominence of emotions in new teacher discourse found in the EPL project data is such that it merits inclusion in any model of early professional learning. Yet it is a dimension that is comparatively neglected in the standards documents of the two recent teacher induction policies in England (TTA 2002) and Scotland (GTCS 2002). However, arguing for such inclusion generally in teaching and learning is neither new nor straightforward, for what also matters is how an emotional dimension might be conceptualized and for what purpose. Moreover, there are also issues around the affective in relation to cognition and values, as well as processes involving self and identity in early professional learning. What also needs to be addressed is the place of emotions in any model proposed by the EPL project, given its aim is to promote 'enhanced competence-based learning': in particular, what might be the nature of such enhancement?

Existing academic literature has largely focused on experienced teachers, while this chapter concerns emotional aspects of new teachers and their induction. Though there are commonalities, there are also distinctive features for those 'at the threshold' of the profession (GTCS 2002). The Scottish Standard for Full Registration (SFR) offers a model of new teachers and their 'expected features' (competences) as well as how they might be supported in their learning. Some comparative data is included here from new teachers in England working to a similar model in the requirements of their standards document. For both countries, key policy concerns were not only the political arithmetic of unacceptable rates of attrition and variable quality of induction, but also the continued promotion of policies defining teacher professionalism. The focus here is on the transition between the initial stage and subsequent lifelong learning. Yet in both countries, except for obligatory recording and assessment points, most new teachers did not keenly engage with their standard as a working document. There was, however, more widespread approval of several features of the formal induction arrangements, all the more so where existing collegial and interpersonal practices were conducive.

Given this, the EPL project retains a commitment to explore the possibilities of 'an enhanced-competence based' approach to early professional learning, though it seems clear from the project data on responses to the standard that just adding more, such as 'emotional' is not in itself the point. Thus, the possible nature of any such 'enhancement' is one of the three main concerns in this chapter. Another is to present evidence concerning the ways emotions seem significantly implicated in the processes of early professional learning. This is related to a third concern, which is to make clear the approach to emotions offered here.

Emotions and teaching

There has been increasing attention paid to the importance of emotions in teaching and similar 'people-centred' work since the 1980s, and beyond that, little agreement as to why and with what possible consequences. Indeed, for pupils and students it already seems that 'emotional literacy has become big business' (Ecclestone 2007). 'Emotion' is now yoked with a range of major concepts against which it was formerly contrasted, whether as emotional labour (Hochschild 1983), emotional intelligence (Goleman 1995), emotional judgement (Bullough and Young 2002), politics of emotions (Hayes 2003) or emotional management (Hartley 2004). Such pairings seek to give emotion a renewed significance, even as sited 'at the heart of teaching' itself (Hargreaves 1998: 835), and winning hearts has huge consequences for minds, ethics and actions. The possibilities are uncertain and might be polarized along a 'good-bad' continuum, from seeking to foster learning and teaching or as refining micromanagement control as 'technologies of the self' (Burman 2006).

Whatever the ends, research highlighting the emotions of experienced teachers has seen them as essential to processes of identity and self in becoming and being a teacher (Nias 1986; Day et al.

2006). Even where emotions are not the major focus of most research, and this is more often the case, they are noted as highly significant casualties, whether in the context of the demotivating effects of policy-driven auditing (Kelchtermans 1996; Woods and Jeffrey 1996; Day *et al.* 2006), or at least fraught consequences of particular reforms and policy innovations (Nias 1996; Stronach *et al.* 2002; Schmidt and Datnow 2005). Although such approaches importantly concern the impact of recent externally driven changes, some tensions pre-date these, such as the fact that schooling (for nearly all in practice) is compulsory, and that pupils are variably keen, resistant and anxious about learning. For there is discomfort as well as comfort in the learning process itself (Salzberger-Wittenberg *et al.* 1983). So as well as compassion for learners and passion for teaching (Day 2004), there is also fear, anger and stress, some attributable to outside causes, some inherent in teaching itself. How to become the sort of teacher who can cope with such tensions has a distinctively high profile in early professional learning. As one new teacher succinctly put it: 'How do I function effectively as a person in class?'(Richard).

The EPL approach to emotion

One of the most concise definitions of emotion is Koestler's: 'mental states accompanied by intense feeling and (which involve) bodily changes' (in Hargreaves 1998: 835). There are three features of this definition with strong implications for the approach taken in this chapter. Hargreaves refers to the Latin origin of the word as 'emovere: to move out, to stir up' (ibid.), pointing up a dual movement, out of and into the person. First, rather than simply individualize emotions, they are linked to possible wider social, structural and political contexts. Examples might include the rate of policy initiatives, workload and pupil behaviour as major sources of dissatisfaction and teacher attrition (Smithers and Robinson 2003: 92). The EPL project's own quantitative survey of job satisfaction in Chapter 8 highlights the distinctive importance to new teachers of relationships with pupils and colleagues. In Scotland, the report from which the new induction policy followed also highlighted a structural matter, the 'scandalous' discontinuity of new-teacher experiences in short-term supply posts (McCrone Report 2000).

The reference to 'mental states' also challenges any simple 'cognitive-affective' opposition, in line with neurological evidence for emotional arousal as a 'mental evaluative process' (Zembylas 2003: 233) and not just as reactions to but also interpretations of the world and the self in it. They are also not just 'moods' that tend to occlude thought. Though emotions only 'accompany' cognition, they 'can become objects of reflection' (Solomon, in Bullough and Young 2002: 418) and are thus educable (Golby 1996: 425). Finally, the reference to 'bodily changes' signals the links between emotions and the person as embodied, a feature of approaches to identity formation and the teacher self. It is at these points that some discursive intersections with the standard open up, though not by explicit reference to emotions but rather by including self (as 'self-evaluation' and 'reflective practice'), 'personal style' and evaluative judgements (as 'commitments and values'). These necessarily invoke the teacher as person.

Such connections are important to the case developed here for, despite its focus, the aim is not to end up with competence as 'enhanced' by including 'a discourse of disclosure of feeling as an endpoint' (Burman 2006: 322). The aim concerns learning in context, rather than simply as the 'personalized remedies' of a therapeutic discourse in education (Nolan, in Hayes 2003: 40). It is equally important not to deal with emotions in what Hartley sees as an emerging managerialist framing, whereby 'more of "the person" – the emotions – is being held up for "skilling", recording and assessment' (2004: 591).

Methodology

For this chapter, the present author has analysed Scottish and English transcripts of interviews with new teachers specifically in relation to emotions (quotations used here are from the Scottish data, unless 'E' appears after the new teacher pseudonym). Where it seemed that 'feel' was used more or less synonymously with 'think', these were not included (unless they clearly had affective content, as in 'feeling very disillusioned'). Examples include the straightforward use of words such as 'agitated', 'enjoy', 'love', 'calm', 'upset' and 'shock'. Those implying emotion were also included: 'fantastic', 'she's lovely', 'tough as old boots'. Longer formulations can also imply the affective: 'we've been treated like cattle', 'he's gonna be such a nightmare', 'they see you as an ogre'. Also there is emotional content to references to the person: 'not take things personal', 'then your personality can come out'. The relational also seems significant: 'I feel more confident, so they feel more confident', 'they see you as a person, not just as somebody there to teach them', 'pupils come in with different moods' and 'I feel part of a community'. They are also implicated in values and commitments: 'my values have changed ... to fit in with the curriculum, which is really sad', 'I enjoy teaching ... . I don't think I would be doing it if it didn't personally matter'.

It was clear that emotions were always about something and flowed effortlessly into other categories, and this was a significant feature of new-teacher discourse. Besides this flow there was also flux, underpinning the importance of rapid and uncertain change as key dynamics in the early experiences of becoming a teacher. Flux and flow demand more extended illustration. Here, Richard recalls his initial 'conciliatory model' of professional self:

> I went in trying to be democratic [...] you know 'What do you think?' [...] the kids just wiped the floor with me [...] I learnt from that [...] I was a lot more assertive and directive. That worked. I built on that even more [...] I'm a lot more confident. Not only that, I think that's also tinged with – and I've discussed this with my colleagues in the department – I don't have any fear because teaching was never my be all and end all [...] I'm very easy going, very fair, but I set very strict boundaries [...] throw people out [...] I realize that was probably against the rules. I realize this conversation is confidential.

In this lengthy passage, shortened here by bracketed omissions to reveal the sinews of his thinking, his account effortlessly flows through dimensions such as the emotional ('confident', 'fear'), the temporal ('I went in', 'built on that'), the ethical ('fair', 'democratic)', the relational ('discussed with colleagues', 'assertive'), the cognitive ('I learnt from that') and the structural ('department', 'rules'). These are six of the seven dimensions of the EPL model. Several of these, though named differently, overlap with those guiding the formal induction process. The reference to 'confidential' obviously concerns the quality of teacher-researcher relationship to new teachers, an instance of the regular confirmation of the methodological aim to be seen as separate from formal and even some collegial aspects of assessment. It indicates a qualitatively different relationship, in terms of power and the possible consequences of such narratives. This and the discursive features of flow and flux were repeated aspects in the data, even though Richard's guarded commitment to a career in teaching was unusual (though he did 'love his subject').

Initial findings from EPL research

At this point it is worth noting some relevant overall findings from our data on new teachers and the formal induction documents. We found no resistance to any specific 'Standard' item, nor to the notion of standards or even competence as such:

> Yes standardization would be a good idea after all this is supposed to be a national initiative throughout Scotland and sharing good practice would be helpful.
>
> (Geller)

> I think the [standards] document is really useful, but obviously it depends on how you use it. Luckily we've got Ann [induction coordinator] who's spot on with everything.
>
> (Frances, E)

The emphasis though is on its use with and for others. In itself, it is seen as 'such a dull document' (Linda), and either as 'too much to read' (Ann) or too little to capture learning experiences and instead something to 'fit in with' (Geller). In Scotland in particular there was antipathy to the associated profile recording of themselves as not useful for sharing practice and as too reductive: 'all very much ticking boxes with numbers' (Diane), 'it doesn't tell them anything at all about me as a teacher' (Lewis).

A fuller quotation illustrates new-teacher discourse on the SFR and emotions:

> I found [the SFR] really dry. I would be reading and half way through I would give up in disgust … It wasn't seeking to find out anything about me personally as a teacher, about my learning styles and that's what the whole point of teaching is […] it's about tapping into the learning styles of your pupils.
>
> (Rachael)

First it is worth noting that Rachael's comment involves modelling, and includes components such as the emotional, relational, ethical and cognitive. Secondly, the emotional force of 'disgust' indicates the significance of the SFR's main failing for her, not just to support for her self-evaluation, but its perceived lack of interest in doing so: what 'it wasn't seeking to find out'. Yet the SFR competences do refer to values and commitment: for example, that she 'can evaluate and justify [her] approaches to teaching and learning and take action to improve the impact on pupils'.

If it is not modelling as such, why does the SFR not generate more enthusiasm? It may be its relentless and overwhelming detail. Yet some new teachers did complain about the very lack of detail its related profiling allowed. Perhaps what is more crucial is not to lose the thread between detail and more holistic new-teacher priorities. For example, Rachael wants more about her learning style and those of her pupils, because at this stage she sees this relational exploration as 'the whole point of teaching'. The EPL model's comparative brevity may make it easier to attempt such connections. Of course, this is not all she has to say on the 'Standard':

> it was something that had to be done ... and made sure I was meeting those targets and made me aware of different aspects of teaching.
>
> (Rachael)

There is ambivalence here, conveying both a sense of reduced agency mixed with some appreciation of its possible value beyond her own current priorities. The fullness of the SFR's detail has a strength here, hence its comment that it may take five years to acquire its competences, even if its triple timescale (one year, five and 'lifelong') can be felt as problematic in relation to immediate priorities and assessment deadlines. Even the mundane and unexciting can be accepted as intrinsic to the learning process:

> Obviously as I come more used to the school and procedures and stuff and that's just part of the learning process. I don't know if that's me getting more professional or just something that has to be done.
>
> (George)

What seems more important is not whether something is particular or holistic, mundane or inspirational: there is ready mobility between such contrasts, shifting according to new-teacher priorities as they see them at that stage.

To return to the main concerns of this chapter, Rachael's comments reveal that engaging with any model requires extra work, and the quality of this may be where enhancement is constructed. Three aspects of this are noted. Her words suggest the particular involvement of emotion in 'providing meaning to experiences' (Zembylas 2003: 222), here in her 'disgust' about the mismatch between its apparent purpose and hers. The same can be said where a discursive flow is afforded between different aspects of what she finds significant (here between the emotional, ethical, relational, structural and cognitive). The significance of any particular competence is in its connections, not in its isolation. A third feature seems to relate to the qualities of other people, their formal use of the documents and, importantly, more informal support. Rachael spoke highly of these features in her school, though not every new teacher felt as fortunate. Such aspects are constitutive rather than just 'extra' to enhancement. They are also evident in the English data:

> The observations are good, and the feedback is good, and chatting to senior members of staff ... We've covered the necessary paperwork, it's there, it has to be done, it's not really intruded on my first year, so I'm glad about that ... I enjoy setting the targets, it gives you something to aim for each term.
>
> (Hugh, E)

Again there is an emotional ambivalence here: support for learning with and from others is valued, whether formal or informal; even documentation ('paperwork') can be valued ('enjoyed' as 'targets' for learning), or not (as potential 'intrusion' on what really matters).

Such ambivalence suggests that the SFR's competences are constantly being held up to something more pressing or important to new teachers. Exploring beyond the fact that she finds the SFR 'an incredibly dull read' and admitting 'I have not used it', Avril elaborates:

> I think I would have been too scared [to use PowerPoint in classroom teaching] and I convinced myself that I'm a technophobe ... but because I knew it was in the [standard's] benchmarks if you like, I thought that I've got to overcome this, so probably I wouldn't have done that had it not been there. So yes, in that respect it probably helps [...] a lot of what is in it

is motivated for the right reasons, so you would [...] probably cover most of it anyway.

(Avril)

'Motivated for the right reasons' turns out to be because of her commitment to pupil learning, and not just bureaucratic 'full registration' procedure. Yet she does also admit to an SFR role in helping her overcome fears about using ICT in her pedagogy. We next focus more on the emotional not just as aspects of induction, but as part of a deeper process in the desire to become a teacher. We begin with a basic form of modelling: the teacher as person.

Emotion and process

Embodied models: 're/member pedagogical work as inescapably corporeal'.

(McWilliam 1996: 367)

For some older entrants, memories of their teachers as embodied persons are emotionally fresher and, in a sense, initially fuel their desire to become a teacher:

I think ever since I had a really, really inspiring teacher, I thought 'That's what I want to do, I want to be able to inspire kids'.

(Carla, E)

New-teacher learning can continue this emphasis:

my mentor has been fantastic this year ... but we talk informally as well, it's given me a person.

(Nadine, E)

Older new teachers are less likely to invoke such embodiments as much as anticipate personal emotional rewards denied them in previous work, a chance to counter boredom, isolation, and lack of worthwhile purpose. In both cases the past informs commitment.

Embodied aspects such as age, gender, and ethnicity, crop up repeatedly, and feature in the process of resculpting new-teacher corporeality, sometimes in surprising ways:

They do see you like a father figure in some ways, even though I'm only 26 ... they just go to you, naturally assume it's your responsibility.

(Matthew, E)

I don't mind [being] female, I don't mind being you know ... a minority, but the kids are bigger. And I'm not as strong in the voice ... and I try to work on not being so strict with the class.

(Gwen, E)

The implications of embodiment for early professional learning are immediate. And however unexpected, they are not as much of a shock as a kind of disembodiment that is sometimes experienced:

I had one class that were behaving as if I really wasn't there and they were shocked to begin with that I wasn't their old teacher.

(Linda)

Over time, having been deprived of a physical presence, comes the pleasure of becoming unexpectedly made flesh again:

students who I don't even know will go 'Oh hiya Miss' as you're walking past them, whereas before they'd just ignore you.

(Nadine, E)

The realization of having accomplished a physical presence in the classroom can lead to a seeming 'out of body' emotional reward:

I see me jumping around the classroom and there is no way I would have done that in the first lessons [...] I mean the staff at my old school wouldn't recognize me.

(Lewis)

And it is not only others who might find it difficult to recognize the developing 'self':

I have a very working class accent I'm trying to filter out ... It's very weird, almost like an out of body experience ... stepping back and looking at myself and thinking 'What the hell are you doing?'

(Lewis)

It also becomes obvious that there is an 'emotional geography' for the body in the classroom, which recognizes 'its socio-spatial mediation [...] rather than as entirely interiorised' (Bondi, in Burman 2006: 317):

I think having your own room makes a huge difference ... It makes you feel more like a qualified teacher ... it's done a lot for my confidence.

(Linda)

The body can be made to appear and disappear for cognitive and discipline purposes:

I was someone who constantly walked around ... now I flip between walking ... and maybe sitting and also just standing at the back observing them without them seeing me and I've actually found that quite informative.

(Rachael)

It can be extended out of the classroom:

You can't distance yourself, you do become attached to the children, and the people who work in the school, and the building and everything else.

(Frances, E)

I think the biggest thing is my confidence within and out of school ... I feel I get more respect from people ... Even emotionally I feel more mature, I feel I should be somebody the kids can look up to.

(Ann)

In such ways it is clear that the process of becoming a teacher involves learning as embodied persons, and as such entails the emotions in both senses of the relational, inwards and outwards to others, in the classroom, the school and the socio-economic context beyond. The salience of the emotional importance of developing 'confidence' is apparent and much repeated. And distinctively for new teachers, they seem to be shape-shifters in novel and unanticipated ways. This can be both exciting and disconcerting, and perhaps partly explains why getting a 'reputation' over time is a recurrent theme in early professional learning, as it affords a comforting sense of professional solidity. This process depends of course on continuity, whether afforded by permanent appointment in England or new induction arrangements for year-long 'placement' in Scotland.

The emotional labour: the process of becoming 'strictly nice'

Once in post, the simply inspiring teacher, recollected as pupil, is seen in a more emotionally problematic way. Richard's experience of being shocked into a move from 'conciliatory' to 'assertive' is reiterated. The trick seems to be neither 'ogre' nor 'best friend' (Geller), but there is no obvious set of techniques for doing so. Experienced teachers are scrutinized for clues as to how they personify what appear to be impossibly simultaneous practices of both control and affection:

> Seeing her in a lesson with year ten boys and how she controlled them ... not harsh by any means ... she's still really nice ... but she had very clear boundaries and rules which they all seemed to know.
>
> (Laura, E)

> She had discipline but she makes the kids want to do well for her and I think that's the kind of teacher I want to be ... although you've got to keep a boundary there.
>
> (Ann)

> He can have kids in tears ... get them interested ... this perfect routine ... behaviour is not an issue ... and it works because of who the teacher is.
>
> (Martin, E)

In this growing but surprising awareness, the new teacher is to become not simply 'inspiring', but also concerned with 'boundary' and 'routine'; even more surprising, these self-conflicting qualities become somehow holistically reconciled in the person – 'because of who the teacher is'.

This 'strict–nice' tension becomes a theme in the informal affective curriculum of new-teacher discourse, and is a key aspect of the emotional labour of early professional learning. What's more, the emotions of pupils as well as those of the teacher become more important as a relational feature of early professional learning, and are seen as interdependent more than largely as adversarial or charismatic givens. But it is a long haul, unstable and precariously achieved, lost and retrieved. Different teachers have different starting points:

> I went in at the start too softly and tightening up has been quite a steep learning curve … The major thing I've found is kids really want you to set boundaries.
>
> (Ann)

> I've learnt not to be quite so harsh … I've lightened up a little bit and I think I've learnt from them.
>
> (Linda)

The emotional order of the classroom seems to connect easily with an ethic of both self and pupils as learners, yet with teacher as ultimately responsible for that learning. This involves moving beyond any simple desire – 'I just want to be me, teaching' (Shreya, E) – to something more inflected. It is sometimes important to explore ways of being someone you dislike (Nias 1986) for learning ends:

> They're not staying focused as much as they should … I then have to be the nagging, moaning teacher in a bad mood all the time, or as far as they are concerned anyway, which is not nice for me, it's a necessary evil.
>
> (Lewis)

Different 'sides' to self are developed, some as essential to sustain commitment, others acquired just for tactical display.

These more complex selves are discovered, often by 'trial and error', moving between 'faking in good faith' (Ashforth and Humphrey 1993: 93) and an emotional truth to commitments. How this is done is not always visible nor easily articulated as technique:

My [mentor] just has to walk in a room and silence descends
... he admitted he doesn't know how he does it. So I just hope
one day that will happen to me and your reputation goes before
you and you're known as a fair teacher.

(Rachael)

Three months later, Rachael feels something of this has happened
to her:

I think one of the nicest compliments I had was, yes I was a
nice teacher but boy could I give a shout, could I be mean ... I
think they like that ... they know where they stand.

(Rachael)

It is nice to be 'mean' for good reason, and it is essentially relational,
gifted by pupils as well as actively sought by new-teacher 'trial and
error'. For Rachael and others who achieved it, the transformation is essentially about establishing a relationship over time, but
also includes particular actions and tactics, culled from a variety
of sources, including 'tips' or observations of colleagues (from
clapping hands for attention, standing on a chair in a crowded
laboratory, chatting on school trips, lunchtimes, in school clubs,
notes to parents, use of detention time, and so on). There are such
things to learn and try out, in an overall context of extended contact, and involving past inspiration, gradually formed reputation
and renewed commitment.

Such a seemingly paradoxical combination, desirable/undesir-
able and accomplished/gifted, does not lend itself to a discourse
of standards, yet it is meaningful in new-teacher narratives. Fixed
acquisition of competence cannot be assumed:

I think it's up and down, that's day-to-day, not even week-to-
week.

(Shabana, E)

I thought all kids are the same, they're not, [they're] all totally
different, what will work for one child will not work for
another.

(Ann)

The emotional economy is not one of fixed exchanges when pupils 'come in with different moods', and with one class a 'friendly face' can be worn and the next 'the visor goes up'.

Proofing, proving and the teacher self

Becoming both 'nice and strict' seems to involve a process of emotional labour, especially learning to proof the self against an initial vulnerability:

> It is a very challenging school ... for example a boy threw a chair at another boy ... but – ha! Almost now that doesn't shock me any more ... I deal with it.
>
> (Anna, E)

> I don't take things personally any more ... . I can just step back, think about the situation, analyse it and think about how I am going to deal with it.
>
> (Lewis)

Emotional responses can become objects of reflection, then turned outwards to link with other kinds of knowledge, such as knowing how to make use of school discipline procedures or developing personal classroom practices. Both aspects become intrinsic not only to a new competence to deal with the initial upset, but a new emotional quality, a growing confidence.

Becoming more 'relaxed', 'resilient' and 'confident' were important to early professional learners, as they countered certain 'dark emotions' of fear, shock, dislike, and self-doubt (Winograd 2003). Yet other 'light' emotions may need to be nurtured rather than overcome:

> obviously day-to-day things get you down and you think 'Ohh I shouldn't be here, and I shouldn't be teaching' but I enjoy what I do ... I see kids getting something out of what I do ... it just sort of blocks everything else out and fills up the holes.
>
> (Frances, E)

There is a renegotiated emotional economy here, in which some occasional rewards are linked to a sustained and renewed commitment which serves to 'block everything else out' – at least until the next time. If the completely proofed teacher is suspected as illusory, then some legitimate doubting might be incorporated into the teacher self:

> No you wouldn't be a good teacher if you didn't have the doubts, because if you become complacent I don't think you teach to your ability.
>
> (Frances, E)

There was some comfort in seeing that more experienced teachers might have problems as well as inspirational qualities. What was important was dealing with the practical and emotional aspects of this, not pretending they do not exist. Although nobody sought incompetence, lengthy lists of competences as implicitly exhaustive and exclusive of conflict and tensions do not ring true to the process of becoming a teacher. Indeed, rather than always measuring themselves against experienced colleagues, some new teachers regarded contacts with recently qualified teachers, fresh from similar experiences, as valuable to their own learning.

The following extract highlights the learning potential of risk and failure, with the emotional in relation to cognitive development, especially here in its pedagogic aspect:

> I've also taken a few risks in class, like my colouring the protoplast synthesis day when I did these cartoons [...] I put the overhead up and I remember going bright red and feeling so nervous and thinking either this will succeed or fail in an absolute ... you know foulest [manner] and everything. And it succeeded so well and because I had taken that wee risk and shown your personality a bit, then they really respond to that ... . And it's learning to experiment and to have the confidence to fail and that's okay and actually the kids warm to you. And I think that's the main way I have learned anything since I've come.
>
> (Avril)

Avril's reference to developing 'confidence' is another recurrent aspect of new-teacher emotionality, and it seems to be fuelled or depleted in many ways, some seemingly trivial, some major, and related both to formal and other aspects of induction. Avril's account of her introducing what she termed the 'the magic ingredient' of personal feelings and learning style into her pedagogy clearly relates both to the EPL and SFR models. Examples from the

SFR competences include: development of pedagogic techniques, use of different media, adaptation of communication style to her pupils as well as a commitment to learning and reflective practice/self-evaluation. She admitted however that she found the SFR 'an incredibly dull read' and only used it retrospectively when profiling herself to see 'where it fitted in' (and despite having instanced her proactive use of it to develop ICT competence).

It is clear that the gap between how new teachers talked about their learning experiences and how they were presented in standards documents cannot be relied upon to spontaneously bridge itself, even in relation to an event with apparent relevance to both discourses. It is also important to note that new-teacher narratives themselves do not necessarily guarantee a productive link between emotions, or any other dimensions, and the possibilities for learning. This is clear in the following account from Shreya, in which she comments on what happened when she had been to fetch her induction tutor (Rose) to help her with a troublesome class:

> I can't remember what she did or said but they'll listen to Rose because she's been here a while, not only because she's senior, because she's lovely and they like her and they've probably got that sort of relationship with her ... they know that she's nice and they know that if they get on the wrong side of her, god help you. So it's just about that. I see that class twice a week, once on a Friday, period five, I'm knackered, they're knackered. See I don't think it's individual kids, they're just a problem together, they're not rude or anything, not horrible to me, they just don't listen. I was thinking 'I've done this and I've done this' and I just thought 'I'm going to cry in a minute, I'm not staying here'.
>
> (Shreya, E)

The model in Shreya's account here is quite complicated: it includes the structural (e.g. timetabling, Rose's status), the relational (e.g. 'strict–nice' relationship), the temporal (e.g. 'been here a while', 'twice a week'), the cognitive (e.g. thinking 'I've done this') and the emotional. However, for her nothing of this analytic breakdown implies anything she could learn from and this characterized her reflections on a stressful year for her. Shreya was the only new teacher in the EPL cohort who failed the induction year (she was offered a deferment but left shortly into the new term).

Conclusion

As with all the new teachers quoted from here, there was a wider biographical backstory to the outcome for Shreya. The point here is that no model of early professional learning of itself, whether implicit in new-teacher discourse, or more explicit in academic or formal policy proposals, will necessarily lead to learning unless it is seen as a resource for further dialogue and action. This involves an interplay between individual, institutional and national policy factors. The role of others is crucial in this: 'it all depends on how it is used' (new teacher). No policy can fully standardize the variations encountered by new teachers, whether at the level of individual colleagues, the department, the school, the catchment area or the LEA. New teachers commented on the significance of changes they experienced in all of these, or made comparisons with peers in other contexts, either celebrating or lamenting their luck of the draw. They were all working to, and being assessed by, the same set of competences, but there was a double refraction at play here: the first is that of the particular priorities for new teachers, and the second the contextual mix they encountered in their particular cases. For new teachers, the contexts in which they found themselves were the first crucial 'enhancements' for competence development.

Both SFR and EPL project models have something to offer, though the claim here is that the latter's grounding in new-teacher discourse offers something distinctively closer to their stage-critical priorities. These are largely to do with processes of getting to know and be known by pupils, initially to establish discipline, and later to improve pedagogy. Developing 'confidence' and 'reputation' are seen as intrinsic outcomes, the emotional underpinning of which seems to be a matter of proofing, of becoming less emotionally reactive in one sense, by being 'more resilient' and 'taking things less personally', while in another sense, fostering and sustaining personally felt commitments to pupils and learning. Such emphases and processes are also more in tune with the important way the induction year is not simply a narrative of triumphs and the SFR's relentless linearity of consolidation, extension and addition, but is also about fear of failure, the risk of trial and error and self-exposure, as well as the precariousness and unpredictability of working in classrooms. A second kind of enhancement then is the way in which new teachers felt their priorities were recognized and catered for in competence development.

As Barbelet says (in Day *et al.* 2006: 613), 'without the emotions category, accounts of situated actions would be fragmentary and incomplete'. The importance of emotions is not to contain within the individual whatever they signal, but to acknowledge them wherever it is felt they can contribute to new-teacher learning. Such learning is highly context dependent. The emphasis here has been to see this as an argument for the inclusion but not the dominance of the emotional in early professional learning, for this chapter has also sought to emphasize a multiple constitutive flow not just between various dimensions, but also between the particulars of accounts and more holistic judgements about what really matters ('the main way I've learned'). These features are seen as enhancing discretely analysable items, whether as 'standard' competences or more broadly drawn EPL dimensions. The SFR competences do not need adding to. They do relate to the accounts of new teachers in the EPL data, but the latter expresses and prioritizes them differently, seeking constantly to connect as well as atomize, and to see them as partial, contingent and precarious rather than as totally embedded. A third 'enhancement' concerns the degree to which dimensions such as the emotional and relational are drawn on where appropriate to learning, including the way they may be linked to more formally expressed competences.

What's more, some of the learning that has taken place has engaged with 'dark emotions' and negative aspects of relationships and circumstances, often kept hidden from formal procedures and assessments. The quality of support offered by some colleagues, family, friends and peers has been crucial here. This is a fourth form of enhancement in becoming a teacher. The quality of the teacher-researcher and new-teacher relationship has been important here in creating a context in which certain kinds of things could be said. Although this cannot be entirely reproduced within the formal induction process, not least because it avoided the tension between assessment and development, new teachers did comment on whether the formal process 'gave me a person' (Nadine, E) or someone less committed to the personal and developmental aspects of the role. This calls on a high level of skill and judgement on the part of those with formal roles in the induction process, and is a crucial element in the degree to which competences might be seen as 'enhanced'.

References

Ashforth, B. E. and Humphrey, R. H. (1993) 'Emotional labor in service roles: the influence of identity', *Academy of Management Review*, 18:88–115.

Bullough, R. V. and Young, J. (2002) 'Learning to teach as an intern: the emotions and the self', *Teacher Development*, 6:417–31.

Burman, E. (2005) 'Beyond emotional literacy in feminist research', paper presented at the ESRC/TLRP/RCBN Seminar: The Educational Future and Innovative and International Research: International Perspectives, Manchester Metropolitan University.

Burman, E. (2006) 'Emotions and reflexivity in feminised action research', *Educational Action Research*, 14:315–32.

Day, C. (2004) *A Passion for Teaching*, London: RoutledgeFalmer.

Day, C., Kingston, A., Stobart, G. and Sammons, P. (2006) 'The personal and professional selves of teachers: stable and unstable identities', *British Educational Research Journal*, 42:601–16.

Ecclestone, K. (2007) 'All in the mind', *Education Guardian*, 27.02.07:1–2.

Golby, M. (1996) 'Teachers' emotions: an illustrated discussion', *Cambridge Journal of Education*, 26:423–34.

Goleman, D. P. (1995) *Emotional Intelligence: Why it can Matter More than IQ for Character, Health and Lifelong Achievement*, New York: Bantam Books.

GTCS (2002) *The Standard for Full Registration*, Edinburgh: GTC Scotland.

Hargreaves, A. (1998) 'The emotional practice of teaching', *Teaching and Teacher Education*, 14:835–54.

Hartley, D. (2004) 'Management, leadership and the emotional order of the school', *Journal of Education Policy*, 19:583–94.

Hayes, D. (2003) 'New labour, new professionalism' in J. Satterthwaite, E. Atkinson and K. Gale (eds) *Discourse, Power and Resistance: Challenging the Rhetoric of Contemporary Education*, Stoke: Trentham Books.

Hochschild, A. R. (1983) *The Managed Heart: Commercialization of Human Feeling*, Berkeley: University of California Press.

Kelchtermans, G. (1996) 'Teacher vulnerability: understanding its moral and political roots', *Cambridge Journal of Education*, 26:307–23.

McCrone Report (2000) *A Teaching Profession for the 21st Century: The Report of the Committee of Inquiry into Professional Conditions of Service for Teachers*, Edinburgh: SEED.

McNally, J. (2001) *The Induction of New Teachers in Scotland: A Report for the General Teaching Council of Scotland*, Edinburgh: GTC Scotland.

McWilliam, E. (1996) 'Admitting impediments: or things to do with bodies in the classroom', *Cambridge Journal of Education*, 26(3):367–78.

Nias, J. (1986) 'What it is to feel like a teacher', paper presented at the symposium: Becoming and Being a Teacher, BERA Conference, Bristol.

Nias, J. (1996) 'Thinking about feeling: the emotions and teaching', *Cambridge Journal of Education*, 26:293–306.

Salzberger-Wittenberg, I., Henry, G. and Osborne, E. (1983) *The Emotional Experience of Teaching*, London: Routledge & Kegan Paul.

Schmidt, M. and Datnow, A. (2005) 'Teachers' sense-making about comprehensive school reforms', *Teaching and Teacher Education*, 21:949–63.

Smithers, A. and Robinson, P. (2003) *Factors Affecting Teachers' Decisions to Leave the Profession*, Nottingham: DfES.

Stronach, I., Corbin, B., McNamara, O., Stark, S. and Warne, T. (2002) 'Towards an uncertain politics of professionalism: teacher and nurse identities in flux', *Journal of Educational Policy*, 17:109–38.

TTA (2002) *Qualifying to Teach (Professional Standards for Qualified Teacher Status and Requirements for Initial Teacher Training)*, London: DfES.

Winograd, K. (2003) 'The functions of teacher emotions: the good, the bad and the ugly', *Teachers College Record*, 105:1641–73.

Woods, P. and Jeffrey, R. (1996) *Teachable Moments: The Art of Teaching in Primary School*, Buckingham: Open University Press.

Zembylas, M. (2003) 'Emotions and teacher identity: a poststructuralist perspective', *Teachers and Teaching: Theory and Practice*, 9:213–38.

Chapter 5

Who can you count on?
The relational dimension of new-teacher learning

Jim McNally

Introduction

The social dimension of human development is nothing new. Even in a professional context, we accept that our relationships with other people matter. We know from experience that this is the case but the importance of the social in professional development is also well supported in the literature, often it seems from a need to strike a balance against models that are overly cognitive in emphasis. Even our small-scale initial explorations into the experience of beginners in teaching revealed the prominent place in that experience of relationships with others. Although no straightforward link to any specific kinds of learning were apparent, it was evident that interaction with others was nevertheless central and this empirical position was represented more accurately as 'relational' rather than as social, a term often seen as rather amorphous and unconvincing to the more clinically inclined. The relational or social conveys, it seems, a more 'informal' sense of learning, something that is not reducible to the strictly rational and predictable, or indeed cognitive, connecting instead to the emotions as well as the processes and stages of identity formation. This chapter presents our extended exploration of the relational, its connection to the emotions and what it means in the context of beginning teaching: the people, their roles, informal learning and what ties it to identity and purpose.

Informal learning

The fundamental question of the research prior to and during the project was to reach a deeper understanding of what and how beginning teachers learned. It was clear from earlier studies that there was much more going on in the experience of becoming a teacher than was being caught by competence-based standards (McNally *et al.* 1994) and formal structures of support such as appointed mentors (McNally 1994). The notion of informal learning served to open up a much wider sense of what that learning might be. It was a tentative term that served its purpose as an initial conceptual base but one that has received more explicit recognition in recent years (Coffield 2000; Eraut 2004). We know that much of what teachers know and do is tacit and is not easily caught by an observer or interviewer. Teachers themselves, as with many other professional contexts (Schön 1987), are rarely able to explain their expertise or how it developed. According to Rachael, for example, her mentor 'just has to walk in[to] a room and silence descends ... he admitted he doesn't know how he does it. So I just hope one day that will happen to me'. Is it surprising to think therefore, that whatever is learned from veterans by the neophyte in teaching may not be consciously acquired? 'I don't think it's a conscious thing but I do believe that I've picked up skills of ... of, eh ... of being settled quicker, getting to know the kids quicker and things like that' (Ann). For the researcher as well, it is a process that eludes easy understanding, or articulation.

Eraut's (2000) work has helped to elevate informal learning above its misconstrual as some kind of casual and incidental, peripheral process. As we are not yet clear on what is actually being learned informally by new teachers, it is perhaps too early to know whether Eraut's theorization, his typology of implicit, reactive and deliberative learning, and the distinction between informal and non-formal can illuminate understanding. Our particular description of the early learning of teachers does not readily belong to any categorizations that stem from attempts to circumscribe and define what is informal and what is not. Though our attempts to impose some clarity of definition do at least recognize that crucial learning takes place in ways that would not be described as formal, or simply (that is unthinkingly or dispassionately) cognitive.

Our use of informal includes both the everyday and the structured and is consistent with the notion of informal education as interactions with friends, family and work colleagues. The review of informal education espoused by Smith (2009) does suggest features that would find support from our earlier data: the range of opportunities for learning that arise in everyday settings; the importance of relationships; people's experiences and feelings; and probably the central form of conversation. His review also indicates that such informality has a purpose: running through it is a concern to build the sorts of communities and relationships in which people can be happy and fulfilled. The everyday lives of new teachers in schools have this implicit essence of purpose, highlighting the relational within the informal.

Informal learning may, of course, have different meanings in different contexts; for example, lifelong learning, workplace learning, organizational learning and other professions. Although our use of the term emerged in grounded theory as a counterpoint to the formal, there was no intention of generalization or claim for parity of status across all learning contexts. In learning a new language or specific craft skills, for example, it is acknowledged that the support of a formal structure is superior to more informal experiences. Whatever the balance may be in different contexts, the extensive study of informal learning in the workplace by Eraut (2004: 255) concludes that 'relationships play a critical role in workplace learning'.

Studies that focus on the impact of induction programmes, as in, for example, the recent systematic review by Totterdell et al. (2004), tend to systematically exclude informal learning. According to Gorard et al. (1999), informal learning has been neglected in official policy statements and standards in the field of lifelong learning too, and also in the narrow definitions of learning present in literature on the same. There appears, however, to be a weight of evidence supporting a strong informal, social or relational dimension in workplace learning. The informal learning of new teachers in school may be seen as a specific illustration of this. It is intimately linked with relationships. Indeed Lohman (2000) has suggested that an environment that hinders such informal engagement actually serves as an inhibitor to learning. It is a claim that finds further support from philosophical fundamentals, for example in friendship and the formation of human bonds (Almond 1988; White 1990), which are seen as universally important, especially in new situations where we are individually more vulnerable.

Relationships with pupils

The informal and relational are also imbued with the emotional. Early evidence showed that 'affective engagement with colleagues and classes taught was of paramount importance' (McNally *et al.* 1997: 486), and a number of commentaries by the project's teacher-researchers contained fresh examples:

> The week before school started Rachael felt nervous of the unknown [...] The probationers' day, the week before school started, was when reality set in and she felt nervous, very nervous. Apparently others felt the same. On the in-service day at school she felt more relaxed but on the pupils' first day she had never been so nervous in all her life. She couldn't stop it and the more she worried the more nervous she felt. By Thursday the feeling of physical sickness had gone and being here began to feel like her job [...] She has been pleased at the pupils' response to her lessons and she liked being recognized by them in the corridors. One other aim this year is to build up relationships with her pupils and to learn about their family networks within the school.

> Over the summer Linda thought about her classes a lot. What if they are really bad? What if I can't control them? What if I feel horrible about myself? Can I handle classes?

> Ann described her first week as a 'roller coaster' and 'bizarre' experience. She had half expected it to be like a student placement but it was so different because they are 'your classes'. As a student 'you knew you could hand them back' [...] Already she feels torn between the good pupils and the more challenging ones. She can see she's spending more time with a minority in some classes. She has been waking up at two or three in the morning thinking about the quieter pupils she hasn't spoken to.

Within this last emotional response to 'her classes', we do see early signs in Ann of a cognitive dimension in her learning. The recognition of difference within her class – between the good and the challenging and on time spent with the quieter pupils – tends to be the main indication of cognitive development across some of the narratives. This is no simplistic application of theory, though we might infer awareness of a concept of differentiation and related approaches, but a sense of actual difference needs to be considered and that stems from the fundamental nature of an inevitable and even deep-seated relational engagement.

Extreme feelings can clearly take the form of anxious anticipation before the job has even started. This arises mainly from what defines the job – the pupils in the classes actually taught by the new teacher – and whether it is being done well enough. The answer tends to lie in how the same pupils respond, both in and out of class. Rachael, for example, has been pleased at the pupils' response to her lessons and she liked being recognized by them in the corridors, and her aim is to continue to build up relationships with them. For some, this defining experience is associated with a sense of whether they will be able to do the job. For Ann at least, any such doubts have been resolved within the first week or two:

> After the first day she felt like not coming back and thought to her self 'What have I done?' But the week got better and better. Now she is learning names […] After her first observed lesson during which four boys had dominated the class, Ann felt 'pretty disheartened about the whole thing'. By the following week she wasn't so totally disheartened because she realized there were lots of strategies to try. She now felt she had most of the class with her […] She felt as if it wasn't a 'brick wall', and if she could turn round two pupils it would be a good class and she would be happier.

For another beginner, the doubt was gone, so it appears, on the first day:

> [My concerns were] mostly dispelled, a positive first day. The pupils responded well to my personal style, which includes humour! When I met my classes they were friendly and respectful and I was able to have a laugh with them without them taking advantage. Some tried it on a bit to see how the new teacher would react but they were left in no doubt that I was in charge and they accepted that.

The emotional nature of the starting phase stems from the concern about whether a working relationship can be established in the classroom. This concern is not exclusively about controlling pupil behaviour. It is a more complex question of acceptance by them as their teacher and of being recognized as such.

Early professional learning involves often uneasy and fragile moves from the unregarded stranger to acceptance (or not) as a 'proper' teacher. The acceptance is layered, perhaps beginning with a recognition that the newcomer is here to stay:

> Once they realized that I was here to stay, the atmosphere changed quite considerably, they actually started listening to what I had to say.

Relationship building takes time, and it is needed to solve discipline problems. Disciplinary action, on the other hand, can inhibit relationship building. Over time, the teacher usually gains a 'reputation', and learns to square the circle of discipline and pedagogy:

> It is quite strange. You think you are making progress in terms of relationship building and then something happens and a spanner is thrown in the works. It happened to me today with one of my classes. I was quite shocked by their behaviour, you know, and the way they had spoken to me and I thought I had developed a relationship of respect, you know, and it turned out two or three people didn't have quite the same idea on relationship.

> If you are good at teaching your subject you won't have behaviour problems though behaviour management has been my priority first term, hoping that next term I really want to focus on the subject and how I'm delivering the subject.

Such 'reputations' are not so much a matter of strictness or friendliness or the elusive balance between these as a more cumulative getting-to-know the other.

> And they see you [in the corridor] and say 'Oh miss' and they start telling you stuff and that's really useful because when you see them in the lesson they know you've taken an interest in them outside of the classroom and you can have more of a relationship with them.

> I think the longer you are here the more of a reputation you get, not like, 'Oh yeah, sir's really strict' or whatever. I think it's more as a, you know, a teacher, not just a supply.

Like the example of Rachael's mentor, who 'doesn't know how he does it', this point possibly indicates the limits of the usefulness of 'observation' of experienced and competent teachers. The 'discipline' question was less often a matter of where to go or what to do, but of how to get there. And that was a puzzling invisibility in any and all observation.

Nor is the situation totally informal, it should be said. There is a formal structure in which the experience takes place and which necessarily requires learning to happen: the timetable of classes, for example, and lesson planning. The formal-informal distinction may not even be helpful in understanding what is happening. What is clear is that the experience is largely affective in nature and explicit examples of learning – other than learning that one is becoming accepted – are generally absent from new teachers' accounts. As we suggest in our discussion of the cognitive dimension in Chapter 7, while it is reasonable to suppose that new teachers are learning in the sense of developing their competence in classroom management skills and curriculum knowledge, and so on, evidence of this in any explicit terms is hard to elicit. Rather, it is as if the cognitive is taken as being less problematic, or somehow predictable, and therefore rarely mentioned, or (as in the example of the teacher above who hopes to focus on his subject next term) deferred in the face of the considerable demand in the emotional domain. It is within the prominence of the relational in the data that we find affirmation of our findings from Eraut (2004) who claims that the emotional dimension of professional work is much more significant than is often recognized. Hargreaves (1998) too, sees the emotions of teaching as not just a sentimental adornment but as fundamental in and of themselves.

Relationships with colleagues

If relationships with pupils are definitively important, then so too are those with colleagues at this early stage. The feeling of having support at hand is of enormous importance, both from individuals and in a collective sense, as in staffrooms, for example:

> Going up to the staffroom at interval and lunchtime was a double-edged situation. Rachael knew it was a good way of getting to know people and hearing about what was going on but she also felt the need to be ready for her classes and there was planning to do.

Such experience describes a 'socio-professional context' within which the individual text of the new teacher's development itself begins to appear. This could be viewed as a dynamic kind of equilibrium, the balance shifting between solitary reflection and practice and a strongly felt need for the support of others. Disequilibrium could occur at the extremes of total abandonment to one's own resources or a rigidly controlled, stifling support. In one case a principal teacher (PT) had given out his home telephone number and, in another, the new teacher had been taken 'under the wing' of a colleague:

> I had been nervous and not sleeping well. The PT had given me his home phone number so I called him on Monday night. He put me completely at ease. I felt he was friendly and supportive. I still didn't sleep well but felt more relaxed about my first day.

> Great atmosphere in the school department and classroom – one teacher has taken me under her wing and is very supportive. At the end of the day I was relaxed and very positive about the future. One big help had been that the department were friendly and helpful.

It is often the case in schools that there is a natural mentoring of the beginner that involves a few people, typically from the department, but sometimes a supportive relationship can be struck up with a teacher from elsewhere in the school. Other beginners, or recent entrants, whatever their department (for secondary) or stage (for primary), are often significant players as mutual peer mentors within a more or less general mentoring environment within the school as a whole.

> Linda had been out for lunch with another probationer and some of this probationer's department. It had been reassuring when they had said that they hadn't heard her voice carrying into the corridor. She had worried about how she could meet people on the staff when she worked in a two-person department. She felt awkward about sitting down somewhere in the staffroom.

Linda's experience corresponds with those who have found

teacher development to be intimately dependent on relationships. Hargreaves (1992: 217), for example, states that:

> The way teachers relate to their colleagues has profound implications for their classroom teaching, how they evolve and develop as teachers and the sorts of teachers they become [...] what goes on in a teacher's classroom cannot be divorced from the relations that are forged outside it.

Yet it is perhaps when a significant relationship does not work so well that the importance of the relational is most emphatic:

> As we put it, we feel over-supported; I mean it is good to have the support but when you are over-supported in everything ...
>
> (Gavin)

> [...] I feel like I am still a student quite frankly, that is how I feel [...] Every single class I take is getting checked up on, you know, she [the appointed mentor] is popping in, or she is asking me about it later on or she has heard me shouting and she wants to know who I shouted at and why I didn't give them a punishment exercise.
>
> (Katie)

Again, we find ourselves in agreement with Eraut's (2004) observation that informal support from people on the spot tends to be more important for learning than that from formally designated helpers or mentors. This may be the case even in a school that is 'very good at doing the mentoring. We have three hours of it a week which is quite a lot ... but maybe I am inherently cautious, I wouldn't necessarily reveal everything about what I am feeling to anybody' (Laura). It is a point also made by Gavin, whose appointed mentor is a departmental colleague, meaning that there are 'times that you find you cannot approach her to [...] talk things through. I feel a mentor should be someone not within that department so that you can feel as if you can go and chat to them'.

As we have suggested, the narrative evidence is permeated with the relational; indeed even those questions that probe for more specific learning often tend to lead back to the relational and its affective impact:

Interviewer	Can you think of any other situations or anything else where you think I definitely learned something or I've changed because I've learned something?
Linda	I was just thinking about the way I put things across. I've learnt not to be quite so harsh […] and now I'm starting to learn to ease up slightly […] Before I thought you've got to be on task 24/7 you're not allowed to stop working or chat about something […]. They've [classes] shown me, well, yes we can actually be better; we get more work done if we know we can speak to you about something that isn't the subject right now.

I guess I learnt a few things, simple things, I guess cumulatively just walking past some of my colleagues' doors […] nipping in to pick up a book, you learn a lot of things that way, a lot of how other teachers conduct themselves […] I was at the photocopier and doing some work and I was chatting away to an English teacher [who had] overheard a conversation I was having with another probationer about some particular boys in my class giving me trouble […] she said, 'Don't worry about it, I've been teaching for 45 years or whatever and they are one of the worst [classes] I've ever seen in my career', and it was just so reassuring and made me feel so much better to have somebody like that with so much experience just to say, 'Don't worry about it. It's not you' […] I guess I've learnt that you should share these things with everyone cause I think everyone feels these things about behaviour at sometime or another.

(Ann)

'*Ad hoc* interaction' within subject departments and conversations in staffrooms and bases appear then to mean as much to beginners as planned events, such as the observation of experienced teachers. It is evident that beginners learn about teaching in indirect ways and, in a much wider sense, through contact with teachers as persons outside the classroom. And in the example of Ann especially, we can see the demand in the emotional domain for that spontaneous, informal, personal interaction between teachers that occurs 'mainly in the interstices of school life; in the corridor conversations and exchanged glances that weld teachers and their school together in a working community' (Hargreaves 1992: 233).

Indicators of interaction

We were mindful in designing the EPL project of the accusation often levelled at educational research, that it is too often based on soft data. As well as probing deeply into an area of professional learning and exploring more innovatively the somewhat well-trodden qualitative route to understanding, we also incorporated a quantitative element. The relational was therefore operational-ized as INTERACT, one of the project's five quantitative indicators of new-teacher performance. This indicator (discussed at greater length in Chapter 10) provided a fairly rudimentary but nonetheless persuasive indication of the extent to which relationships count. It showed the range of relationships with others within which the interactions of new teachers took place, their general order of importance and also in what ways they were important. Briefly, the results tended to reflect the significance to new teachers of the affective domain in their relationships with pupils and fellow teachers more so than with mentors and line managers.

If you look hard enough at relationships, of course, you may be likely to discover their importance. Hence, we reiterate, INTERACT was developed because of the dominance of the relational theme in the project's early narrative data. But the place of relationality is not confined solely to INTERACT and the corroborating data here. For example, the statistical analysis of our job satisfaction instrument in Chapter 8 identifies the main source of job satisfaction among new teachers as being relational in nature. A further telling statistic reveals that as much as 41 per cent of the variation in new teachers' overall job satisfaction is attributable to their working relationships with colleagues in the same departments ($\rho = 0.642$, $p<0.01$, N $= 29$).

The importance of teacher-pupil relationships was likewise suggested by the statistical analysis of the project's classroom environment survey. The components of classroom experience that emerged from the exploratory factor analysis of these results (using principal component analysis[1]) can be summarized as follows: quality of teaching-relationships; quality of teaching-explanation; pupil engagement; pupil cooperation; equity/fairness. The personal qualities of teachers expressed through their interaction with pupils came out as the most significant aspect of the classroom environ-ment. That is to say, quality of teaching relationships accounted for 31.4 per cent of the 49 per cent of the variance in the results that could be explained by the five components, and included such survey variables as 'the teacher makes lessons interesting', 'the teacher makes lessons fun', 'the teacher knows the class well' and 'the teacher knows my name'.

A relational self-as-teacher identity

It is clear that the support that new teachers need cannot be confined to the conventional epistemological base of subject knowledge, pedagogical content knowledge, localized information, and so on. There is a considerable need or demand in the emotional domain, met through a range of different persons and roles in a variety of relationships. The indication from INTERACT, within the EPL sample, is that out of 236 recorded conversations with colleagues, new teachers felt better as a result on 43 per cent (N = 102) of occasions. This kind of broad psychosocial support (Jacobi 1991) stems from the intrinsic emotional nature of the experience. It is also consistent with the key role of emotions in the construction of identity (Zembylas 2003). We have indeed tended within the project to refer to the 'emotional-relational dimension' of early professional learning (McNally *et al.* 2008) as they are often intertwined or inseparable in a given interaction. Barbalet (2002: 4) too, writes about emotion as 'a necessary link between social structure and social actor', that 'without the emotions category, accounts of situated actions would be fragmentary and incomplete'. The interactions of new teachers (as actors) support and illustrate this view.

There is then a need to think beyond the conventional epistemological constraints of a knowledge and skills base in understanding the experience of new teachers, and to acknowledge this in their preparation in courses of initial teacher education. Without taking the argument too far into an ontological case, analysis of the indicator and interview data does reveal a complexity of support and interpersonal interactions that raises questions of insecurity, vulnerability and uncertainty. These are, it appears, ineluctably experienced by new teachers.

New teachers are aware they are changing as persons. This is partly caught in their interactions with significant others:

> I've got into trouble from my mum because I used the tone and words I would use to the pupils like, 'Stop speaking to me like that'. And she just looked at me and said, 'You're not a teacher

here'. And I said, 'What?' because I didn't realize I was doing it and my boyfriend's always on at me saying 'stop treating me like one of your pupils'.

The kind of development or learning which is taking place is clearly transformational and so, grounded in the narrative data, is a strong sense of identity formation. This is validated further by theories of learning that recognize transformation. Illeris (2004: 84), for example, acknowledges the presence of:

> a far-reaching type of learning, implying what could be termed *personality change* and characterised by simultaneous restructuring in the cognitive, the emotional, and the social dimensions. This typically occurs as the result of a crisis-like situation caused by challenges experienced as urgent and unavoidable. Such processes have traditionally not been conceived of as learning, but they are well known in the field of psychotherapy, right back to the Freudian concept of catharsis.

This sense of a changing self permeates the narratives and is consistent with the equation of the development of self and identity to learning as an inherently emotional process embedded within a relational context (Bosma and Kunnen 2001). In exploring the place of 'self' in connection to relationality (based on the view that the narratives in themselves are powerful individual entities as well as data for thematic analysis), there is support for the concept of 'biographicity' (Alheit and Dausien 1999), the capacity that people have that could not be taught by experts and their uniqueness as a resource for building new relationships:

Ann	I was someone who liked to socialize at parties and things like that. Now I kind of feel, not past it … it's hard to put into words how I feel about it. I kind of feel like I shouldn't be doing it because I've got this respectable job but kind of … I don't know, I feel I should be somebody the kids can look up to. Conduct myself in a way that is respectful.
Interviewer	Like you're teaching all the time by the way you behave, by the way you do things?
Ann	I do feel like a teacher all of the time. I feel like a teacher at the weekends, I feel like a teacher during

the holidays. You know because of the way you got to conduct yourself. It's a bit daft really because your job and your life should be separate but this is a unique job.

Relationality is therefore more than some warm, vague notion of idle friendliness in the workplace. Hinchliffe (2004), for example, argues that there is an ethical nexus inscribed in relations with others in the workplace, that this is inescapable and bound up with technical skills and, furthermore, that it is important for human flourishing and for the quality of work that is done. And why else would Ann come awake in the early hours 'thinking about the quieter pupils she hasn't spoken to'?

Our concept of relationality extends to a strong sense of mutuality. The 'pure relationship' is one that depends on mutual trust (Giddens 1991) and it is possible to idealize teacher-pupil interdependence as a pure relationship. Giddens writes of the ontological security pupils gain through relationships with their teachers. Yet it is clear new teachers are dependent on their pupils for a sense of professional purpose, for their very acceptance as a teacher. The interdependence in this early stage of development is, therefore, one of reciprocal ontological security. We would suggest that this interdependent mutuality is fundamental to the new teachers' experience, to their forming an identity as a teacher, and it transcends the meeting of a professional 'standard'.

Self is thus in the data. It is a mightily contested concept, of course, but our grounded concept resonates with the 'relational self' (Schibbye 2002). This conveys a sense of agency and purpose that is consistent with our data – a self that is intrinsically dependent on pupils and colleagues and others for its emergence and expression. As one principal teacher that we interviewed explained:

> Good teachers are very good at interpersonal skills. We manage very often 20 to 30 other individuals every hour. It's a very unique job and sometimes we don't get a chance to stop and reflect on how unique it is. The interpersonal skill thing is not just between teacher and pupil. It can be between teacher and teacher [... it] can be a huge stumbling block if you get somebody who thinks they can just ride roughshod over everybody.

Bakhtin's (Holquist 1990) philosophy is that 'self' can never be a self-sufficient construct and he emphasizes particularity and situatedness, arguing that abstract questions about selfhood can only be pursued as specific questions about location. The scope of this chapter and the book as a whole limits discussion of these philosophical connections and so we can only recommend them as worthy of further reading in relation to this and perhaps other contexts of professional learning.

Even though our research findings probably belong in a fairly long tradition of teacher learning and becoming (e.g. Lortie 1975), it is not until recently that the relational and informal (and emotional) have resurfaced as crucial to early professional development. Smith (2009) recognizes a purpose in informal learning that is a concern to build the sorts of communities in which people can be happy and fulfilled. Straka (2004), however, has cautioned that informal learning is a problematic term suffering from a lack of systematically and empirically grounded valid evidence – a challenge that this project has sought to address. In identifying dimensional themes from typically integrated experiences, our year-long tracking of new teachers has revealed that the dimensions change in intensity over time and in relation to context, and this multidimensionality of professional learning is key to understanding identity formation in the beginner: a fundamental process that incorporates relationality, emotionality and a sense of a changing self. Perhaps no illustration is more graphic than this valedictory catharsis by email to one of the project's teacher-researchers:

Hi Phil

Thanks for the e-mail and sorry for the delay in the reply – life has been pretty hectic recently. I have been busy finishing work on a flat that needed gutted and have bought another one as well as settled into a new job. Lochside is 100 per cent better than Eastmuir. At least you can teach and the PT is pleasant which makes all the difference. I have a nice interactive board – no more chalk that you have to lick! My room was also painted over the holidays and so I have been able to put out all the artefacts and posters that I would never have risked putting out in Eastmuir.

As far as keeping in touch with anybody from there – I don't see anybody except Kat, the geography probationer, who almost left teaching but is now having a much better experience at another school and so is giving it another go. I also hear from some in the learning support department now and again. It certainly wasn't a sad day when I left. As soon as the bell went I had all my belongings already packed in the car and I was out of there within two minutes.

Last year I had a dreadful skin rash and that has now completely gone so I am sure it was the stress of Irene (my PT) that caused it. Since leaving, I have only had one nightmare about her – I'm afraid it has been a recurring nightmare, which involves me running her down and I always wake up when she is spread out over the windscreen!!! I have to laugh at it really. She was a very insecure lady.

Anyway, I hope all is well with you. Are you doing the surveys again this year with the probationers?

Garibaldi

References

Alheit, P. and Dausien, B. (1999) '"Biographicity" as a basic resource of lifelong learning,' paper presented at the European Conference on Lifelong Learning, University of Bremen.

Almond, B. (1988) 'Human bonds', *Journal of Applied Philosophy*, 5:3–16.

Barbalet, J. (2002) 'Introduction: why emotions are crucial' in J. Barbalet (ed.) *Emotional Sociology*, London: Blackwell.

Bosma, H. A. and Kunnen, E. S. (2001) *Identity and Emotion*, Cambridge: Cambridge University Press.

Coffield, F. (ed.) (2000) *The Necessity of Informal Learning*, ESRC report, Bristol: Policy Press.

Eraut, M. (2000) 'Non-formal learning, implicit knowledge and tacit knowledge in professional work' in F. Coffield (ed.) *The Necessity of Informal Learning*, ESRC report, Bristol: Policy Press.

Eraut, M. (2004) 'Informal learning in the workplace', *Studies in Continuing Education*, 26:247–73.

Giddens, A. (1991) *Modernity and Self-Identity*, Cambridge: Polity Press.

Gorard, S., Fevre, R. and Rees, G. (1999) 'The apparent decline of informal learning', *Oxford Review of Education*, 25:437–54.

Hargreaves, A. (1992) 'Cultures of teaching: a focus for change' in A. Hargreaves and M. Fullan (eds) *Understanding Teacher Development*, London: Cassell.

Hargreaves, A. (1998) 'The emotional politics of teacher development', keynote address to AERA, San Diego.

Hinchliffe, G. (2004) 'Work and human flourishing', *Educational Philosophy and Theory*, 36:535–47.

Holquist, M. (1990) *Dialogism: Bakhtin and his World*, New York: Routledge.

Illeris, K. (2004) 'Transformative learning in the perspective of a comprehensive learning theory', *Journal of Transformative Education*, 2:79–89.

Jacobi, M. (1991) 'Mentoring and undergraduate academic success: a literature review', *Review of Educational Research*, 61:505–32.

Lohman, M. C. (2000) 'Environmental inhibitors to informal learning in the workplace: a case study of public school teachers', *Adult Education Quarterly*, 50:83–101.

Lortie, D. C. (1975) *Schoolteacher: A Sociological Study*, Chicago: The University of Chicago Press.

McNally, J. (1994) 'Students, schools and a matter of mentors', *The International Journal of Educational Management*, 8:18–23.

McNally, J., Blake, A., Corbin, B. and Gray, P. (2008) 'Finding an identity and meeting a standard: connecting the conflicting in teacher induction', *Journal of Education Policy*, 23:287–98.

McNally, J., Cope, P., Inglis, W. and Stronach, I. (1994) 'Current realities in the student teaching experience', *Teaching and Teacher Education*, 10:219–30.

McNally, J., Cope, P., Inglis, W. and Stronach, I. (1997) 'The student teacher in school: conditions for development', *Teaching and Teacher Education*, 13:485–98.

Pallant, J. (2007) *SPSS Survival Manual* (3rd edn), Maidenhead, UK: McGraw-Hill.

Schibbye, A. L. L. (2002) *En Dialektisk Relasjonsforståelse i Psykoterapi med Individ, Par og Familie* [A dialectical understanding of relationships in therapy with individuals, couples and families], Oslo: Universitetsforlaget.

Schön, D. (1987) *Educating the Reflective Practitioner*, San Francisco: Jossey-Bass.

Smith, M. K. (2009) 'Introducing informal education'. Available online at http://www.infed.org/i–intro.htm (accessed 10 March 2009).

Straka, G. (2004) 'Informal learning: genealogy, concepts, antagonisms and questions', occasional paper, Universitat Bremen.

Totterdell, M., Bubb, S., Woodroffe, L. and Hanrahan, K. (2004) 'The impact of NQT induction programmes on the enhancement of teacher expertise, professional development, job satisfaction or retention rates: a systematic review of research rates on induction', *Research Evidence in Education Library*, London: Institute of Education.

White, P. (1990) 'Friendship and education', *Journal of Philosophy of Education*, 24: 81–91.

Zembylas, M. (2003) 'Interrogating "teacher identity": emotion, resistance, and self-formation', *Educational Theory*, 53:107–27.

Note

1 A correlation matrix determined the presence of a majority of coefficients of value 0.3 and above, p<0.05, which indeed suggested the presence of one or more investigative components. In addition, the Kaiser-Meyer-Olkin Measure of Sampling Adequacy was 0.96, exceeding the recommended value of 0.6, and Bartlett's Test of Sphericity was statistically significant, again supporting the factorability of the correlation matrix (Pallant 2007).

Chapter 6

Making room for new teachers

The material dimension in beginning teaching

Phil Swierczek

Introduction

The relationship between new teachers and their material (or physical) surroundings has a significant impact on their ability to develop the personal and professional skills that are required for effective learning and teaching during the guaranteed placement year. As with all the dimensions identified by the research as impinging on the beginner's experience, the material exerts influence on, and is influenced by, several of the others; the relational, emotional and temporal, for example, are particularly evident in the accounts that follow. Anxious as they were to establish and maintain constructive professional relationships within schools, new teachers were often reluctant to be critical at the outset of their careers about poor or insufficient resources or accommodation; despite, in some cases, a continuing lack of basic essentials some months into the post, such as the swipe cards that were required to gain entry into the school, or passwords for access to computer technology. Some new teachers were frustrated by out-of-date resources or by a shortage of materials that had then to be shared between pupils and classes. Others still experienced a drop in confidence and self-esteem as their classroom management skills were undermined by books and audio visual aids that were uninspiring or simply irrelevant to twenty-first century teaching and learning. The allocation of teaching accommodation in particular was found to have a profound effect on the quality of the induction year, positively so in the experience of many new teachers, but of worryingly negative impact for a few.

Accommodation

In the evidence of this chapter, 'claiming the classroom' was highly important as a kind of marking out of a personal territory, with student work on the wall, a name on the door, a set of expectations about what kind of behaviour and relationship could be expected in that environment:

> Generally being able to say, I teach at Forth Academy, to say it's my job. And having my own classroom and being able to put my stamp on my classroom and have desks and room the way I want it and put up displays. Just now I have [a wall display] and I didn't think I had to ask anyone's permission for it, I can just do it and I think that's definitely helped.

In this forest of personal pronouns, the layers of the 'real' can be seen most clearly in the demarcations new teachers made between placement, graduate trainee apprenticeship and probationer status, and a perception of a reality that all of these were lacking in some aspect. For all the phases of preparation and induction, the material dimension provided tangible evidence that the 'real' was in a state of postponement.

Postponement of a very real kind was a problem for those new teachers who were not issued with pass cards to afford entry into the school itself (quite apart from a classroom) until after they had been in post for a number of weeks. Having to ring for entry tended to erode their status as teachers and made them feel more like visitors to the school rather than members of staff. For new teachers trying to establish their identities, this had a detrimental effect. Indeed, the statistical analysis of the project's structured interview schedule for secondary schools (which investigated the induction process, accommodation and resources, pupil behaviour, relationships with staff and pupils, policy initiatives, the SFR and career issues), revealed a moderate, positive correlation between the efficacy of the school at providing new teachers with basic information and access and how new teachers rated themselves as practitioners at the end of their first year ($\rho = 0.312$, $p < 0.05$, N = 59). That is, the better the quality of information and the level of access provided by the school (entry cards, room keys, computer passwords, and so on), the more positively new teachers tended to regard their own development.

Access to classrooms created difficulties for some. Although Linda, at least, was in the fortunate position of having been allocated 'her own classroom' and she was aware of the advantage:

> I think having your own room makes a huge difference. If you didn't have your own room it would make you feel that in effect you were a student teacher and a probationer teacher. It makes you feel more like a qualified teacher. Without having a room you would find it difficult to see that change and you would always feel that you were in effect still a student teacher and I think it's done a lot for my confidence to know that, yes, this is my classroom, this is my room, this is where I can stamp my authority.
>
> (Linda 2005)

Classroom allocation often depended on whether or not the new teacher was filling an actual vacancy or had been appointed in a supernumerary status. Afforded their own classroom, new teachers could arrange the room to suit their teaching style and their pupils' needs; importantly, this often meant that they had a set of keys to the room. To some, this might seem insignificant; however, being in possession of the keys to a classroom had an impact beyond immediate perception. If a new teacher had no keys, they had to rely on someone else for access. If this person did not arrive promptly, the pupils became restless, their behaviour deteriorated and the new teacher experienced a loss of status as a 'real teacher'. Thereafter, they would have to spend time re-establishing a suitable teaching and learning ethos before beginning the lesson. Their confidence often suffered as a result.

There was evidence too that in a shared classroom, the occupying teacher could be reluctant to concede ownership of 'their' space, often spending their preparation time in the classroom during the new teacher's lessons, which was found to be distracting and uncomfortable. Many new teachers felt that they were already subject to an inordinate amount of official scrutiny and that it was unacceptable to have to work in the presence of unofficial observers as well. They were worried that if a lesson did not go as well as expected, it might become the subject of 'staffroom chat'. In this situation the material dimension, in the form of the allocation of physical space, had a direct impact on the emotional well-being of new teachers as well as on their relationships with colleagues:

You saw for yourself when you came into my room how things are. She [the other teacher] came in to work on the computer at the back of the room while I was trying to teach, then her pal came in and they had a loud conversation. It's not as if they can't work anywhere else: there's the base with a computer in it.

(Geller)

This situation also meant that some new teachers were not allowed to reposition desks in the room and were given access to only limited storage facilities or wall space for display purposes. This made them feel tolerated rather than welcomed as colleagues, and many found it inhibited their ability to develop a personal style and approach:

Having your own classroom to me is the ultimate, it would be fabulous and I know there is all this stuff that teachers shouldn't be tied to a classroom – absolute rot, it is fantastic having your own classroom, the kids like it and you can just be very creative in a classroom in a way that I haven't been able to. I mean I have had displays and stuff but I have got loads of ideas of what I would do in a classroom if I had one which was mine for all my classes.

(Kate)

But worse even than being denied a single room of your own, was being denied seven:

Having to organize seven different rooms and find out where everything is, where I'm going to find a Bunsen burner, test tubes. I mean every room is laid out differently. So seven classrooms ... yeah and you can customize your whiteboard with things that you need ... [but] you need to do that in seven classrooms ... like if I've been doing an experiment then I'll turn up late for my next class because you have to clear away properly and you can't leave someone else's room in a mess – which is quite hard.

(Trixie)

Indeed, perhaps one of the most concerning findings from the data emerged in those cases of new teachers who had to work in multiple rooms. Teachers in this situation (and in one example, a teacher was in ten different rooms in the course of a week) found it difficult to be well organized for their classes, particularly if they were teaching practical subjects such as science. They reported that the location of resources was different in every room, to say nothing of the fact that it could be difficult to arrive on time to the next classroom if they had to move through the school between classes when the corridors were crowded. This left some new teachers struggling to establish discipline at the beginning of the lesson because the pupils had been left unattended outside the classroom.

In the case of one new teacher in a small department that could only occasionally make available a classroom (depending on the non-teaching time of the other members of staff), it became necessary to collect pupils and escort them through the school until an available space could be found in which to conduct the lesson. This caused stress and anxiety, because she was acutely aware of the disruption that was caused by having to take pupils on a tour of the school when other classes were settling to work:

> I haven't got a space that is just specifically mine … . However, drama is struggling with accommodation; on the days when we can muddle … through and we can sort of swap the classes about I can get a drama studio, that's fine. But for example on a Thursday we have a fifth year, now obviously a fifth year takes precedence over a first year so then I have to find alternative accommodation [for the first year]. I find that quite difficult because the kids are sort of walking across school and you don't know what might happen on the way to this alternative accommodation. I've had problems before when something quite dramatic has happened on the way to this other accommodation, this other room. The kids then get involved or they get sort of excited by what's happened, by the time they get to my class, through no fault of my own, they are not half as focused and not half as on the ball as they would have been. There's a nicer room I can go to and if I can get that, great, because it's more confined and it's just more conducive to learn in – but at a push I have to go up to the sort of porch area which isn't really … it's more like an assembly sort of room. It's either too hot or too cold; we have to move furniture around before we can start. So yeah, that is a problem.
>
> (Fran)

This is a telling example of the knock-on effects of what might seem to be the minor inconvenience of having to escort a class to distant accommodation in the absence of a dedicated teaching space. Here the material, temporal, relational and emotional dimensions combine. Time is wasted on the journey to the detriment of the pupil behaviour; the pupil-teacher relationship is affected when the pupils begin to drift out of control before the lesson even begins. The new teacher suffers emotionally as a result of the worry about the disruption to other classes and the possibility that they will be judged professionally inadequate as a result. The fact that the new space is often at the wrong temperature and that more time is lost through moving furniture adds to the frustration of the new teacher.

In the third year of the project (2006/07) the teacher-researchers visited primary schools throughout Scotland and observed the open-plan arrangement of classrooms, which was not a feature in the secondary school sector. New teachers interviewed in open-plan schools expressed a range of opinions, both positive and negative, about teaching in such areas. On the one hand other teachers of the same stage were usually close by to offer help and advice if required; on the other hand, some teachers felt inhibited at the beginning of the year by concerns over making visible mistakes, or felt self-conscious about being overheard during lessons that did not go according to plan, with some fearing they may be judged as lacking in skills or knowledge as a result. However, the overriding impact of open-plan teaching was a high noise level resulting in distraction for both pupils and teachers.

In several accounts, new teachers reported problems with voice strain as a result of having to compete with neighbouring classes for the attention of their pupils:

> The noise level is unbelievable. I can see it affecting the children's concentration and mine just goes as well. I have to speak so much louder than I want and I have to suck throat sweets all weekend so that I have a voice again for Monday morning. It affects totally what I can do. I have tried very quiet teaching to keep the children calm and listening but I had to give up, as they couldn't hear me. Don't get me wrong, this is not a criticism of the other teacher because I am sometimes aware of the noise in my area and I look around to see who is chatting – who is shouting. Really though they're not. They're just working,

moving around and talking to each other when they do group work, just getting involved and enthusiastic.

(Rory)

Indeed, during one observation, a new teacher had to instruct her pupils thus: 'Use your playground voices, boys and girls, otherwise I can't hear your answers.' This is the antithesis of normal classroom management, in which teachers often have to discourage pupils from talking at playground volume in class.

Although there was evidence of new teachers and classes working in harmony with their counterparts in open-plan classrooms, this was not true for all. One new teacher was adjacent to a noisy and disruptive group of pupils, whose teacher focused on one group of pupils at a time to the exclusion of all and everyone else in the room. The new teacher was on occasion forced to respond to the behaviour of pupils in the other group, who, having escaped the notice of their own teacher, were disrupting the beginner's lesson. But the absence of a dividing line or wall was not the only problem that the researchers encountered; in one school the space afforded to the new teacher doubled as an accessway to another part of the building. The storage facilities for pupil work and the display areas were on one side of (in effect) the passageway, and the pupils and desks on the other. There was a constant movement of children and adults through this area that the pupils and teacher had somehow learned to 'tune out'.

The focus on teaching accommodation has thus far suggested the links that exist between the material, relational and emotional dimensions; however, the characteristics of school environs were of consequence in the temporal dimension also. For example, the conditions of service outlined in *A Teaching Profession for the 21st Century* (McCrone Report 2000) ensured that no new teacher on the guaranteed placement scheme should have more than 0.7 days of class contact time. But a problem encountered by many new teachers, particularly those in the primary sector, was the lack of areas set aside for preparation and CPD. Many new teachers therefore spent their allocated preparation time moving around the school in search of a quiet and suitably equipped area in which to work:

Nobody has a place to work in their preparation time. There's a desk in the staffroom but there are always people moving in and out so it's hard to concentrate. The computer in the staffroom doesn't work so it's hard even to fill in our profile forms. We could use the computer room and the pupil support base but the problem is they are timetabled for classes and are basically never free.

(Laura)

Only a small number of new teachers reported that they felt confident in requesting permission to sign out of school to work in another venue (which is a right within the conditions of service). As a result, many felt that their guaranteed preparation time was largely wasted, with the bulk of preparation, assessment and marking being undertaken either at the end of the school day, or at home, with the inevitable impact on their work and life balance.

Resources

The provision of relevant and effective teaching and learning resources was surprisingly poor in some schools, both primary and secondary. In one primary school, new teachers were without jotters, pencils, board markers or play materials for younger classes during the first three weeks of the year. Reluctant as they were to 'make trouble' in the early days of their new careers, their solution was to beg, borrow and buy the required items. This situation was not the result of any negative feeling towards the new teachers, but the consequence of a poor management of resources and a lack of communication with new members of staff:

When I came into my room I had tables and chairs and nothing else. No pencils, crayons, jotters or play items. I need play items because I teach primary two but there was nothing. I brought in some of my own children's toys, begged more from family and friends and bought the rest at charity shops and car boot sales. How can I meet the criteria for the *Curriculum for Excellence* [Scottish Executive 2004] with no suitable resources?

(Rory)

Many teachers were unable to access suitable materials and had to spend time at the outset of their induction year producing or adapting materials for their classes. There was, moreover, reluctance on the part of some experienced, and indeed promoted staff, to share resources, to accept the limitations of existing materials or even acknowledge the diligence of beginners:

> My PT here is just [...] not interested and she is using stuff sent out by the region in 1980; so black pictures you can't even see, typewritten stuff, I mean today I just had my fourth years and we were all trying to read it, and we couldn't read it, no wonder there is disruption when the resources are like this and I spent the whole of my October holidays making up a new unit, two new units, and I told her I have made a new unit and she said, 'Well it can't be any different from the ones we have got'. And I was like, look at it. And no she didn't even want to see it.
>
> (Garibaldi)

Linda also encountered problems with resources that were sufficiently out of date to cause her pupils to treat them with contempt. Linda felt that being forced to use these resources reflected badly on her as a teacher and did not provide the pupils with sufficient stimulation to maintain their interest in the topic of the lesson. Their boredom inevitably led to a disintegration of behaviour and a reduction in Linda's confidence:

> I know the fourth year just weren't responding to a video that I had to use and I said to my PT, 'They are misbehaving because they are bored. They are not interested', and she said 'What do you mean?' and I said, 'The video is so out of date it's one of those boring documentaries from the 80s or something and they are sitting there thinking, "I'm going to laugh, I'm not going to sit and listen to this"'. It's black-and-white and so old they you could barely even hear what was being said. I have to admit I was bored sitting watching and if I'm bored sitting watching it that usually means the kids are going to be bored stiff.
>
> (Linda 2007)

Indeed, turning again to the analysis of the project's structured interview schedule for secondary schools, both the availability and the quality of teaching materials and resources correlated positively (albeit moderately) with how new teachers rated themselves as teachers at the end of the first year (respectively, $\rho = 0.360$, $p<0.01$, N = 58; $\rho = 0.329$, $p<0.05$, N = 58).

Conclusion

Not all of the material problems that new teachers faced can be solved effortlessly. Space in schools is finite and must be allocated to meet the needs of the pupils; but classroom provision could be evaluated to ensure that new teachers, especially, are not subject to unnecessary stress at what is a vulnerable stage in their careers. As our evidence suggests, teaching in up to ten rooms in one week, or, worse, seven rooms in one day, can diminish the teacher's ability to manage behaviour and resources. If it is necessary to accommodate new teachers in classrooms or buildings that are removed from the main body of the school, then it must be ensured that they do not feel isolated but do have access to support and advice when required. Equipping new teachers with entry cards and network access should be a priority of school managers at the beginning of the session to thus contribute to beginners' feelings of professional acceptance and counter their sense of feeling to be students on extended placements. Of equal importance is the new teacher's ability to negotiate the school environs; in large secondary schools particularly, a tour of the school and the familiarization with procedures should take place as early as possible, with responsibility for this duty being allocated to a specific, identifiable person.

The impact of poor material resources should not be underestimated either, nor the extent of the time spent updating or reinvigorating them. There are new teachers who prefer to compile their own materials, a task that they feel gives them ownership over, and therefore greater confidence in, their delivery of lessons. Nevertheless, the obligation to create new resources in the face of illegible scripts is a burden that can interfere with an appropriate work–life balance. Many new teachers confirmed that they had been invited to bid for new resources as and when finances allowed, resulting in a commensurate improvement in their ability to deliver stimulating lessons. Some were less fortunate, however, and as this final quotation suggests, at the mercy of less democratic managers, the difficulties of the material dimension can appear to become those of materialism itself:

> At the departmental consult we were asked what we needed most from next year's budget. We all agreed we needed grammar books for two of the languages – the ones we've got are from the year dot. So at the next meeting we asked 'Did you

get the books?'. 'No,' he said, 'but I got you 30 MP3 players'! It's just a gimmick – we're all on minimum non-contact so nobody has the time to download stuff even if we knew where to find it. You can have all the technology in the world but it's no use if you don't have the basics. We are trying to negotiate with him to return 25 of the players and buy the books!

(Geller)

References

McCrone Report (2000) *A Teaching Profession for the 21st Century: The Report of the Committee of Inquiry into professional conditions of service for teachers.* Edinburgh: SEED.
Scottish Executive (2004) *A Curriculum for Excellence*, Edinburgh: Scottish Executive.

Chapter 7

The temporal, structural, cognitive and ethical dimensions of early professional learning

Brian Corbin, Allan Blake, Ian Stronach and Jim McNally

The temporal dimension: learning at the speed of life

If early professional learning can be said to begin on time, that is to say it is 'early', when does it end? In posing so playful a question of the temporal dimension, we recognize, of course, that new teachers are afforded a one-year probationary period in which to establish their efficacy as educators against state-approved, competence-based descriptions of early teacher development that make no real provision for 'notion[s] of autonomy or self-actualisation' (McNally *et al.* 2004: 1). Yet, as McNally *et al.* (ibid.) also note, contact with practitioners in the field suggests that teachers' knowledge is personal, context-rich and elusive (Russell and Bullock 1999). Specifically, McNally *et al.* (2004) stress the importance of the informal, socio-emotional dimension to the experience of beginning teaching, which they say is neglected within a paradigm of formal competence whose decontextualized sense of time cannot account for the recursive ways in which new teachers form their professional identities (Britzman 2000). Probationary teaching, it could be said, is bound by a teleology whose linear sense of development cannot altogether account for the dynamic processes of identity formation.

For new teachers, the time of identity formation, of 'becoming', is strange and uneven, moments of liminality interspersed with breakdowns and breakthroughs. School time may be metronomic, marked by bells, periods and timetables, but new-teacher time is mercurial:

'days going in a blur'
'It feels like I have been here forever'
'time is actually flying by'
'can't believe it's October'
'it feels like I have been here for months and in other ways it feels like I have been here a long time'
'I can't believe it's November already'
'I just thought, it was a matter of getting through this 35 minutes'
'the last five minutes of the lesson I was so excited thinking any minute now the bell is going to ring, but it is nothing like that now'
'Another 148 days to go, then I can go.'

These are all teachers in their turbulent first term of teaching, who experienced time in many different and paradoxical ways:

> It feels like I have been here for months and in other ways it feels like it is the first couple of days and [I'm] still taking time to get used to the routine and to get used to feeling, like, I am a proper teacher.

Sometimes time elongates, making the beginning of the week seem very distant: 'Monday seems so far away now.' And at other times it compresses into a future time that seems to be hurtling towards them: 'amazing, watching the days go by – I'll be retiring before you know it.'
    At other times, it crashes ominously down:

> I've seen the full thing flash in front of my eyes – no show, no this, no that, and no the next thing. And I thought they won't even panic until 24 hours before their show, so why am I panicking for you just now?
>
> (drama teacher)

Accelerating, stopping, dragging, elongating, jumping forward, turning back on itself – this 'time' of becoming a teacher seems to be contradictory and strange in another sort of way. It is both vivid and forgettable. Past selves are uncertainly recalled:

> It's difficult to analyse what you were like six weeks ago.

It's hard to think back and think, 'What was my idea about being a teacher?' like a year ago.

Oh, it's very difficult to remember now, the last couple of weeks have just blurred into one.

Sometimes we drew a complete blank:

Interviewer What were your feelings the night before you started?
Respondent I can't remember.
Interviewer I know we should have done this within two weeks of you starting.
Respondent I can't remember […] I just can't remember, honestly, I just can't remember.

The disordering of time seems to result in, or at least be accompanied by, a disordering of memory. But why such disorderings? It seems to us now that the beginning teachers were simultaneously undergoing an *induction* and an *initiation* (a theory that is explored more fully in Chapter 13). These are different kinds of thing, largely process versus event, sustained by a necessary gap across which the performance of bridging – in itself a very personal engineering – constructs professional practices, ends, motivations and values.

Inductions have an ideal logic of means and ends; they are smooth and progressive, expressing a learning curve and a continuous sense of time. They are a cumulative *knowledge-for-action*. Both initial teacher education and probationer new-teacher training have these features, and indeed, can probably have no other. Initiation however is discontinuous, emotional, incommensurable and full of trials, false starts, endings, ordeals and confrontations with past selves and unrealized future selves. It is, quite inherently, *knowledge-after-action*. This section will argue an irony: that however 'training'-oriented preparation is, it is nevertheless often evaluated as abstract and theoretical by beginning teachers in relation to subsequent 'real' practice. It is not that there is no substitute for practice (for practice too is criticized in the data as 'not real'); there is instead no substitute for performance, in the fullest sense of enduring and *responsible* work. To this extent, we could sum up early professional learning as a rather unpredictable and individualistic collision of foreknowledge and afterthought wherein forewarned is never quite forearmed.

Induction and initiation are not only disjunctive, they split the self into past, present and future shards:

> At the end of uni that book's closed, this is now your working life.

> Even emotionally I feel more mature […] I don't know, I feel I should be someone that the kids look up to […] I guess for the first time ever I see myself as a professional person.

The disjunctions and shifts are many and various, even involving the uncontrolled expansion of the young teacher self into problematic areas, or into forms of over-investment where 'it has completely taken over my life':

> I see my boyfriend at the weekend and […] I'm sitting on the bed like that, dropping off and he's getting mad with me and I'm like, 'I'm not joking, I'm tired.'

> I've got into trouble from my mum because I used the tone and words I would use to the pupils like, 'Stop speaking to me like that.' And she just looked at me and said, 'You're not a teacher here.' And I said, 'What?' because I didn't realize I was doing it and my boyfriend's always on at me saying, 'Stop treating me like one of your pupils'.

These emergent and discrepant selves can look at each other in dismay or frustration, but also sometimes very positively: 'But then sometimes I take a step back and look at myself, in the third person, and think, "Is that really me?" Ha!'

The metaphors employed by the new teachers clearly suggest the experiential domination of initiation – the 'roller coaster', all those watery metaphors of 'plunging', 'treading water', 'keep my head above water', being 'swept along', 'sink or swim', 'thrown in' and 'dumped in at the deep end'. Initiation and induction birth discrepant selves, whose arguments and negotiations originate professional 'moments': the more fraught the initiation, the more likely that the props of induction seem inadequate to the beginners. If initiation dominates induction, and simultaneously reveals gaps between them, this is inevitable in a negative sense: in any initial preparation for complex work there will be shortfalls in knowledge, expertise, performance.

But we also argue that these gaps are necessary in a positive sense: it is in the gaps *between* the necessary limits of preparation and the excessive demands of performance that new teachers largely and to a neglected sense in the literature *invent* themselves through processes of what they usually refer to in the data as 'trial and error'. We are not interested here in whether preparation is more or less adequate; our interest is in arguing that there is a *necessary* gap between the possibilities of induction and the experiences of initiation that opens up a space for both the failure and success of emergent professional selves (and this is the place of invention on which Chapter 13 centres). This is the liminal *and* subliminal learning of teachers. And now we can see the disordering of time and memory is symbolic of a deeper existential confrontation, as the ordered limits of induction are contested by the disordering excesses of initiation. And it is not surprising that in such a collision it is the limits of 'training' itself that are reached:

> A kid last week told me to 'fuck off', [and that] he was going to kill me … . There's no training you could go through to prepare you for that.

The structural, cognitive and ethical dimensions: a matter of professional learning

At first sight of the transcripts of teacher-research interviews with probationers, the metaphor of 'big bang' was suggested to capture what seemed to come across as an explosion of overwhelming activity when new teachers first encountered their schools. While the cosmological metaphor looked back from the present of an expanding universe to its conjectured beginning as an infinitesimally small 'singularity', the transcripts were often witness to a turbulent beginning, with possible professional expansion yet to come. A history of all too frequent initial turbulence was also the warrant for the discourse of the structural dimension itself, most especially in new teachers' expression of the formal induction process, with its key policy terms of 'standardization', 'transition', 'consolidation' and 'extension', with the professional as 'lifelong learner', negotiating change by collaboration, reflection and self-evaluation.

One conceptualization of such movement has seen new-teacher professionalism as contextually formed, and like a cooling and forming from inchoate matter, settling by processes of situated learning: 'Specifically, the teachers, especially good ones, drift towards routinization and consistency' (Leinhardt 1988: 147). However, 'drift' seems rather a serene description for probationer accounts that can be fraught and thus betray something of the contested nature of the new teacher's professional identity. At best, Bernstein sees this professional 'self' as embroiled in an '"arena", which creates a sense of drama and struggle' (Bernstein and Solomon 1999: 269); at worst it is increasingly being vacuumed altogether of ethical commitment or subject expertise, and instead forever to be responsive to political direction. In the following short case, the analysis draws especially on the tensions, dilemmas and movements referred to above: of role, boundaries and the importance of time in constructing a sense of the professional self within the structures (and fractures) of induction.

Geller and the structural dimension: 'real education' in the 'exam factory'

Geller is a language teacher who, on a pre-probationary short-term supply post, was forewarned that it was likely to be a 'roller coaster' ride. With no full induction support, so it turned out:

> When you arrived to take a class for absent teachers you were slow handclapped, booed and hissed. I felt that the pupils did not know me yet.

After such mortifying encounters, his subsequently supported probationary status in his next school revives him. He begins to clarify how he sees his role in relation to both pupils and another teacher:

> I've got a shared S1 class ... the teaching styles are completely different ... but they'll realize when they're in my class they'll do things my way ... . Some of them said, 'But we like you Sir, why can't we have you all the time?' Maybe I'm doing something right after all!

Later in the same month, he continues to define his professional self against rather than with immediate colleagues, this time the development of his subject expertise denied by being cloned into the curriculum scheme of an unsympathetic head of department. He offers a new metaphor:

> I feel like I'm in a pool of water and one day I will break the surface and be able to breathe more easily.

After this near-death by drowning, by October, things are improving, but only within the constructed context of the classroom rather than in the school as a whole:

> I feel a lot more confident in the classrooms now ... but I feel as if I'm not really being treated as a proper member of staff. I feel like an extra ... just the probationer and I just have my classes to worry about but I would much rather get involved in the school and have a say.

Denied 'expansive' engagement, sidelined as a non-acting 'extra', he continues to question collegial practices, a reminder that tensions are not just between discourses of 'occupational' and organizational 'professionalism'. Later in the same month, induction observations help his personal clarification of the teacher role:

> I saw teachers doing things in different ways. I am quite stern with them ... a lot of teachers took a far more light-hearted approach and the kids seem to respond to that ... . I come across unprofessionalism every day ... they maybe side with the kids and then the kids look on you [that is, Geller] as an ogre. When I was at school and you had a strict teacher you did learn from them ... . I don't want to be their best friend.

This is a key learning issue for him, though experienced as a role paradox: 'unprofessionalism' works. The problem of what he might become leads him from present to past collegial practices: as a pupil what kind of teaching enabled him to learn? His discourse of professionalism centres on a commitment to learning, and now its paradox becomes a still difficult but workable problem: How to be strict yet neither 'best friend' nor 'ogre'?

Well into his first term, and struggling between remembrance and aspiration, he addresses an SFR competence, that he 'is sensitive to the impact of [his] personal style … on pupils'. Yet these personal reflections are not just an issue of 'therapeutic process' against subject knowledge, nor is his concern with self at the expense of the wider context:

> Most schools are exam factories at the end of the day and interested in statistics. I don't agree with any of that but at the end of the day I will be accountable … . I think for the first time I have seen the negative side of this job.

The future is no longer aspiration but suddenly collapsed into what is nigh, 'the end of the day', and he is already a 'dead man walking', condemned to imminent death by numbers. It is a wider dilemma, between his commitment to learning and how he sees accountability. This is the time of his Interim Profile Report and he feels unable to make these doubts transparent to this formal process (as he has to the teacher-researcher). He has to keep going, and the LEA promises a job next year 'with the proviso' he gets the school's imprimatur.

Next term, he feels better that he is learning a more inflected professionalism, somewhere between 'ogre' and 'best friend':

> Basically if the pupils can, in between direct teaching, … tell you a joke or tell you something that happened outside school then … that is a good indicator that they see you as person not just as somebody there to teach them … . I try really hard to be fair and consistent.

What has helped is that he has 'broken away' from his original mentor and, discovering that although collegiality is not universal, he has found some other teachers helpful – and then 'you get a completely different picture'. Two months later, he observes an experienced teacher who combines her personal teaching style, which though not for him, is compatible with his ideals of learning:

> In a lot of ways I think you can get away with a lot of things if you have been here for ages … . Yeah, you learn to know when you can let go and just be yourself.

The experienced teacher has achieved the sort of relationship with pupils that his initial encounters denied him ('they don't know me yet'). Time, induction arrangements for observation, and his commitment to his subject, his personal style and his relationship to his pupils all seem to be gelling more favourably.

In getting to this point he has loosened up his view on ways of being a teacher and seen both possibilities and constraints afforded by collegiality and external pressures:

> I feel that in this school … it is an exam factory. There is no real education going on … . I normally put up a case but I find that I have had to keep my mouth shut this year.

His comments specify 'this school' and 'this year', and he resurrects his aspirations that his professional dilemmas will in future, if not resolve then at least oscillate with a healthier pulse:

> The values that I had when I became a probationer or even a student are totally changed … but I have had to change them in order to fit into the curriculum, which is really sad I think and going to be an issue for me.

So he gets on with it, though in a way he feels has to be invisible to formal profiling. By now, it is decision time. He would feel more secure with a permanent post, and is torn between the uncertainty of moving on or staying in the 'exam factory', in a polluted context but where at least he is getting established, because 'the kids now know me' and he is 'building up a reputation'. He gets through his induction and accepts a post at the school.

Geller's story is presented here not as an exemplar case of 'the new teacher and induction', and even in our data his narrative both shares with and differs from those of other new teachers. For example, he made more consistent use of the SFR standards than most, and seemed more unfortunate in the collegiality he experienced. Yet his 'personal-professional' role dilemma, and the troubled engagement between subject commitment and 'standards discourse' were often shared. The specifics of his school made for a highly textured and shifting context: a staff whose 'morale is rock bottom', capable both of 'unprofessionalism' and support; pupils who are 'fantastic' but with 'deep-rooted problems'; his idealization of education as learning pitched against 'exam factory' accountability; and an induction process both restrictive (feeling he must 'try to fit into the Standard') as well as potentially expansive.

Britzman has warned against any tendency to see 'competency as the absence of conflict' (2003: 7), and its possibility is addressed in official induction guidance to schools. For example:

> The personal code of practice of the probationer in the classroom should be compatible with that of school/department. It should be established and put into practice from day one.
>
> (GTCS 2001: 29)

Geller's year-long struggle is at odds with the discursive tenor here and raises several questions. Its deadline of 'day one' assumes summary resolution rather than issues for reflection. Yet how clear to new teachers is their own 'personal code of practice'? Or the school's? How long might it take for the two to be made 'compatible'? How would this be displayed in competence discourse – as outward acquiescence? In the case of Geller we see an instance of a new teacher's performative display of 'compatibility', but only by putting his deeply felt commitment 'on hold'.

Competence in the cognitive dimension: reflection as therapeutic or expansive?

The format of the profile report seemed to have caused problems in that there was 'nothing that personalized about it' (Linda). Yet this often-repeated appeal is not simply as reflective therapy, but can be discoursed as of pedagogic benefits for the learning of others:

> It wasn't seeking to find out anything about me personally about my learning styles ... and that's what the whole point of teaching is ... it's about tapping into the learning styles of your pupils.
>
> (Rachael)

Rachael also thought that probationers might 'share what each other got on these forms' but their 'ticky box' format prevented 'expansive' use, as no specific details could be included. Lewis also links the personal with collegial:

> It doesn't tell them very much at all about me as a teacher.

I guess that comes from [experienced teachers] in their sections [of the report].

(Lewis)

The uneasy discursive relationship with the documentation often contrasted with probationer experiences of the induction arrangements as a whole:

It's a great introduction to first time teaching ... time to coordinate and to learn and to bounce ideas off other members of staff.

(Richard)

Opportunities for learning-focused dialogue as well as stress-releasing therapy of 'letting off steam' with peers were appreciated. But there were structural factors outside the school that made a significant impact on new teachers, too. In one interview, Rachael expressed dismay at the inflexibility of the induction scheme: disbelief at getting fifth-choice location out of five; despair at having no choice but to take the post offered; financial problems incurred due to travel; not being able to understand how the probationers were allocated to positions; the hassle of arranging all the transport and how this added to her feeling of nerves for the first day: 'It was eight o'clock in the morning, I thought I've already been up and, like, at it for two hours and I've not got even to work yet.'

The SRF is intended to inform the processes of reflection and self-evaluation as well as assessment of fitness for full registration. But when the competences of the SFR are consulted, there can be specific criticisms. For Ann, not only is there 'too much to get your head around', but taken point by point there is a further problem:

It's impossible to actually look at each point and ... know if you've even completed it. How do you know if you're working cooperatively with other professionals and adults? You don't know yourself. Only the people you're working with know.

(Ann)

She sees the SFR as asking too much of self-auditing and takes a more collegial view, especially as novice professional. A senior teacher put succinctly what many felt:

The actual Standard I think is not a user-friendly document. I know that mentors toil over just exactly what some parts mean and obviously so do the actual probationers ... reading between the lines and saying, 'Well, I could make that fit'.

(Induction Supporter)

Added to local interpretation, time is also an issue:

I do think what is behind the document is important though ... . I don't think you could fulfil all these things in one year as a probationer ... so it shouldn't just stop after you are fully registered.

(Ann)

It should be noted that this longer-term developmental view is exactly how the SFR sees itself, but the new teachers wanted it more clearly differentiated from immediate issues of coping with 'the big bang' of classroom and curriculum issues.

It is a policy concern that new teachers tended to make little or no reference to the SFR, other than occasional, brief mention of the bureaucratic requirement to complete the interim report based on the SFR. The weak connection between the cognitive development of beginners and the official SFR that purports to govern the experience is also of some concern across the policy and practice communities, although some research has indeed been critical of the apparent absence of a more substantial pedagogical focus in mentoring dialogue (Edwards and Prothero 2003). It is important to recall that this project was initially about learning – the question of what and how new teachers were learning – and later associated with the more philosophically aware question of learning as becoming. It is reasonable to suppose that new teachers would be learning in the sense of developing their competence in classroom management skills and curriculum knowledge, for example. But evidence in any explicit cognitive terms about what and how they are learning (such as the example that follows) is not substantial:

I witnessed an experienced teacher dictating absolutely everything to the pupils, which they later regurgitated. The pupils had a poor learning experience and although he got good results the pupils did not enjoy the experience. This strategy was used partly to keep pupils quiet and under control and

partly because he was lazy. This is one role model I have no
intention of emulating.

(Logan)

This may be a methodological issue, of course: has the conventional
interview-based method been too limited in its capacity to make
cognitive detail more explicit, or would a more focused and imagi-
native method elicit further insights into how new teachers 'learn'
their professional craft?

We do not believe that such 'cognitive' development is absent.
Rather it may be submerged in the ontologically intense formation
of a teaching identity; epistemologically, new teachers feel secure
enough to get through as they find their new selves in a new world,
that of a teacher in a school. Insofar as we have some indications of
beginners' reference to cognitive aspects of development, such as
differentiation (McNally *et al.* 2008), they tend, as in the quotation
above, to be bound up in developing knowledge of, and relationships with, children, both as individuals and collectively as a class
– 'good results' are not in themselves enough. And even though
this may be an additional imperative for the clearer articulation of
informal learning, it is, if Richard is correct, equally a call for a new
critique of competence:

> I think that being trained to be a teacher isn't about 'head
> knowledge' necessarily; it's not about academia [...] it's all
> about behaviour management, about a psychology, classroom
> management. It's a lot more practical. But I felt [... that in ITE]
> the accent was too much on 'head knowledge' and academic
> knowledge than it was on actually functioning effectively as a
> person in a class.

Professionalism and values: the ethical dimension

Professionalism also entails ethical issues, acknowledged by the
SFR as underpinning practice in two ways: by statements of 'values'
such as the commitments to social justice and taking responsibility
for professional learning; and second by reference to inner processes of 'self-evaluation' and 'reflection'. Rightly so, as these are
'an integral part of teaching' (Arthur 2002: 317), but not either as
self-evident in themselves nor straightforward in their relationship
to everyday practice for probationers. They are always contextually

embedded in power relationships and, as with Geller, they can be both a remembered ideal and an aspiration, only occasionally realized in the here-and-now.

However, values may not always be self-evident and ready to summon as a basis for action:

> My priority in class is just that everyone is participating and doing the best they are capable of. That hasn't changed ... . I'm not sure that my values have changed all that much to be honest. I'm not sure what my values are which is one of the difficulties.
>
> (Lewis)

> I still feel my ideas and ideals about being a teacher have stayed the same but they might have changed ... it's something that's difficult because they would be developing gradually so it's hard to think back and think, 'What were my ideas about being a teacher like a year ago?'
>
> (Linda)

Becoming a teacher can be an uncertain process though always focused around their own and pupil learning, even if there is a shift in what exactly is to be valued about the supposed purpose of learning and what might sustain a commitment to it:

> I increasingly think I'm not just here to teach biology and I would far rather that at the end of the school time the kids were leaving socially competent adults ... that's more important than whether they get a 1 or 5 in their biology.
>
> (Avril)

Like Geller, Avril is losing interest not in her subject so much as what happens to it in the 'delivery' discourse. Yet unlike him she begins to shift her core role commitment to what might become compatible with a 'therapeutic' subjectivity, within which she experiences meaning and purpose. Not through an espousal of values, but through relationships with others, her engagement in an enterprise with fellow travellers taking them somewhere that matters. For it is then and there that the 'ethical nexus inscribed in relations with others' (Hinchliffe 2004: 536) becomes important in itself as a performance end as much as a means.

In exploring the temporal, structural, cognitive and ethical dimensions of our model of early professional learning, evidence of different kinds of tension has been offered, some inevitable and necessarily related to the nature of professional discourse, and the complex process of induction and teacher education itself. The good news is new teachers are often discoursed by more established teachers as learners requiring support, and probationers see themselves as such, and that at least there are uncertainties and struggles in 'self-formation' which are seen as extending well beyond the initial year. Less productive have been assumptions of continuity and of a 'standardization' impervious to contextual uncertainties, collegiality, sympathetic management and compatibility with a 'delivery' discourse. The success of formal arrangements is seen to depend on how they are used and such use cannot be removed either from the pressures schools are under, nor their occupational cultures or values. The mistake of policy is in thinking that standards-driven professional development can be more than a public statement to which teachers are accountable; to think that it can actually guide or govern practice; to fail to see that the SFR is a set of contextualizing professional statements but not itself the text of that professional development, which is written in the experience of the individual, represented imperfectly in each new teacher's narrative as a simulacrum of the experience.

References

Arthur, J. (2002) 'Editorial: professional value commitments', *British Journal of Educational Studies*, 51:317–19.

Bernstein, B. and Solomon, J. (1999) 'Pedagogy, identity and the construction of a theory of symbolic control: Basil Bernstein questioned by Joseph Solomon', *British Journal of Sociology of Education*, 20:265–79.

Britzman, D. P. (2000) '"The question of belief": writing poststructuralist ethnography' in E. A. St. Pierre and W. S. Pillow (eds) *Working the Ruins: Feminist Poststructuralist Theory and Methods in Education*, London: Routledge.

Britzman, D. P. (2003) *Practice Makes Practice*, New York: State University of New York Press.

Edwards, A. and Prothero, L. (2003) 'Learning to see in classrooms: what are student teachers learning about teaching and learning while learning to teach in schools?', *British Educational Research Journal*, 29:227–42.

GTCS (2001) *The Standard for Full Registration*, Edinburgh: GTC Scotland.

Hinchliffe, G. (2004) 'Work and human flourishing', *Educational Philosophy and Theory*, 36:535–47.

Leinhardt, G. (1988) 'Situated knowledge and expertise in teaching' in J. Calderhead (ed.) *Teachers' Professional Learning*, London: Falmer Press.

McNally, J., Boreham, N. and Cope, P. (2004) 'Showdown at the last chance saloon: research meets policy in early professional learning', paper presented at the Annual ECER Conference, Crete.

McNally, J., Blake, A., Corbin, B. and Gray, P. (2008) 'Finding an identity and meeting a standard: connecting the conflicting in teacher induction', *Journal of Education Policy*, 23:287–98.

Russell, T. and Bullock, S. (1999) 'Discovering our professional knowledge as teachers: critical dialogues about learning from experience' in J. Loughran (ed.) *Researching Teaching: Methodologies and Practices for Understanding Pedagogy*, London: Falmer Press.

Chapter 8

Job satisfaction among newly qualified teachers in Scotland

Nick Boreham

Introduction

Job satisfaction is an important outcome of the induction year – to complete probation successfully, new teachers should end that momentous period with positive feelings about the work that they do. However, like most other people in employment, teachers experience varying degrees of satisfaction or dissatisfaction with their jobs. The issue of job satisfaction became prominent in the 1960s and since then many studies have been carried out across the economy – for example, questions about job satisfaction are often included in national household panel surveys. Job satisfaction is closely linked to motivation, in the sense that any factors that undermine job satisfaction are also likely to undermine the extent to which one throws oneself into one's work. Research has also shown that a significant level of job *dis*satisfaction is associated with resignation, always an unsatisfactory outcome and a problem for teacher supply (Wright 2006).

This chapter describes the questionnaire we developed to measure this outcome of early professional learning, and reports results obtained by administering it to new teachers throughout Scotland. Although numerous studies have been carried out into teachers' job satisfaction, as far as we can establish, only one (Fraser *et al.* 1998) included probationers, and that study did not report separate results for them. Moreover, it preceded the restructuring of the teaching profession and the introduction of the new induction year in Scotland. A further gap in the literature is that previous research on teacher job satisfaction has tended to use instruments, frequently American in origin, that were not designed for completion by probationers. Consequently, in order to measure new teachers' job satisfaction within the new induction framework, we developed an instrument specifically designed for the purpose. It is called JOBSAT.

Job satisfaction and its measurement

The construction of JOBSAT was based on the following assumptions: a job can be decomposed into several elements known variously as facets, job factors, job dimensions or job characteristics. For example, a teacher's job might include the dimensions of marking and administrative paperwork. Individuals are consciously aware of feelings of satisfaction or dissatisfaction with each of these dimensions, as well as satisfaction or dissatisfaction with their job as a whole. These feelings can be measured by asking individuals to report them using a rating scale such as very satisfied, moderately satisfied, neither satisfied nor dissatisfied, moderately dissatisfied, very dissatisfied.

What lies behind the ratings thus obtained? The classic view in occupational psychology is that different personality types find fulfilment through different kinds of work, and that job satisfaction reflects the goodness of fit between the person and the job. This hypothesis was tested for the teaching profession by McDonald (1981), who found that serving teachers' ratings of their job satisfaction were significantly correlated with their personalities as measured by Cattell's 16PF test (N = 68). It was estimated that 37 per cent of the variance in teacher job satisfaction was explained by variance in personality scores, although the small sample size makes this finding indicative rather than conclusive.

An important theoretical contribution to our understanding of job satisfaction is Herzberg et al.'s (1959) study of the motivation of industrial engineers and accountants in the US. This research reported the job factors that gave people satisfaction were different from those that made them feel dissatisfied. Herzberg et al. called the former 'motivators' and the latter 'hygiene factors'. Job satisfaction arose from factors intrinsic to the work itself (the motivators). When people were dissatisfied, Herzberg et al. found that this was due to factors extrinsic to the work, such as salary and conditions. The important practical implication is that improving hygiene factors will not make people feel satisfied about their work. It will just make them less *dissatisfied*. Herzberg's two-factor theory has been challenged many times since it was first published, but overall it has stood the test of time. It has, for example, been broadly confirmed in studies of teacher job satisfaction, including Bowen and Radhakrishna (1991) and De Nobile and McCormick (2005).

In the present study, our model of new-teacher job satisfaction has at its centre a probationer who wants to work with children and seeks professional fulfilment by helping them learn and overcome their problems. However, the sense of professional worth and well-being obtained in this way can be undermined by a number of 'dissatisfiers'. Previous job satisfaction studies in teaching suggest that the major sources of dissatisfaction are school leadership, salary, the way the profession and the particular school are perceived in the community, pupil discipline and infrastructure (Dinham and Scott 1998; Fraser *et al.* 1998; Nias 1981; Poppleton 1989; McNally *et al.* 1994).

Method

The job satisfaction of new teachers in Scotland was studied by a combination of ethnographic and psychometric methods. We drew two samples – 25 new teachers in the six schools who participated in the ethnographic study, and 150 new teachers from ten Scottish local authorities who participated in the psychometric study.

Ethnographic study

Six teacher-researchers of the EPL project undertook ethnographic research during the 2004/05 academic year. Each followed the progress of a small number of probationary teachers (on average, three) through the induction year in his or her own school. Data were gathered by observation of new teachers at work and a series of in-depth interviews. The interviews were transcribed by the teacher-researchers and written up alongside observations about the context of the school. Among other things, the ethnographic study gave the teacher-researchers rich insights into those dimensions of the new teachers' experiences that related to their feelings of job satisfaction and dissatisfaction. These insights were the source of our identification of the dimensions of the probationer's job that we included in the JOBSAT questionnaire.

Individually, each of the six teacher-researchers made a list of those dimensions of the probationary teacher's job that they judged likely to provoke feelings of job satisfaction or dissatisfaction.

'Satisfiers' and 'dissatisfiers' were listed separately. This resulted in a total of 57 items, which contained numerous duplications. Two teams, each comprising three teacher-educators and one of the teacher-researchers, separately reviewed the list and grouped the items into a reduced number of categories. These two lists were then compared in a consensus meeting, and a final combined list of job dimensions was agreed.

The consensus list was compared with four comparator studies, Van Saane *et al.* (2003), Dinham and Scott (1998), Fraser *et al.* (1998) and Nias (1981). The first of these was a meta-analysis of studies of job satisfaction in the helping professions. The next two were large psychometric studies of job satisfaction among teachers, and the last was a naturalistic study of job satisfaction among primary school teachers carried out by unstructured interviewing. The comparison with our own list revealed a high degree of overlap, i.e. most of the job dimensions identified in previous studies had emerged in our own investigation. However, three job dimensions cited in the previous literature were not represented. Financial reward/salary occurred in both Van Saane *et al.* (2003) and Fraser *et al.* (1998) but not in the consensus list. Ability to exert influence over school policies/procedures occurred in both Fraser *et al.* (1998) and Nias (1981) but not in the consensus list. Likewise, promotion/career prospects occurred in all four comparators but not in the consensus list. While it is easy to understand why these factors might not have impacted on the job satisfaction of probationers, to ensure as much convergent validity as possible with previous studies, new items were constructed for inclusion in JOBSAT (e.g. 'Your salary as a probationary teacher', 'The availability of permanent posts in your subject').

The dimensions of the work of the probationary teacher that relate to job satisfaction and dissatisfaction (including the additional items) were finalized as follows:

1 The support you get from the head of your school;
2 The support you get from the head of your department or faculty (if applicable);
3 The support you get from your official supporter or mentor (if different from the above);
4 The support you get from your subject supporter or mentor (if applicable);
5 The support you get from other colleagues;

6   The support you get from non-teaching staff;
7   Opportunity to meet and exchange experiences with new teachers from your school (if applicable);
8   Opportunity to meet and exchange experiences with new teachers from other schools;
9   Recognition of your status as a teacher by the head of your school;
10 Recognition of your status as a teacher by other management team members in your school (if applicable);
11 Recognition of your status as a teacher by other teachers in your school;
12 Recognition of your status as a teacher by pupils;
13 Working relationships with colleagues;
14 The help you have been given in finding out about school procedures;
15 The degree of warmth with which you have been received;
16 The ease of asking apparently trivial questions within the school;
17 The willingness of experienced colleagues to let you observe them teach;
18 The amount of collaborative work you do with colleagues;
19 Your colleagues' willingness to listen to what you have to say;
20 The way other teachers relate to you in the staffroom;
21 Your relationship with pupils in the classroom;
22 The way pupils respond to your lessons;
23 Your level of competence in the classroom, given the amount of teaching you have done so far;
24 The opportunities you have to help children achieve or to overcome their problems;
25 Pupil behaviour in your school;
26 Your personal capacity to manage pupil behaviour;
27 School support for managing pupil behaviour;
28 Your relationships with parents at your school;
29 The teaching accommodation allocated to you;
30 Availability of material resources for teaching;
31 Your current workload overall;
32 Opportunities to get involved in extra-curricular activities;
33 The balance you are able to maintain between work and private life;
34 Formal communications with your local authority (e.g. over arrangements concerning your induction);

35 The local authority induction support programme;
36 Formal review of your progress (e.g. interim report) (if applicable);
37 Opportunities for professional development provided by the local authority;
38 Opportunities for professional development provided by the school;
39 The availability of permanent posts in your subject;
40 Your salary as a new teacher.

Construction of the JOBSAT instrument

These items were compiled into a research instrument that conformed to the standard format for job satisfaction questionnaires. Each item was followed by a rating scale: Very Satisfied, Satisfied, Neither Satisfied nor Dissatisfied, Dissatisfied, Very Dissatisfied. At the end of the questionnaire, we added a standard single-item measure of overall job satisfaction, item 41: 'Overall, how satisfied or dissatisfied are you with your job as a new teacher?' The JOBSAT instrument takes about 20 minutes to complete and in the EPL research this was done anonymously. Data were also collected on age and gender, sector (primary/secondary) and whether the respondent was a direct entrant into teacher training from university (not counting vacation jobs) or whether s/he had followed another career before entering the teaching profession.

Although JOBSAT includes all the job dimensions which previous research has found relevant to job satisfaction/dissatisfaction in teaching and the helping professions generally, it differs from previous instruments in two ways. First, it is specific to the probationary year of teaching, citing factors that occur only in that context (such as support from the official mentor). Second, it has a finer granularity than most previous instruments. Thus, instead of one generic item on 'communication', it covers different aspects of communication in school: for example, 'the way other teachers relate to you in the staffroom', 'your colleagues' willingness to listen to what you have to say', 'the ease of asking apparently trivial questions within the school'. In fact, we found that the new teachers reported different levels of satisfaction with specific job dimensions that are often lumped together in other instruments.

The psychometric study

The JOBSAT instrument was administered to 150 new teachers in ten Scottish local authorities while they were attending study days organized by their authorities as part of the induction scheme. Authorities were selected randomly from the complete list of around 30. Data collection began late in 2004, towards the end of the first term, and continued in 2005 through the first half of the second term. Thus it began after the initial settling-in period, and was completed before the beginning of the formal assessment against the SFR, and before any of the probationers could have secured permanent posts.

The sample breakdown is given in Tables 8.1, 8.2 and 8.3.

Results

Overall job satisfaction

Satisfaction with the job as a whole tended to be high, with 82 per cent of respondents expressing satisfaction and only 7 per cent expressing dissatisfaction (Table 8.4). This is consistent with

Table 8.1 Breakdown of sample by sector

Sector	No.	%
Primary	61	41
Secondary	89	59
Total	150	100

Table 8.2 Breakdown of sample by gender

Gender	No.	%
Female	85	72
Male	33	28
Total	118	100
Missing information	32	—
Total	150	—

Table 8.3 Breakdown of sample by entry route

Entry route	No.	%
Direct from university into teacher training	37	30
Mature entrant from previous career pathway	85	70
Total	122	100
Missing information	28	—
Total	150	—

Table 8.4 Overall job satisfaction scores

	1	2	3	4	5	Total	Missing	Total
No.	39	85	14	9	1	148	2	150
%	26	57	9	6	1	99	1	100

Mean 1.97, SD 0.816, N = 148
1 = very satisfied, 2 = satisfied, 3 = neither satisfied or dissatisfied, 4 = dissatisfied,
   5 = very dissatisfied

another (unpublished) study carried out in one Scottish local authority at the same time by the present writer, which also found high levels of job satisfaction among probationers.

However, there were some significant areas of dissatisfaction.

Satisfaction and dissatisfaction with the dimensions of the probationary teacher's job

Table 8.5 provides the means and standard deviations for all 40 job dimensions. The five dimensions with which the probationers were most satisfied were (most satisfying first) *recognition by the pupils of your status as a teacher, your working relationship with your departmental colleagues, support from your subject mentor, support from other colleagues in the department* and *your relationship with pupils in the classroom*. These results suggest that it is the relational aspect of the job that provides the most job satisfaction, including relationships with both pupils and colleagues.

The five dimensions with which the new teachers were most dissatisfied were (most dissatisfying first) *the availability of permanent posts in your subject, pupil behaviour in the school, the balance between work and private life, your salary as a probationary teacher, the availability of material resources for teaching.* These are predominantly the kind of hygiene factors identified by Herzberg *et al.* (1959).

The third column in Table 8.5 reveals variations in satisfaction/

Table 8.5 Satisfaction with the 40 dimensions of the probationer's job

Rank	Mean score	SD	Job dimension
1	1.53	0.587	Recognition of your status as a teacher by pupils
2	1.66	0.901	Working relationships with colleagues
3	1.68	0.948	The support you get from your subject supporter or mentor (if applicable)
4	1.71	0.870	The support you get from other colleagues
5	1.72	0.698	Your relationship with pupils in the classroom
6.5	1.82	1.063	The support you get from your official supporter or mentor
6.5	1.82	0.929	The degree of warmth with which you have been received
8	1.85	1.007	The support you get from the head of your department or faculty (if applicable)
9.9	1.93	0.976	Recognition of your status as a teacher by other management team members in your school (if applicable)
9.9	1.93	0.871	Your colleagues' willingness to listen to what you have to say
11	1.96	0.866	Recognition of your status as a teacher by other teachers in your school
12.5	1.97	1.006	The ease of asking apparently trivial questions within the school
12.5	1.97	0.680	The way pupils respond to your lessons

(continued)

Rank	Mean score	SD	Job dimension
14.5	1.99	0.838	The way other teachers relate to you in the staff room
14.5	1.99	0.716	Opportunities for professional development provided by the local authority
16	2.04	0.650	Your level of competence in the classroom, given the amount of teaching you have done so far
17	2.05	0.868	The support you get from non-teaching staff
18	2.07	0.839	The local authority induction support programme
19	2.10	1.029	The willingness of experienced colleagues to let you observe them teach
20.5	2.12	1.036	Recognition of your status as a teacher by the head of your school
20.5	2.12	1.036	The support you get from the head of your school
22	2.15	0.952	Opportunity to meet and exchange experiences with new teachers from your school (if applicable)
23	2.28	0.879	Opportunities to get involved in extra-curricular activities
24	2.31	1.049	The help you have been given in finding out about school procedures
25	2.33	0.914	Opportunities for professional development provided by the school
26	2.34	1.069	School support for managing pupil behaviour
27	2.38	0.939	Opportunity to meet and exchange experiences with new teachers from other schools
28	2.38	0.801	Your personal capacity to manage pupil behaviour
29	2.39	0.764	Formal review of your progress (e.g. interim report) (if applicable)

Rank	Mean score	SD	Job dimension
30	2.45	1.207	The teaching accommodation allocated to you
31	2.46	0.914	Formal communications with your local authority (e.g. over arrangements concerning your induction)
32	2.47	0.818	The opportunities you have to help children achieve or to overcome their problems
33.5	2.49	0.760	Your relationships with parents at your school
33.5	2.49	0.986	Your current workload overall
35	2.51	0.986	The amount of collaborative work you do with colleagues
36	2.52	1.143	Availability of material resources for teaching
37	2.61	1.028	Your salary as a new teacher
38	2.66	1.100	The balance you are able to maintain between work and private life
39	2.68	1.140	Pupil behaviour in your school
40	2.96	1.101	The availability of permanent posts in your subject

1 = very satisfied, 2 = satisfied, 3 = neither satisfied or dissatisfied, 4 = dissatisfied, 5 = very dissatisfied

dissatisfaction. Space restrictions do not allow us to print a separate frequency table for each item, but inspection of the standard deviations shows that some new teachers were far more satisfied than other new teachers with some of the dimensions of their job. An example is the teaching accommodation allocated. Many of these factors will be within the school's control.

A correlational analysis was undertaken to estimate how far variations in satisfaction with the probationer job as a whole were related to variations in satisfaction with particular dimensions of the job. Factor analysis was not attempted because of the small sample size and the presence of heteroscedasticity in the data due to the inclusion of both satisfiers and dissatisfiers. Instead, rank order correlation coefficients were calculated (using SPSS 14.0) between each job dimension and satisfaction with the job as a whole. Table 8.6 provides the top ten correlations between individual job dimensions and overall job satisfaction.

In this table, a significant correlation coefficient means three things: first, that there was variation between the new teachers in their level of satisfaction with their job as a whole (as revealed in Table 8.4); second, that there was variation in their level of satisfaction with the job dimension in question (as measured by the standard deviations in Table 8.5); and third, that across individuals, satisfaction with the former rose and fell in line with satisfaction with the latter. The higher the correlation coefficient, the closer the alignment. While a statistical correlation does not prove causality, a significant correlation does provide *prima facie* evidence that the two factors might be related in some way.

Table 8.6 Top ten rank order correlations (Spearman's rho) between job dimensions and overall job satisfaction (2004)

Rank	Rho	No.	Job dimension
1	0.525	148	Your current workload overall
2	0.512	149	The ease of asking apparently trivial questions within the school
3	0.464	147	The degree of warmth with which you have been received
4	0.456	150	Recognition of your status as a teacher by other teachers in your school
5	0.436	118	Recognition of your status as a teacher by the management team members in your school other than the head
6	0.418	149	Your colleagues' willingness to listen to what you have to say
7	0.413	150	Recognition of your status as a teacher by the head of your school
8	0.410	140	Availability of material resources for teaching
9	0.404	134	Working relationships with colleagues
10	0.402	149	The balance you are able to maintain between work and private life

Correlations are significant at $p < 0.01$ (2-tailed)

The correlations in Table 8.6 provide additional support for the way our theory of early teacher development foregrounds relationality (McNally and Gray 2006). Overall job satisfaction varied most in line with relational factors such as the degree of warmth with which the new teacher was received and the extent to which his or her status was recognized, although material resources and workload also came into the picture.

Discussion

The findings from JOBSAT break new ground by identifying the main source of job satisfaction among probationers as relational – a friendly welcome into the school community, recognition of the probationer's status as a teacher, the establishment of good working relationships with pupils and colleagues, and so on. Thus the main challenge facing probationers (as far as achieving job satisfaction is concerned) is forming good working relationships, becoming assimilated into the school community and having their identity as teachers recognized. The extent to which this occurs will reflect the openness of the school's culture as well as the new teacher's willingness to accommodate him or herself to it. Worryingly, the moderately large correlation coefficients in Table 8.6 and the often quite large standard deviations in Table 8.5 suggest that schools vary a lot in this respect. Detailed examination of the degree of satisfaction for particular job dimensions, and differences between sub-groups, offer practical suggestions for making the induction year a more satisfying experience for probationers (suggestions that we make in Chapter 12).

Although statistical correlations in themselves do not prove causation, they can be read in conjunction with the personal narratives and the sense of individual identity formation obtained from reading the transcripts of the new teachers' interviews with the teacher-researchers. For example, the analysis of the narrative data of one teacher, one of the few to record outright dissatisfaction with her job on JOBSAT, reveals how her negativity was rooted in the way she was undermined by other teachers in the department:

> I don't have my own room so I am in and out of other people's classrooms and I feel that certainly I am being undermined at times when people [other teachers] come into the classroom and make comments in front of pupils about the way I am teaching

or the way things are being done and I don't necessarily think that is the way it should be done. I think perhaps that it should be said at a different time and certainly not in front of pupils.

(Butterkist)

References

Bowen, B. B. and Radhakrishna, R. B. (1991) 'Job satisfaction of agricultural education faculty: a constant phenomena', *Journal of Agricultural Education*, Summer:16–22.

De Nobile, J. J. and McCormick, J. (2005) 'Job satisfaction and occupational stress in Catholic primary schools', paper presented at the Annual Conference of the Australian Association for Research in Education, Sydney.

Dinham, S. and Scott, C. (1998) 'A three domain model of teacher and school executive career satisfaction', *Journal of Educational Administration*, 36:362–78.

Fraser, H., Draper, J. and Taylor, W. (1998) 'The quality of teachers' professional lives: teachers and job satisfaction', *Evaluation and Research in Education*, 12:61–71.

Herzberg, F., Mausner, B. and Snyderman, B. (1959) *The Motivation to Work*, New York: Wiley.

Jacobi, M. (1991) 'Mentoring and undergraduate academic success', *Review of Educational Research*, 61:505–32.

McDonald, J. (1981) 'Personality correlates of job satisfaction among school teachers', unpublished M.Phil. thesis, University of Aston, Birmingham.

McNally, J. and Gray, P. (2006) 'Finding an identity or meeting a standard? Conflicting discourses in becoming a teacher', paper presented at the Annual European Conference on Educational Research, Geneva.

McNally, J., Cope, P., Inglis, B. and Stronach, I. (1994) 'Current realities in the student teaching experience: a preliminary inquiry', *Teaching and Teacher Education*, 10:219–30.

Nias, J. (1981) 'Teacher satisfaction and dissatisfaction: Herzberg's "two factor" hypothesis revisited', *British Journal of Sociology of Education*, 2:235–46.

Poppleton, P. K. (1989) 'Rewards and values in secondary teachers' perceptions of their job satisfaction', *Research Papers in Education*, 4:71–94.

Van Saane, N., Sluiter, J. Verbeek, J., and Frings-Dresen, M. (2003) 'Reliability and validity of instruments measuring job satisfaction – a systematic review', *Occupational Medicine*, 53:191–200.

Wright, T. A. (2006) 'The emergence of job satisfaction in organisational behaviour: a historical overview of the dawn of job attitude research', *Journal of Management History*, 12:262–77.

Chapter 9

Fun in theory and practice

New teachers, pupil opinion and classroom environments

Peter Gray

Introduction

Fun as an educational concept is widely misunderstood, largely because little effort has been expended in trying to understand what it means and whether it can be a useful tool for teachers. There have been many attempts to attach 'fun' to schoolwork. Around 1970, a new textbook came into use called *Physics is Fun*. Needless to say, it was not. In their rush for a snappy title, the publishers had condensed the real version: *Physics is a Complex and Difficult Subject Which Involves Lots of Mathematics: Only a Few Experiments Might Be Considered Fun, and These Are Usually Not Allowed in Class*. A recent EU research programme, also called 'Physics is Fun' (Physfun 2006) attempted a similar feat, that of demonstrating that 'physics is easy and fun'. This chapter attempts to remedy the gap in fun research, using data from the EPL project and in particular the pupil opinion data gathered from the project's pupil opinion instrument.

Teaching and learning are increasingly defined in terms of outcomes, whether simply as examination results or in the four dimensions of *A Curriculum for Excellence* (LTS 2008). The EPL data, however, provide evidence for the basic nature of teaching as relational. That is, teaching is often ineffective unless a positive working relationship has been established with pupils and colleagues, a relationship in which reciprocal communication can take place and in which the identities of both parties are established and respected (Smyth and Fasoli 2007). This relationship can be explored through studying the classroom environment, and its ecology of teaching and learning. Fun is part of this ecology, whether teachers participate in its creation or otherwise. Unlike 'play' or 'games', however, fun as applied to teaching and learning is not the purpose of the activity, but part of the process. Fun is a state (probably an embodied state) whereas play is an activity and games are rule-bound activities, although learning and fun can, of course, arise from both.

In the EPL project, we were concerned with the measurement of new teachers' development in their induction year. As part of this measurement process, we wanted to measure classroom environment (Fraser 1994; 1986), on the basis that studies had shown correlation between positive classroom environment and pupil achievement (Dorman 2002; Bandura 1997). The resulting CEPSATI (Classroom Environment, Pupil Satisfaction and Achievement Instrument) was completed by 3,697 secondary pupils across a range of ages and topics in Scotland and England.

CEPSATI was designed to measure what helps children learn and how teachers can make that learning easier. The intention was to provide

> a formal but non-threatening [...] channel for feedback via a relatively simple survey instrument [...] In order to implement this non-threatening instrument, it was decided to opt for an oblique approach focusing on teaching and learning activity in the classroom rather than on 'the teacher' as such.
>
> (Gray *et al.* 2006: 2–3)

In order to build on existing classroom environment research in this field, we sought permission to adapt CEPSATI from an existing Australian indicator of classroom environment – WIHIC (What Is Happening In this Classroom?), developed by Fraser *et al.* (1996) – revising the EPL iteration according to the experience of experts in the UK context. The experts in question were six teacher-researchers, seconded to the project, who tested the indicator with approximately 200 pupils in their own schools. Changes to the Australian model were made by eliciting descriptions from these pupils about their new teachers, what their teachers did to help them to learn or what they did that inhibited learning. Although WIHIC was used with more-advanced age groups in different linguistic contexts to Scottish secondary schools, we felt that it was broadly applicable to classroom practice. We also took account of a critique of WIHIC by Taylor *et al.* (1997) from a constructivist perspective, and, combined with the advice of the teacher-researchers, a number of items were removed or adapted for the UK classroom environment.

CEPSATI identified 47 items of classroom experience according to a 4-point scale (1-almost always, 2-often, 3-sometimes, 4-hardly ever) and took 20 minutes to complete. In the space provided, the comments of pupils in both the pilot and survey proper suggested that it had been taken seriously, with a number usefully commenting on the scales used and the length of the form:

> I think when we first got it, it looked a bit long but it was really quite short.

> It was shorter than I thought it was and I could understand it fine.

> Easy to understand. There is not too many questions, it is a good amount.

> I have a comment about this quiz – it is too long and takes away learning time that we cannot get back.

There was, nevertheless, some apprehension about collecting pupil opinion data and the effects this might have on new teachers' morale and so it was agreed that completed forms would be returned in sealed envelopes under pseudonyms, without being made available to senior management in schools. Later evidence in fact revealed that some participating teachers used their class results to effect self-evaluation, in some cases changing their practice according to pupil responses (McNally *et al.* 2008).

CEPSATI was administered at three points, more or less equally spaced, throughout the school year, with new teachers being asked to choose two of their classes to participate. For practical reasons we could not insist on specific numbers of pupils or on particular classes; nor was it considered feasible to track pupils longitudinally across the three rounds, since most of the new teachers involved tended to rotate around a number of different classes. It was also felt that it would be as useful to obtain the views of a different 'audience' at a later stage, as it would have been to get the same pupils' views for a second and third time. As we have noted, 'there may well be inconsistencies, bias and repetition of the views of others in pupils' comments and responses, but their core view will have been formed over a period of time and as a result of multiple interactions' (Gray *et al.* 2006: 2). In this chapter, we extract from CEPSATI what pupils have told us about fun in the classroom, but first we need to establish its theoretical basis.

Fun in theory

We suggest that developing a theory of fun is essential to under- standing teaching and learning in schools, partly because of an increasing aversion to boredom in children's lives generally, in which the term 'boring!' has become a term of disparagement. Boredom occurs when nothing solicits our attention (Heidegger 1995), while for teachers, the desire for pupils' attention in the course of learning produces pedagogy (Zembylas 2007). Therefore we might view fun as the enjoyable focusing of attention on a dynamic situation. This is why fun has been theorized by computer-game designers, who have an interest in ensuring that players of their games have as much fun as possible, at least until they can develop a new version. Once players have worked through all the levels, they lose interest, and the game ceases to be fun (Koster 2005). This is, however, a fairly thin description of fun, since it misses the relational aspect. There are circumstances where an activity can be fun because of the inter- action involved rather than the nature of the task itself. Bakhtin's term 'Billingsgate' describes forms of 'low' discourse or badinage as originally used by 'Porters and Fish-women' (Stallybrass and White 1986: 117). This gives a sense of how fun might be conceptualized as something that can be added to an unpleasant activity to make it bearable or more pleasant. The concept of fun is, however, missing from the vocabulary of educational policy-makers, although not from that of educational resource providers. This may be because fun is at the wrong end of a 'frivolous/serious' continuum. Like 'carnival' in relation to everyday life, fun is discursively positioned as destabilizing or transgressive (Stallybrass and White 1986). Education, as part of the State, has to maintain its own 'grandeur' in order to justify its actions (Boltanski and Thévenot 1991), and fun is not a form of symbolic capital (Bourdieu 1991) that can easily be deployed in the service of power. Fun can be allowed or prohibited, but it is not something into which pupils can be coerced, since, as we argue below, it can only arise by mutual consent.

One characteristic of fun in the classroom is that it is usually a collective activity, albeit one that can be disturbed by a minority.

Having fun collectively implies that individuals are having it as well, but there is always the possibility of being excluded from collective fun. Pupils generally referred to themselves as 'we' when discussing fun, or 'working together' but 'I' when experiencing problems. It would be tempting to suggest that fun actually produces the collective 'we', since, as a collective activity, fun necessarily involves interactions and participation. Fun is not something which can be experienced vicariously, and seeing others having fun while failing to experience it oneself is usually irritating, unpleasant or worse. Thus, there is the potential for fun to be divisive unless all members of the class are actively included. This relates to pupils' strong sense of equity and fairness, as expressed in the CEPSATI results, which was upset by disruptions leading to loss of fun (as a privilege). The literature on collective work insists on the importance of shared representations, or mental models, of tasks or situations in order for actors to work efficiently in teams or groups (Grangeat and Gray 2008).

Neither is fun simply about interaction. Draper (1999: 121) explores the relationship of fun to software design and suggests that fun is about intrinsic motivation and is thus related to goals:

> ... fun is not in fact a property of an activity, but a relationship between that activity and the individual's goals at that moment. Most things that you find fun in the middle of a day on holiday you do not find fun when woken in the middle of a night during a work week.

To equate fun with intrinsic motivation emphasizes its temporal rootedness in the present, and Draper is right to point out the relationship between fun, goals and activity, especially in qualifying goals as those of immediate concern, rather than long-term goals for which the motivation may be more complex. We will show below that fun and 'messing about' were not seen as synonymous by pupils and that fun was associated with activities that had identifiable outcomes. Koster (2005: 7), also writing about computer-game design, argues that fun and learning are more or less synonymous: 'I think work and play aren't all that different, to be honest.' We think that fun is conceptually closer to work than to entertainment, since, in having a relationship to goals, it is purposeful, a process rather than a product. There were several comments from pupils that teachers who tried too hard to be entertaining were actually boring as a result, because their stories or jokes had no purpose in relation to the activity in progress.

Conceptualizing fun as a form of motivation that can be 'bolted on' to boring or difficult activities is therefore not enough. Fun also involves what Cziksentmihalyi (1991) refers to as 'flow' and what Heidegger (1962) calls 'transparency'. That is, when activities and/or artifacts (equipment) cease to require conscious attention in themselves, freeing one to concentrate on the associated emotional states or purposes. Draper (1999) makes a useful distinction between 'u-flow', in which one is not focused exclusively on the activity, as in driving a familiar route to work, and 'c-flow', where one is exclusively focused, as in driving in a Grand Prix race. This also has a temporal aspect: *time flies when you're having fun*.

Another problem in developing a coherent theory of fun is the relationship of fun to 'play'. The spatial implications and ambiguous meanings of 'play' are discussed by Heidegger (Inwood 1999: 167). Heidegger identifies four qualities of 'play':

1   It is not a mechanical sequence of events.
2   What matters in play is not what one actually does, but one's state, [...] one's mood.
3   The rules form in the course of play [and] bind us with a special sort of freedom.
4   Playing always creates for itself the space within which it can form and [...] transform itself.

Heidegger has a philosophical role for play as being-in-the-world, and he probably was not thinking about how to have fun in school, but nevertheless the above characteristics seem to fit the comments from CEPSATI that we will discuss below. The paradox of point 1, that rules actually support freedom to act, makes sense in the light of 3, since rules effectively create the world of the game, so long as the players accept and abide by them. Part of the essence of fun is thus that it has boundaries, however fluid these might be. When snowballs have stones in them, fun merges into violence.

The final aspect of fun to be considered here is its role as the representation of a desirable classroom environment. As an emotional state, fun might be thought of as ephemeral. Nevertheless, it can be positioned by teachers as a quality of activity planned for the future ('It will be fun going to the science centre'). Pupils were also able to envision future situations in which they would have fun:

'She [teacher] makes maths fun'; 'I always look forward to English because [teacher's name] makes it fun.' The data suggested that this desirable classroom environment has the following features: a teacher who keeps control of the class (i.e. explains things well; helps pupils with difficulties; is fair to everybody; does not shout or issue excessive punishments); pupils who cooperate (in a wide sense) with the teacher; freedom to work (i.e. freedom from disruption); freedom to enjoy a reasonable level of chat and banter; a comfortable physical layout and conditions; good resources and facilities.

Fun therefore appears to be not just an ephemeral, emotional state, but seems to combine representations of concrete situations with the emotional states associated with them. The pupil statements and responses provide evidence that fun can sometimes be combined with effective learning, at the opposite end of the scale to boring, ineffective learning. It is therefore not surprising that fun is central to pupils' conception of what classes and teaching should be like. It is important to note however that this research was not originally looking for fun (although it was an enjoyable project to work on), but was concerned with the learning processes and professional development of new teachers. This makes the results all the more significant, since fun emerged from the data rather than being an imposed category.

Fun in pupil comments

The following section is based on pupils' voluntary elaborations on the CEPSATI variable, 'The teacher makes lessons fun', together with comments from the open question at the end of the form: 'If you have any comments about the way your class works, please write them in this box.' The percentages of 'Almost always/Often' responses to the 'fun' question were very similar in both countries (Scotland 55.1 per cent, England 54.9 per cent). These were rather low compared with other positive responses, perhaps indicating that this is one of the more difficult problem areas for new teachers.

About 30 per cent of pupils wrote comments for CEPSATI (in the quotations that follow, spellings are as in originals), with issues of classroom management ('control') being the most frequent. There were many comments on fun and these have been largely restricted in what follows to those that actually use the word 'fun', but there were others that implied it. These instruments were, like most surveys, completed on an individual basis. The results, however, indicate that there may be strong feelings of class identity (expressed, for example, in the relative usage of 'we' and 'I'), which affect how relationships with teachers develop over time. Class identity is fostered by teachers who encourage teamwork, treat all pupils fairly and yet are able to differentiate and support pupils as individuals. It also requires effective behaviour management, maintaining a balance between lively interaction, keeping children on task and avoiding disruption. This is not a new finding in itself, and reflects common-sense views of teaching. What is new here is that it comes directly from pupils.

What does fun apply to?

Some comments refer to fun but leave it undeveloped except to say where it might be located as a desirable quality in classroom life:

> More fun things.
> Maybe make it more funner.
> It is fun and I would like it to stay like that.
> The teacher makes things fun.
> I realy like maths it is one of my favourite subjects because the teacher makes the lessons fun.
> I think pupils react differently with some teachers. We do fun things.
> I think Miss is a good techer but could give us less homework or include more fun activities in the lesson.
> Are class is good but we never do have fun.
> Lessons aren't fun.

It thus seems that fun can apply to a range of significant aspects of the classroom environment. Sometimes it is restricted to specific 'activities', but it can gradually expand to cover whole lessons, then to a whole class, then to subjects, then to the teacher herself. So the significance of fun varies as to what it is that can be regarded as its legitimate domain. Its dimensions also vary; it can be: relational (teacher-pupil/class); pedagogic ('makes lessons fun'); curricular (combining the cognitive and emotional – 'I realy like maths [...] because the teacher makes it fun'); temporal ('all the time', 'never').

Interestingly, a perceived shortfall in fun does not prevent a teacher from being thought 'good' or even 'great', although providing it would make her even better. Also, the same class can be seen differently in terms of its fun quota by different pupils. It would be interesting to research the question of homework, since the communal aspect of fun does not usually apply here. The only references to homework were in the preliminary statement bank where 'too much homework' was seen as a hindrance to learning, although 'help with homework' and 'homework clubs' were seen as positive.

What does fun mean to pupils?

Fun can apply to different levels of school phenomena, and some comments go further in specifying what fun might be at some of those levels:

> I like it at the end of the lessons when we do games on the board.
> Could we have a bit more fun things such as playing bingo etc.
> I think about once a week or maybe twice we should do something fun like ICT maths or chocolate maths.
> I would try to make lessons fun and do more group work and don't shout as much.
> Its fun when we use sewing machines and its also good because we don't have set places.
> My History class is fun and enjoyable.
> Miss [name] makes the geography lesson really fun and she allows you to have a laugh now and again.

Fun thus has different meaning for different pupils. Some appreciate it as a modest, occasional activity, contained to specific times and forms, perhaps as an instrumental incentive separate from the learning routine. Others see it as more integral to classroom learning activities ('more group work'), and interwoven into the whole emotional tone of a class (as 'enjoyable'). Broadly speaking, fun seems to be about being active, social and engaged.

Fun has value for pupils in that they are prepared to trade 'fun time' for 'work time' if necessary, where the demands of the work task prevent it being made into fun. In some circumstances, it incurs debts ('you've had your fun, now you will have to pay for it'). Thus, it is metaphorically conceptualized as a commodity which can be 'traded', 'imported' (e.g. watching videos) or which can be created from diverse materials ('she makes maths fun'). As a thing, fun is easily 'damaged' by disruption or by participants being in the wrong mood ('you're no fun this morning, miss'). This, however, was sometimes a positive quality since pupils will tend to safeguard it from the disruptive minority ('Sometimes when we are trying to do fun activities etc people butt in and ruin it'). Although fun can also be metaphorically labelled as 'volatile' or 'unstable' in that it can get out of control, the impression gained from both the CEPSATI survey and the other measures of new-teacher quality, such as classroom observations, was that a class having fun develops 'momentum' and is less likely to be problematic than one which is bored.

If 'games' are synonymous with fun, then even where the term is not used it might be implied:

> We are always writing from books and never do lessons that don't invole writing and do more games.
> Can we have more games.
> I think that Mis trys very hard to make things exciting.

In the next set of comments, fun is given an ethical value as a kind of 'fair' reward in classroom management issues:

> My teacher makes it fair because he says if we get it done or tidy up quickly we can play a game.
> If we behave well we have a fun lesson, if we don't we don't have a fun lesson.

Some comments offer basic contrasts (implying, on the face of it, what fun is not):

> Some lessons are fun but some are hard.
> Do more fun things than just simple work.
> Lessons are usually boring but sometimes can be fun – unusual.

The comments here relate to Koster's observation that 'boredom is always the signal to let you know you've failed' (2005: 46). Draper (1999), drawing on Langer (1997), cautions that adding fun elements as a 'sugar coating' may draw attention to the intrinsic tedium of a task (e.g. verb conjugation), although none of the comments suggested this was the case with the new teachers in the study. The evidence from our study is that fun is undoubtedly part of a continuum of feelings about learning, but that the best teachers were capable of extending the boundaries of fun into the realm of deep engagement.

There is a problem with defining fun from an academic standpoint, however, which is that fun, like fat or bacteria (as one new teacher observes), comes in good and bad varieties:

> It is a very challenging school … for example, a boy threw a chair at another boy … but – ha! almost now that doesn't shock me any more … I deal with it.

The problem here is that it is not clear whether chair-throwers think of themselves as having fun. The evidence from pupil comments is limited. Although no one admitted to chair-throwing, there were frequent comments such as 'I think our class works good but sometimes we are a bit loud'. There was an element of 'owning up' in these comments that suggests collective responsibility, and that in turn suggests a consciousness of boundaries, if not rigid observance. Fun is a bounded condition, where work is neither too easy nor too hard, but somewhere in between. The acknowledgement by pupils that behavioural boundaries exist is implicit in the kinds of comments made. Thus, pupils do not use the term 'fun' to describe malicious activities such as throwing chairs at each other.

This highlights the link between fun and shared representations. At one time it was acceptable to have fun bear-baiting, cock-fighting or smoking in the pub. Nowadays it is not. A shared representation has developed in which these activities are seen as unacceptable and have either died out or are driven underground/outside. Chair throwing is no more acceptable than corporal punishment and the social consensus among most pupils in the schools we surveyed is that violent disruption is contrary to the shared representation of school as work. In the comments it was clear that time spent waiting for classes to be brought under control, or sitting through disruptions, was not fun time for the majority of pupils. Disruption in this case is not fun. Theodosius (2006) uses the example of a nurse reacting to a patient vomiting (sympathy) or a drunk vomiting (anger, disgust) and analyses emotional interactions through a Freudian framework of transference and repression. In the case of teachers we could hypothesize that chair-throwing produces: anger (they can't do that!); guilt (I should be controlling/teaching them better); sympathy (no wonder they feel like that in this dump!); anxiety (what if they throw one at me?); and possibly, though no doubt highly repressed, pleasure (little ******* deserved that!). It is, of course, possible that pupils who engage in chair-throwing would not bother to add a comment to that effect. The almost complete absence of malicious comments (only two mild ones) across the whole exercise is not conclusive but suggests that pupils are capable of having a positive concept of fun as something related to learning and which they are entitled to expect from their teachers. With some new teachers, pupils found even mathematics or modern languages fun, which suggests that the teaching rather than the topic is crucial.

Fun: intrinsic or extrinsic to learning?

Some of the above comments begin to suggest how 'school life', its relationships, purpose and curricula, might be implicitly regarded. For some, it is in the nature of things that school is tedious, so fun is an extrinsic reward in this limited 'economy of performance'. Fun is thus part of some implicit contract: if teachers relieve the tedium, pupils will be better motivated to work. If the teacher fails to supply this resource, it may not be disastrous, as we have seen ('Are class is good but we never do have fun'), but failure to combine this with the ability to control the class spells real trouble:

> The class is naughty and sir cannot control them. people mess about every lesson we hardly learn.

In such instances, pupils might coin their own counterfeit version of fun ('mess about'), although it is significant that this pupil refers to (other) 'people' and not 'we'. If the teacher is failing to be the 'adult' authority in such instances, some pupil discourse can become more teacher-like:

> It would be better if the pupils were quieter and did more work and the teacher would be stricter and more serious.

Fun then can be a serious business, and an important and perhaps even central component of the learning process. But fun is not always seen as being just down to the teacher. Some pupils also see that they have some responsibility for achieving the right classroom mix of 'fun as learning' and 'fun as light relief':

> I think my class does quite well except for some people getting giddy at times.

For others, fun can have a more intrinsic role in the underlying 'ecology of practice' of classroom life. Fun can be seen as integral to collaborative learning, rather than just an added extra to sweeten the pill. It might even be a valuable part of a more engaging pedagogy for learning (including 'harder things'):

> We would like to do more games to help us with our learning. Do things with more fun learn harder things.

Further, fun can be integral to a more holistic judgement about being a good teacher and the overall feel of a class:

> This class works really well, the teacher is fun, good at teaching us stuff and being helpful.

So, fun on whose terms? It seems it has a relational dimension: at best, one in which teachers and pupils work together in constructing it as part of the learning process, or at least as a relief from the tedium of routine work or unengaging pedagogies.

Conclusion

New teachers are typically the least well positioned, as professionals, to influence curricula, relationships with peers and resource allocations in schools. They are also being assessed as to whether they are fit to teach in accordance with the Standard for Full Registration (Scotland) or Core Standards (England).

The use of competence statements as in the SFR has shifted attention away from the collective nature of teaching and learning, towards an approach that embeds all the required qualities in the individual teacher (McNally *et al.* 2008). Fun is rarely possible on an individual basis since that would lead to negative emotions of jealousy, feelings of unfairness, etc. (again as per CEPSATI), so it has to be collective in order to avoid these developing. On the other hand fun is inimical to hierarchy and control. The closest the SFR comes to mentioning fun is 'celebrate success' and to 'ensure learning tasks are varied in form' or 'take action to improve the impact on pupils'. Registered teachers:

> Can use of [*sic*] a variety of communicative styles, strategies and media to capture and sustain pupil interest
> (GTCS 2001: 2.1.2)

They have, however, limited experience, and are still learning so much about pedagogy, classroom management, procedures, pupils and school curricula. In all this uncertainty and newness, they are trying to invent themselves as professionals, so finding out by trial and error what kind of teacher they might be, and in that process establishing relationships and reputation with pupils, colleagues and senior staff. As fun can be important to pupil judgements about what kind of a teacher they may have, it can be at the heart of the early stages of teachers inventing themselves. So it can move from being just a matter of pedagogic technique to other levels, not only as a relational pupil-teacher dimension but also as part of the process whereby new teachers are inventing themselves as teachers and constructing professional identities. More broadly still, fun begins to open up issues concerning the purpose of education, the possibilities for collaborative learning, and the degree to which pupils may be 'ventriloquized' and limited in their expectations of school by assessment and control regimes.

The characteristics or dimensions of fun in school (i.e. both classroom-based and non-classroom activities such as physical education or drama) might thus be as follows: it is collective; it is reciprocal; it is interactive; it involves control (possibly collective control) rather than loss of control; it is equitable; it should not have a downside (e.g. future punishment, work time to be made up). The relational aspect of emotions comes through very clearly in the pupil comments. Fun in this context is experienced individually and collectively, and it is the collective aspect that good teaching seeks to promote. Perhaps paradoxically, it is the ability to differentiate pupils, and then to make lessons fun collectively for a whole class, which makes a difference. This is achieved by creating a shared representation of what has to be done (tasks, goals, targets, etc.). One of the salient features of such shared representations is that they have to extend spatially and temporally across the relevant field of activity in order to integrate task and purpose, so merely giving a class a passage to copy from the board is insufficient. Spatially, this provides somewhere for attention to wander into, most likely promoting the well-known negative emotion of boredom. Fun is therefore possible within a space which is bounded in such a way that pupils' full attention is within its horizon, but at the same time is informed by a collective purpose.

What we have done here is to examine the concept of fun itself, through both theoretical and empirical lenses. We have not attempted to specify what fun might mean in particular curricular contexts, since this would require several volumes. In any case, there are already many 'fun-packed' resources (in a wide sense) available to teachers, on the Web and elsewhere. It would be useful to conduct further research at a practical level, unpacking some of these resources and following teachers as they deploy them in the classroom. It might also be worth pursuing the links developed between fun, learning and game design, as suggested by Koster (2005). It is likely that ICT applications which are represented as 'fun activities' for learning are related in various ways to computer games (Richards 2008). Given the commercial context of game design, however, games will tend to be ahead of learning activities in both technical sophistication and their potential as fun. It would be nice to think that learning could get ahead of the game.

References

Bandura, A. (1997) *Self-efficacy: The Exercise of Control*, New York: Freeman.

Boltanski, L. and Thévenot, L. (1991) *De la Justification: Les Économies de la Grandeur*, Paris: Gallimard.

Bourdieu, P. (1991) *Language and Symbolic Power*, Harvard: Harvard University Press.

Cziksentmihalyi, M. (1991) *Flow: The Psychology of Optimal Experience*, New York: Harper.

Dorman, J. P. (2002) 'Classroom environment research: progress and possibilities', *Queensland Journal of Educational Research*, 18:112–40.

Draper, S. (1999) 'Analysing fun as a candidate software requirement', *Personal Technology*, 3:117–22.

Fraser, B. J. (1986) *Classroom Environment*, London: Croom Helm.

Fraser, B. J. (1994) 'Research on classroom and school climate' in D. L. Gabel (ed.) *Handbook of Research on Science Teaching*, New York: Macmillan Publishers.

Fraser, B., Fisher, D. and McRobbie, C. (1996) 'Development, validation and use of personal and class forms of a new classroom environment instrument', paper presented at the AERA Conference, New York.

Grangeat, M. and Gray, P. (2008) 'Teaching as a collective work: analysis, current research and implications for teacher education', *Journal of Education for Teaching*, 34:177–89.

Gray, P., Blake, A. and McNally, J., (2006) '"She is the best teacher in the world": surveying pupil opinion in Scottish secondary schools', paper presented at the Annual BERA Conference, Warwick.

GTCS (2001) *The Standard for Full Registration*, Edinburgh: GTC Scotland.

Heidegger, M. (1962) *Being and Time*, trans. John MacQuarrie and Edward Robinson, San Francisco: Harper.

Heidegger, M. (1995) *The Fundamental Concepts of Metaphysics*, trans. William McNeill and Nicholas Walker, Bloomington: Indiana University Press.

Inwood, M. (1999) *A Heidegger Dictionary*, Oxford: Blackwell.

Koster, R. (2005) *A Theory of Fun*, Scottsdale: Paraglyph Press.

Langer, E. J. (1997) *The Power of Mindful Learning*, New York: Addison-Wesley.

LTS (2008) 'Assessment for learning: introduction'. Available online at http://www.ltscotland.org.uk/assess/for/intro.asp (accessed 3 February 2009).

McNally, J., Blake, A., Corbin, B. and Gray, P. (2008) 'Finding an identity and meeting a standard: connecting the conflicting in teacher induction', *Journal of Educational Policy*, 23: 287–98.

Physfun (2006) 'Physics is fun'. Available online at http://cordis.europa.eu/search/index.cfm?fuseaction=proj.document&PJ_RCN=9437935 (accessed 12 March 2009).

Richards, J. (2008) 'Will the lights stay on?: Glow and embedding ICT into secondary school curriculum subjects: a quantitative and qualitative design-based classroom study', Edinburgh: GTC Scotland. Available online at http://www.gtcs.org.uk/Research_/TeacherResearcherProgramme/TeacherResearcherReports/will_the_lights_stay_on.aspx (accessed 12 March 2009).

Smyth, J. and Fasoli, L. (2007) 'Climbing over the rocks in the road to student engagement and learning in a challenging high school', *Australia Educational Research*, 49:273–95.

Stallybrass, P. and White, A. (1986) *The Politics and Poetics of Transgression*, New York: Cornell University Press.

Taylor, P. C., Fraser, B. J. and Fisher, D. L. (1997) 'Monitoring constructivist classroom learning environments', *International Journal of Educational Research*, 27:293–302.

Theodosius, C. (2006) 'Recovering emotion from emotion management', *Sociology*, 40:893–910.

Zembylas, M. (2007) *Five Pedagogies, a Thousand Possibilities: Struggling for Hope and Transformation in Education*, Rotterdam: SensePublishers.

Chapter 10

Design of the times

Measuring interactivity, expert judgement and pupil development in the Early Professional Learning project

Allan Blake

Introduction

The methodological design of the EPL project was conceived in 2003, at a time when the government funding of educational research was thought to have reached a critical stage. The view of those close to the purse strings seemed to be that educational research was becoming increasingly irrelevant to policy development. The then Secretary of State for Education and Employment had only recently challenged the ability of social science to improve government or face becoming 'ever more detached and irrelevant to the real debates which affect people's life chances' (Hammersley 2002: 7). Consequently, in a political climate of best value for money, the allocation of funding for research tended to be accompanied by criteria that required, for example, engagement with users, measured impact and knowledge transformation. The widespread impression was that funding was accompanied by an implicit ultimatum to make a positive impact on policy. Educational researchers, it was said, were drinking at the last chance saloon (McNally *et al.* 2004).

In the light of such thinking, it was felt that an extensive grounded theory of early professional learning, however robust its qualitative base and practitioner support, might not ultimately be enough to persuade those looking for 'hard' evidence as a basis for policy. A research-based model of early teacher learning which was to be adopted by the profession and its regulatory bodies, would therefore be expected to demonstrate how it could improve on current practice. In what ways, for example, would new teachers whose experience conformed to such a model benefit in relation to their 'unsupported' counterparts? The quasi-experimental design that was initially envisaged therefore included a battery of five indices, or indicators, of new-teacher performance that would cover the informal dimension of professional learning as well as more behavioural dimensions of teaching.

Our initial conceptualization of early professional learning was built on earlier, small-scale research findings of our own, combined with those from others writing in the same field, though often from different disciplines. It was from these findings that five important areas were identified for which quantitative indicators of new-teacher performance were designed. These were job satisfaction, and children's views, which are discussed in Chapters 8 and 9, and interaction with significant others (INTERACT), expert judgement of teaching performance (EXJUDGE), and pupil development (PDI), which are discussed in this chapter.

If a defining design tension can be said to have occupied the minds of the research team, then it lay perhaps in the co-existence of qualitative and quantitative methods within the one project. Therefore credibility seemed to rest on their compatibility and ultimate co-productiveness. The design was first and foremost naturalistic in that it depended on humans as instruments, and so was subject to criteria appropriate to naturalistic investigation, for example, transferability, dependability and confirmability (Lincoln and Guba 1985). When this was coupled with the demand for 'measurement' of outcomes and the inclusion of quantitative means, there was the potential for the research design to become problematic. As we explain in Chapter 2, it was because of the difficulty of making sense of the distinction between independent, dependent and controlled variables in the context of a live school setting (on which an experimental design would depend), that we eventually modified the design from experimental to correlational.

The synopsis above is intended to remind readers of the context to the development of the three indicators in the outlines that follow. They were each shaped by the complexities of a mixed methodological design; by the necessity of practicability in a school setting; and with regard to the inconsonance of taking too straightforward a view of human beings as instruments. As you might expect, the last chance saloon was tough going. The stiff drink was not the problem, but rather the thought of coming back for humble pie (McNally et al. 2004).

Interactivity

In response to earlier small-scale research (McNally *et al.* 1997) which found that beginning teaching was an affective transition in which relationships with colleagues were crucial, INTERACT was designed to probe the nature of these relationships and find out more about the actual interactions between beginners and significant others. Existing instruments for social network analysis are often based on generic items that fail to capture the specificity, for example, of an induction process or life in schools. As in embodied realism (Lakoff and Johnson 1999), the project sought to give credence to naturalistic accounts by participants of events or feelings experienced by them in material settings. This involved a trade-off between technical rigour and user engagement, since it was felt that the use of language and concepts grounded in the embodied world of (Scottish) teaching would produce more accurate responses than might have been given had the language been that of, for example, American universities, as was the case with most existing instruments. And although we recognized that interactions covered a range of verbal and non-verbal exchanges, intended and unintended, our operational focus was on the face-to-face conversations that took place. This was by far the most common kind of interaction, and we reasoned that new teachers would recall more readily what it was they had talked about and to whom than a less tangible sense of something that may have been learned during a teaching observation, for example.

Preliminary discussions with the teacher-researchers led to the view that the instrument should not take the form of a questionnaire (there was, it was felt, a risk of survey overload in continually subjecting participants to questionnaires, with a potential impact on their response rate and patience). Version one was therefore designed as a graphic flowchart onto which new teachers could map their significant conversations with others. We settled on a graphic form on the grounds that it could be completed most days in a couple of minutes by busy new teachers with priorities much more pressing and worthwhile than cooperating with researchers. The general rationale was that the foundation for quantitative measures of performance would mainly derive from the important dimensions of our existing qualitative theoretical base. Analysis of interview data indicated the range of people who interacted with new teachers (Another teacher; My mentor/supporter; A faculty head or SMT member; Another new teacher; A pupil (other than in class); A non-teaching member of staff; A friend or family member) and what these interactions were about. The items generated under these headings were grouped and standardized in discussion with the teacher-researchers. It should be emphasized, however, that the headings reflected questions to which a credible answer could be expected rather than empirically derived or literature-based dimensions, for example: to whom did the new teacher talk; what was the reason for the conversation; what was the conversation about; why was the conversation important – or a waste of time.

Following testing by the teacher-researchers in their own schools, 82 new teachers were issued with a book of conversation-recording schedules, and asked to complete one for each 'significant' conversation they experienced during the first three months of teaching in autumn 2005. The instrument advised participants that 'a "significant" conversation [...] is one which mattered to you at the time and which you remember afterwards'.

In the event, INTERACT was not as easy to use in practice as we had presumed. Completed schedules were returned by 19 new teachers, which represented a response rate of only 23 per cent (although lower than anticipated, the participation of these 19 teachers still generated records for 236 conversations).[1] The instrument's visual form was problematic for at least one new teacher, who commented, 'I'm not sure how to fill these in. Can't we have an exemplar?' INTERACT possibly encountered the typical problems of many diary-type instruments, most notably people forgetting or not having enough time. It may have been that during the initial design phase we over-estimated the time available to new teachers to engage with the instrument, and perhaps we should also recognize that the 'significance' of an event is not necessarily, or immediately, transparent to introspection; likewise, the remembrance of things past, if, as Proust (1983: 692) suggests, 'the better part of our memories exists outside us, in a blatter of rain, in the smell of an unaired room or of the first crackling brushwood fire in a cold grate'.

These impressions notwithstanding, we see from Table 10.1 that new teachers interacted most frequently with another teacher; their mentor or supporter; a faculty head or senior management team member; or another new teacher. It would be misleading, of course, to place too great an interpretational emphasis on which person category comes before another in an exercise such as this. For although INTERACT provides a frequency count of conversations, it

Table 10.1 Significant others with whom new teachers interacted by frequency

Person category		Frequency	%
	Another teacher	60	25.4
	My mentor/supporter	45	19.1
	A faculty head or SMT member	39	16.5
	Another new teacher	30	12.7
	A pupil (other than in class)	19	8.1
	A non-teaching member of staff	18	7.6
	A friend or family member	13	5.5
	Other	11	4.7
	Total	235	99.6
Missing		1	0.4
Total		236	100.0

says nothing about the intensity or duration of the encounters that it records, nor does it take into account the difference in sizes of the populations of person categories consulted (for example, there will likely be fewer new teachers in a school than experienced ones).

As to the reasons why conversations were important to new teachers (Table 10.2), 'I felt better' is the explanation most often cited (N = 102, 43.2 per cent), followed by 'I learned something' (N = 82, 34.7 per cent).[2] It is worth noting that it was conversations with another teacher that most often caused new teachers to feel better (N = 28, 46.6 per cent); conversations with a mentor or supporter appeared to be less significant in this regard (N = 16, 35.5 per cent).[3] The emotional and relational dimensions of beginning teaching are developed fully in Chapters 4 and 5; briefly, however, in discussing these findings we to tend to agree with Eraut (2004: 267) in thinking that the emotional dimension of professional work is much more significant than normally recognized, with 'informal support provided by people on the spot' – in this case, other teachers – tending to be more important (or at least opportune) than

Table 10.2 Reasons why conversations were important to new teachers by frequency

	I felt better	The other person felt better	I learned something	The other person learned something	I felt worse	The other person felt worse	Other
Another new teacher	13	3	10	7	1	0	2
Another teacher	28	7	26	6	1	0	5
My mentor/supporter	16	3	16	4	0	0	4
A faculty head or SMT member	16	4	16	9	2	0	3
A pupil (other than in class)	5	2	3	5	1	0	1
A friend or family member	8	1	3	3	0	0	1
A non-teaching member of staff	10	4	5	3	0	0	2
Other	6	1	3	3	0	1	2
Total	102	25	82	40	5	1	20

that from formally designated mentors or supporters (of the 45 occasions when a new teacher sought to speak to their mentor, in 22 per cent (N = 10) of those intended interactions the colleague in question was unavailable). The indication from INTERACT then, within this sample at least, is that in the first three months of teaching the affective component of interactivity ('I felt better') appears to be of moderately greater significance to new teachers than the cognitive ('I learned something'), a finding that appears to support the importance of the emotional-relational dimension in the learning of new teachers.

Because the response rate to the first instrument was lower than anticipated, INTERACT was redesigned as a card-sort exercise to be completed as part of the final round of interviews with new teachers in spring 2006. In this version new teachers were asked to place in order of importance the people with whom they interacted and then, in relation to these person categories, the following categories of interactions: exchange information; Get support/reduce anxiety; Have a laugh/offload; Solve a problem; Scheduled meeting. Allowing for changes to some of the categories subject to findings from version one, the combined indicator generated a triangulated database of new teachers' interactions with significant others based first of all on frequency counts of conversations that took place at the start of the induction year, and, secondly, on the conscious ordering in importance of people and conversations as they occurred to new teachers at the conclusion to the induction year.

Given the limited time that was available to deploy and discuss the cards and their arrangement, there is no way to be entirely precise about the exact ranking. Of the 50 new teachers surveyed (a response rate of 61 per cent on this occasion), we can be fairly sure (Table 10.3) that the most significant sets of interactants were (as before) other teachers (in the same department, specifically); a principal teacher or faculty head; a mentor or supporter; and another new teacher.

The important difference between the sets of results concerns new teachers' interactions with pupils. In attempting to sidestep the kind of tautology identified by Wilson *et al.* (2006: 412), who note that 'interaction of some kind is intrinsic to all teaching', we initially targeted pupils 'other than in class' (see Table 10.1). INTERACT was concerned with investigating conversations with pupils that went beyond the strictly pedagogical – though not necessarily, as we first implied, outside the classroom itself. The possibility that we may

Table 10.3 Rank order (1–12) of significant interactants by mean score

Person category	N	Minimum	Maximum	Mean	Std deviation
Teacher in department	46	1	7	2.83	1.539
Pupils taught	44	1	9	2.84	2.145
PT or faculty head	47	1	12	3.21	2.095
Mentor/supporter	46	1	9	3.52	2.178
Other new teacher	46	1	9	4.13	2.072
Teacher in nearby room	39	1	12	4.49	3.128
Family or friends	45	1	11	4.62	2.766
Teacher in other dept	43	1	10	5.70	1.934
Other staff	43	2	11	6.42	2.096
Senior management team	44	1	10	6.64	2.263
LEA staff	29	2	12	8.21	2.731
Other	12	5	12	8.50	2.355

have depressed the number of recorded conversations with pupils by prescribing their presence in class (in version one of INTERACT) as a means of differentiating the personal from the pedagogical could be suggested by the elevated significance of 'pupils taught' in the second set of data. Although the teacher-researchers generally explained that the type of interactions we were interested in were those falling outside the normal course of classroom exchanges (questions and answers on lesson content, behavioural instructions, etc.), new teachers were still able to identify areas where interactions with pupils were what might be termed 'professional' or 'personal' rather than 'pedagogical'. For example, explaining how an interaction with a pupil had the effect of reducing her anxiety, one respondent observed, 'There are days when you can take yourself far too seriously ... there is one girl in my class and ... when you're having a moment of [stress] she just shouts out, "Just relax, Miss", and you are like, "OK"'.

Although we acknowledge that an imprecision on the part of INTERACT may have concealed important interactions with pupils during the first three months of teaching, there remains the possibility that in the results from this second survey, we see evidence (in Table 10.4) of a later-phase formation of new teachers' relationships with pupils, in which the exchange of information

Table 10.4 Rank order (1–5) of top 15 significant interactions by mean score

Person category	Interaction category	N	Minimum	Maximum	Mean	Std deviation
Pupils taught	Exchange information	34	1	3	1.09	0.379
Senior management team	Exchange information	26	1	3	1.35	0.562
Family or friends	Have a laugh/ offload	33	1	4	1.36	0.783
Other staff	Exchange information	28	1	3	1.46	0.637
Teacher in other department	Exchange information	36	1	4	1.59	0.797
Other new teacher	Have a laugh/ offload	36	1	4	1.61	0.934
Teacher in same department	Exchange information	32	1	4	1.65	0.839
PT or faculty head	Solve a problem	33	1	4	1.67	0.777
PT or faculty head	Exchange information	34	1	5	1.68	0.912
Other staff	Solve a problem	22	1	4	1.77	0.922
Senior management team	Solve a problem	24	1	3	1.83	0.702

(continued)

Person category	Interaction category	N	Minimum	Maximum	Mean	Std deviation
Teacher in nearby room	Exchange information	25	1	4	1.84	0.850
Pupils taught	Solve a problem	26	1	3	1.88	0.766
Mentor/ supporter	Solve a problem	36	1	4	1.89	0.820
Teacher in same department	Have a laugh/ offload	32	1	4	1.91	1.058

is (from a quantitative perspective at least) the most significant interaction. Whereas INTERACT first captured the significance of emotional support from colleagues during the first three months of teaching – reflecting a 'traumatic first phase of starting teaching' (McNally et al. 2008: 295) – latterly we see emerging in importance new teachers' interactions with pupils, a phenomenon that we have interpreted previously in the light of an ontological security in which new teachers depend increasingly 'on their pupils, not only for offering a sense of professional purpose, but also for their very acceptance as a teacher' (ibid.: 294).

Fuller et al. (cited in Yandell and Turvey 2007: 547) are critical of situating the learning of new teachers within a 'dyadic newcomer-old timer relationship', and find evidence instead for a model in which all teachers learn 'from one another through their normal work practices'. But even within the restrictions of our own quantitative indicator of interactivity, the question of informal learning appears to invoke the notion of a community of practice that extends further even than Fuller et al. envisage; one that includes other (that is, non-teaching) staff, pupils, and even family and friends, each of whom (as Table 10.4 suggests) were involved in significant interactions with new teachers. It is encouraging to note, for example, that INTERACT recorded few moments in which conversations were a waste of time (N = 15, 6 per cent); few conversations after which new teachers felt worse (N = 5, 2 per cent); and few moments in which no one was available to talk (N = 17, 7 per cent). Indeed, even the new teacher whose classroom was isolated geographically from the rest of his department, and who had little interaction with either his mentor or subject colleagues as a result, was able to say:

> Teachers in other departments help me get through the day ... .
> I do have a good time with some of the management team; we have a chat, which is always a good thing. Also, I have got a good ... rapport with the old jannies [janitors] as well.

INTERACT, we suggest, has revealed the existence of an idealized kind of ecology that, if we may step outside the academe for a moment, might echo the civilized observations of a certain Tristram Shandy on writing and conversation – that as no one who knows what they are about in good company would venture to talk all, so no authority who understands the just boundaries of decorum and good breeding could be presumed to think all (Sterne 2000).

Expert judgement

The EXJUDGE indicator addressed the need for external expert judgement of new teachers' classroom performance. A team of judges comprising four experienced teachers who had worked closely with students and new teachers was assembled to conduct observations of teaching and to record grades and compile reports. We initially considered employing HMIs and head teachers, but given the practical difficulty of releasing either practising inspectors or teachers to visit and observe what could have been as many as 82 new teachers across Scotland, we secured instead the services of four recently retired teachers.

In surveying the literature on the nature of expertise, Farrington-Darby and Wilson (2006: 26) found that a 'commonly used criterion for the selection of experts is that of a *position* held'. Yet this is hardly an infallible standard. We too were aware that our judges' occupations as teachers did not alone certify expertise, nor guarantee the 'type of expertise that may [have been] ... relevant to the investigation' (ibid.). Had any of them been promoted for example, to a largely 'non-operational position', say faculty head, this could have been seen as diminishing their teaching expertise (ibid.), and, by implication, their ability to judge practice. Indeed, Bullough and Baughman (1995: 461) have found that the development of teaching expertise is situated, the 'product of a complex interaction of person and place'. This is a possibility with which we on the project were certainly conversant, and we were careful therefore to select judges with the maximum amount of recent experience of classroom practice. In arriving at our own understanding of expertise, we avoided assuming either that it was static (Farrington-Darby and Wilson 2006) or somehow conferred, and thought about it instead in terms of 'process – as something people do rather than as something they have' (Bereiter and Scardamalia 1993: 4).

The indicator itself combined qualitative and quantitative methods of investigation. Using the commentaries of our (now) expert judges, it first imparted a description of a single lesson as it unfolded. Secondly, it graded the effectiveness of the lesson according to a five-point scale. The grading was based on the expert judges' experience of working with teachers in their first year of practice. Thus 'C' was satisfactory or average performance, 'B' was better than average and 'A' was excellent teaching. 'D' was not quite good enough and 'E' was clearly unsatisfactory.

The purpose of grading was to generate a quantitative indication of the performance of new teachers, as well as give an indication of their rate of development across the year. New teachers were therefore observed halfway through the year (in January/February 2006) and again at the end of the year (in May/June 2006). It had been our intention to begin observations at the start of the school year, however, in our negotiations with schools, we felt that our scrutiny of teaching performance in the first few weeks (however benign the research) would have been a request too far and too early for new teachers in a vulnerable position, and might also have over-stretched the widespread goodwill that we had met in schools.

Regarding the description of the lesson itself, no predetermined criteria were used; the judges were asked instead to comment on those aspects of new teachers' performance that they considered important. We provided oral and written feedback to the new teacher at the end of the lesson, and, because the observation had no role in formal assessment, our advice in those instances focused primarily on positive aspects of performance (nor did we make known the grade). The decision to avoid using performance criteria was consistent with the aim of the project, namely the research-based modification of those fixed standards of specific behaviours that were imposed in beginning teaching. Also, it appeared to us (from our reading of expertise) that the application of standardized criteria would have had more in common with the kind of 'patterns that novices recognize [...] smaller, less articulated, more literal and surface-oriented' (Glaser 1999: 91), and therefore less related to the application of the conceptual, or even intuitive knowledge that was after all our purpose in appointing expert judges. The credibility of this approach is borne out, we believe, in the resulting rich descriptions of new-teacher performance, in which the judges are consistent in articulating their holistic professional judgement of classroom practice, including examples of specific pedagogic competence where required.

The EXJUDGE indicator could reasonably be taken as being inversely proportional to the formal SFR, which only 'grudgingly' accepts that a few examples of

> holistic quality indicators ... [of] ... an individual's capability ... [to engender the] respect of pupils in classes taught; being valued by other members of staff; having a purposeful class ethos; being trusted by parents; enabling pupils to make good progress ... could provide a useful way of supporting judgements made when reviewers are discussing progress with new teachers or completing their reports at the end of the induction period.
>
> (McNally *et al.* 2008: 295)

Readers may detect something of a dialectical interplay here between processes that are difficult to standardize and methods of verification that in reality require the complexity of a narrative structure. Whereas qualitative research into the social and relational dimensions of teaching and learning is thus afforded only a supporting role by the GTCS – an illustrative footnote at the end of the induction period, 'professional in shape and size' but unconscious 'of a more generous tide of blood' (Stevenson 1995: 284, 285) – the following extract from an EXJUDGE report of an observation carried out in February 2006 is typical of the indicator's findings, in that it records evidence of classroom 'atmosphere', which here is 'one of quiet industry and mutual respect':

> You [the new teacher] managed pupil behaviour firmly, fairly and with a quiet non-aggressive manner which pupils responded to.
>
> Classroom displays were interesting and informative – pupil achievement and attainment was recorded and displayed

prominently. There were many gold stars in evidence so I assume pupils are motivated to perform well. Pupil work also well displayed.

Differentiation introduction through use of extension work.

As opposed then to a narrowing analysis based on standard measures of performance, one's eye is drawn instead along a vista of extension in which the particular and the cognitive (behaviour management, attainment, differentiation) can be understood in relation to those context-rich and often elusive 'developmental processes through which performance is attained' (Glaser 1999: 100) – relationality, fairness, motivation – and which we take as being commensurate with the ability of our expert judges to 'perceive large, meaningful patterns. These patterns guide experts' thinking in everyday working activities. Pattern recognition occurs so rapidly that it appears to take on the character of intuition' (ibid.: 91).

For the secondary school phase of the project, 84 EXJUDGE observations were completed: 47 in January/February 2006, and 37 in May/June (see Tables 10.5, 10.6 and 10.7). There were 34 teachers with observations common to both rounds. The judges were of the opinion that the reduction in observations in May and June was likely due to the extra pressure of time generated by the approaching conclusion to the school year. For the purpose of statistical analysis, the grades were converted into numbers as follows: A: one; B: two; C: three, and thereafter submitted to a paired sample t-test (using SPSS 14.0 for Windows) in order to determine if the scores did imply a development in performance during the period of investigation.

Table 10.5 EXJUDGE mean scores

	Jan–Feb	May–June
N	47	37
Mean	1.68	1.24
Std deviation	0.629	0.495
Minimum	1	1
Maximum	3	3

Table 10.6 EXJUDGE grades January/February

Grade	Frequency	%
A	19	40.4
B	24	51.1
C	4	8.5
Total	47	100.0

The t-test examines whether the mean scores for the two rounds of data differ significantly, in the statistical sense, and therefore involves only the grades of those 34 teachers who were observed in both rounds. As far, then, as can be compared, the mean for round one was 1.56 (standard deviation, 0.561), and for round two, 1.21 (sd, 0.479), a reduction of 0.353, significant at $p < 0.002$. In sum, the grades conferred by the judges in May and June were more favourable than those in January and February, thus establishing (in the eyes of the judges at least) a degree of progression in the performance of the teachers observed.

We would be remiss, however, in thinking that such an analysis is unproblematic. For one thing it evinces what Colley (2007: 431) calls a 'highly teleological notion of "progression" as a linear trajectory onward and upward', which in hands other than those of our judges could be seen as part of a positivist tradition of control and standardization in schools which 'deflects responsibility onto the individual for learning and furthering their own career development', with failure to do so being 'construed as a deviant abdication of responsibility which incurs the punitive withdrawal of "rights" – in this case the right to teach'. Consequently, our own

Table 10.7 EXJUDGE grades May/June

Grade	Frequency	%
A	29	78.4
B	7	18.9
C	1	2.7
Total	37	100.0

'alchemic transformation' (Franzosi 2004: 561) of performance into numbers might best remain framed as a technique for 'gaining uses from information fraught with uncertainty, without either denying the uncertainty or losing touch with a basic attitude of scepticism' (Hazelrigg 2004: 104). For example, on what might appear to be a prosaic note, it is the case that the choice of lessons that were observed was determined by new teachers themselves, raising the possibility that the sample of observations was biased in favour of those classes that most advantageously exemplified 'better than average' performance. Then again, we might just as easily be inviting the charge of hubris in thinking that competent new teachers would be unduly influenced in their choice of class for observation for the purpose of academic research, at a stage in their careers when they were in any case researched formally and regularly for the purpose simply of retaining the right to teach.

Pupil development

The aim of the pupil development indicator (PDI) was to form a judgement about pupil progress in specific new teachers' classes in comparison to the progress that might normally be expected for a beginner. This was the simplest of the five indicators in terms of design but posed a number of conceptual questions. Should it measure attainment via test results, and if so, were these to be national tests or tests specifically designed for the project? Should it use samples of pupil work to inform external judgements, and should it incorporate other sources of data, such as pupil targets?

Attainment is assessed as a matter of course by schools and teachers and, on the face of it, determining the impact of new teachers on attainment should not have been problematic. In the context of our anticipated (but ultimately rejected) experimental design, we had hoped to see whether an intervention aimed at improving the development of new teachers could be detected in an improvement in the attainment of their pupils. But this is much more difficult than it sounds. We could not, for example, have used external exam results because not all of our sample would have presented pupils for exams at the end of their first year. Even if they had, we would not have had a baseline and so we would have had to compare overall attainment of pupils in the intervention group with a control group. The other problem with using external exams is determining how much of the pupils' attainment to attribute to the new teacher;

pupils will have learned some of their course material from previous teachers whose effectiveness might be expected to carry through.

As all of this suggests, the indicator ran into problems over the relative terminological claims of attainment, achievement and development. So although the idea of using standardized classroom attainment tests did receive some consideration, it was felt that issues of ethical and practicable acceptability to schools, and subject-specificity precluded the use of such tests. Given these difficulties, we felt that trying to link pupil attainment to the classroom abilities of new teachers was not likely to provide a reliable indicator of progress. Following consultation with local authority officers, we decided to make development rather than achievement, or attainment the focus and to rely on the judgement of experienced teachers in participating schools as to the evidence used.

Based on consultation with the project's teacher-researchers, PDI used a five-point scale to rate the development of one or more of the new teacher's classes: 5-much better than expected; 4-slightly better than expected; 3-about the same as expected; 2-slightly worse than expected; 1-much worse than expected. Space was provided to record results relating to four classes (including a description of the evidence upon which the rating was based). Though intended for completion by the principal teacher or the person responsible for new teachers within a department, space was also provided for the opinions of up to four colleagues where appropriate. Results were added together and averaged to produce a rating for each new teacher.

PDIs were sent to all the new teachers in the project, it being left to them to decide whether to submit their teaching performance to additional scrutiny by colleagues, or not. Indeed, only 27

Table 10.8 PDI grades

Grade	Frequency	%
5	10	37
4	5	19
3	10	37
2	2	7
Total	27	100

were returned (a response of 33 per cent). Although this is not a large number, the results were sufficient to establish a degree of comparison with those of EXJUDGE. The consistent finding from PDI was that most new teachers were regarded as doing good work and were valued and respected by colleagues. However, although the returns were too few to be conclusive, the slightly lower overall ratings from PDI do perhaps ask if the use of the Standard for Full Registration as a benchmark for observations underestimates the abilities of new teachers as compared, say, to the kind of holistic observations, recorded, for example, by EXJUDGE.

Conclusion

Engagement with users, measured impact and knowledge transformation; these conditions are based perhaps on a preoccupation with ensuring that educational research contributes to existing policy or practice (Hammersley 2002), and probably reflect a fear that the 'greater the number of values and interests that are exposed and legitimated [by research], the greater the demand upon the state to resource their expression' (Pettigrew 1994: 49–50). But the 'human dynamic', according to one new teacher, 'is so unpredictable, [that] one theory does not cover it all'. The challenge then for the EPL project in developing a practical model of new teachers' learning has been to address an activity which is a complex, socially situated process of intuition and implicit theorizing (Shulman 1986), at a time when pluralistic models of evaluation tend to be ignored by policymakers, who favour quantitative measurement over qualitative relativism (Pettigrew 1994). Perhaps, therefore, it is only fitting that the discussion of PDI should have ended on a note of indeterminacy, a cliffhanger as it were; as if in the last chance saloon 'the most heterogeneous ideas are yoked by violence together [...] their learning instructs, and their subtlety surprises; but the reader commonly thinks his improvement dearly bought, and, though he sometimes admires it, is seldom pleased' (Johnson 1993: 2405). If the narrative base of our theory development proves to be more discursive than policymakers can swallow, it may yet reflect more accurately those uncertainties in beginning teaching that require further attention from policy. In this, we have perhaps been less concerned with sustaining the compatibility of qualitative and quantitative methods within the one project, than with improving knowledge in spite of, or perhaps even because of any potential methodological conflagration. If research methods are like language in that they are 'ideological' and therefore 'produce, not just re-produce meaning' (Tseelon, in Malson 2000: 158), then in combining ethnographic substance and experimental-style evidence the EPL project has been fighting talk.

References

Bereiter, C. and Scardamalia, M. (1993) *Surpassing Ourselves: An Inquiry into the Nature and Implications of Expertise, Preface*, Chicago: Open Court Publishing Company. Available online at http://ikit.org/fulltext/1993surpassing/preface.pdf (accessed 28 November 2008).

Bullough, R., and Baughman, K., (1995) 'Changing context and expertise in teaching: first year teacher after seven years', *Teaching and Teacher Education*, 11:461–77.

Colley, H. (2007) 'Understanding time in learning transitions through the lifecourse', *International Studies in the Sociology of Education*, 17:427–43.

Eraut, M. (2004) 'Informal learning in the workplace', *Studies in Continuing Education*, 26:247–73.

Farrington-Darby, T. and Wilson, J. R. (2006) 'The nature of expertise: a review', *Applied Ergonomics*, 37:17–32.

Franzosi, R. P. (2004) 'Content analysis' in M. Hardy and A. Bryman (eds) *Handbook of Data Analysis*, London: Sage.

Glaser, R. (1999) 'Expert knowledge and processes of thinking' in R. McCormick and C. Paechter (eds) *Learning and Knowledge*, London: Sage.

Hammersley, M. (2002) *Educational Research, Policymaking and Practice*, London: Paul Chapman Publishing.

Hazelrigg, L. (2004) 'Inference' in M. Hardy and A. Bryman (eds) *Handbook of Data Analysis*, London: Sage.

Johnson, S. (1993) 'From lives of the poets' in M. H. Abrams (ed.) *The Norton Anthology of English Literature*, vol. 2, New York: W. W. Norton.

Lakoff, G. and Johnson, M. (1999) *Philosophy in the Flesh: The Embodied Mind and its Challenge to Western Thought*, New York: Basic Books.

Lincoln, Y. S. and Guba, E. G. (1985) *Naturalistic Inquiry*, California: Sage.

McNally, J., Blake, A., Corbin, B. and Gray, P. (2008) 'Finding an identity and meeting a standard: connecting the conflicting in teacher induction', *Journal of Education Policy*, 23:287–98.

McNally, J., Boreham. N. and Cope, P. (2004) 'Showdown at the last chance saloon: research meets policy in early professional learning', paper presented at the Annual ECER Conference, Crete.

McNally, J., Cope, P., Inglis, W. and Stronach, I. (1997) 'The student teacher in school: conditions for development', *Teaching and Teacher Education*, 13:485–98.

Malson, H. (2000) 'Fictional(ising) identity? Ontological assumptions and methodological productions of ("anorexic") subjectivities' in M. Andrews *et al.* (eds) *Lines of Narrative: Psychosocial Perspectives*, London: Routledge.

Pettigrew, M. (1994) 'Coming to terms with research: the contract business' in D. Halpin and B. Troyna (eds) *Researching Education Policy: Ethical and Methodological Issues*, London: Falmer Press.

Proust, M. (1983) *The Remembrance of Things Past*, trans. C. K. Scott-Moncrieff and T. Kilmartin, Harmondsworth: Penguin.

Russell, T. and Bullock, S. (1999) 'Discovering our professional knowledge as teachers: critical dialogues about learning from experience' in J. Loughran (ed.) *Researching Teaching: Methodologies and Practices for Understanding Pedagogy*, London: Falmer Press.

Shulman, L. S. (1986) 'Those who understand: knowledge growth in teaching', *Educational Researcher*, 15:4–14.

Sterne, L. (2000) *The Life and Opinions of Tristram Shandy, Gentleman*, London: Everyman.

Stevenson, R. L. (1995) *Markheim, Jekyll and the Merry Men*, Edinburgh: Canongate.

Wilson, L., Andrew, C. and Below, J. (2006) 'A comparison of teacher/pupil interaction within mathematics lessons in St Petersburg, Russia and the north-east of England', *British Educational Research Journal*, 32:411–41.

Yandell, J. and Turvey, A. (2007) 'Standards or communities of practice? Competing models of workplace learning and development', *British Educational Research Journal*, 33:533–50.

Notes

1 The data discussed in this chapter is for Scottish secondary schools with typically over 50 staff; schools with only a few staff (and most primary schools) have fewer relational options.

2 While participants selected only one person category per schedule, no such restrictions applied to the interaction categories. For example, the reasons why conversations were important (N = 275) exceed the number of conversations actually recorded (N = 236). That is to say, following an interaction, a new teacher could both have learned something and felt better.

3 Percentages are expressed in relation to the numbers of conversations with another teacher (N = 60) and mentors or supporters (N = 45), respectively.

Chapter 11

An age at least to every part

A longitudinal perspective on the early professional learning of teachers

David Dodds

Introduction

This chapter explores the professional development of those new teachers who took part in the longitudinal phase of the EPL project. This initial phase of ethnographic case study began in August 2004. It generated sets of sequential interviews with 25 new teachers in six Scottish secondary schools, and was supplemented by ethnographic observations of school culture as a context for learning to teach – equivalent, eventually, to some 540 pages of transcript. From the outset, it was apparent in the data collected that informal learning, emotions, context and identity formation were important dimensions of the experience. Studies which focus on the impact of induction programmes, as in, for example, the recent systematic review by Totterdell *et al.* (2004), tend to exclude such phenomena, perhaps highlighting a lack of empirically grounded evidence (Straka 2004). More generally, an enduring weakness in studies of the early professional development of teachers has been the absence of longitudinal data which might otherwise generate insights on the extent to which there may be stages of early development or indeed discontinuities at such key transitions as 'student to inductee' and 'inductee to fully qualified teacher'. Such evidence would be important for the development of meaningful policy on induction with perhaps a direct bearing on policy relating to teacher retention and career development. It was in order to address this inconsistency in teacher research that the decision was taken to build a longitudinal study into the project's design trajectory, and this chapter now examines the extent to which the dimensions of the EPL model remain true to the experience of beginning teachers beyond the induction year itself.

Of the 25 new teachers with whom the EPL project began in 2004, 12 continued to be interviewed until the conclusion of the study in 2007. By the end of the first year of the project, six of these new teachers had gained permanent posts within their induction schools, and another a post in a different school but within the same local education authority; a further four had gained permanent posts in schools in different authorities. By June 2007, only one of these new teachers had failed to find a permanent post; he was, however, in long-term temporary employment in a school in the local authority in which he had qualified. For the majority of these new teachers at least, the data suggested that the induction scheme was successful in its aim of ensuring that new teachers moved into the profession following successful qualification. The chapter begins, however, with the case study of the teacher for whom the scheme was least conclusive.

Lewis's story: 2005 to 2007

For Lewis, who did not gain a permanent post, uncertainty at the beginning of his third term of the induction year gave way first to frustration and then to disillusionment:

> I don't know. A couple of weeks ago I would probably have sat and ranted about not having a job next year but I've got over it now. It was annoying, it was really frustrating that I had worked my backside off for the history department and then I'd been told, 'Cheers, see you later'.
>
> (April 2005)

> I can see the benefits of [the induction scheme] and I can understand why the scheme was implemented, so that you don't have the situation where you've got people on probation for five years [...] At the end of the day I don't think there's enough in place at the end of it. So you've got the situation that I'm now in, and doubtless others across Scotland are in, whereby the GTC say you shouldn't have a probationer in a department two years running but there's no check to make sure that councils don't do that, so I'm now being replaced next year by another probationer, which leaves me at the dole office. It's something that I feel the scheme fails us on, basically.

It's not just a let down, it's an actual failure, because all the scheme has achieved in that respect is delaying the inevitable [...] despite having completed a very successful probation year, [I'm] in the position where I'm unable to get a job because I don't have experience, so although at some point over the year I have become a proper teacher, so what? It doesn't get me anywhere.

(June 2005)

Despite being highly regarded by his principal teacher, who felt that 'because he's been such a good probationer ... he hasn't actually needed much support' (PT history, June 2005), no permanent appointment was offered to Lewis, and the vacancy that arose in the history department for the following year was (as Lewis indicated) filled by another new teacher. Lewis therefore embarked on a long-term supply post in another authority, a situation that was repeated in the following year.

One year on, and the frustration is again evident in his comments:

In terms of whether I'm here next year or not it's still in the balance. I would have hoped that by this time in the session I would have had at least an inkling of an idea, if not a definite contract signed, so in that respect I don't feel I have been well supported [...] Apart from joining the dole queues at the end of next week things are going well.

(March 2006)

Lewis expressed frustration about the Standard for Full Registration, whose format he felt could not adequately reflect what he had achieved:

What that document tells the GTC is what classes I've taught this year. It doesn't tell them anything about the work I've done with them [the classes] or how I feel the year has gone. I mean there is no way for me to reflect on the form on the way the year has gone.

(May 2005)

Given the importance of the SFR, Lewis felt strongly that it should in some way be able to reflect the quality of his performance as a new teacher; that it should be capable of differentiating between different levels of performance. While it was never intended that the SFR would act as a CV at the end of the induction year, the disappointment expressed is understandable. Given that only approximately 1 per cent of new teachers fail to achieve the SFR means, of course, that 99 per cent are graded at exactly the same level. From the perspective of new teachers, the format of the document permits no detail of their accomplishments as teachers, thus creating the danger of a 'shadow' profile emerging as beginners collate evidence not just of their competence, but also of their 'all-round' quality. In a year that is already challenging, such an additional burden would surely be undesirable; the challenge then for researchers and policymakers would be to re-format the SFR such that it might convey a more comprehensive representation of the new teacher to prospective employers.

At the end of the induction year, new teachers' chances of obtaining a permanent post in the induction school do not then appear to be entirely determined by achieving the SFR, nor determined enough by the quality of their performance during the year. Quite apart from the competition inherent in the job market, the year-on pressure of numbers of new teachers in the induction scheme itself appears to have (in the example of Lewis) conspired to thwart the progress of an inductee whose performance is acknowledged as being better than competent. However, the guaranteed induction scheme can at least be said improve on the old system insofar as new teachers are now fully registered as and when they come up against the job market, and have been spared (as Lewis conceded) the protracted series of supply posts that might previously have been typical of their experience. Nevertheless, Lewis summed up the personal cost of long-term failure to find permanent employment in his final interview:

> I moved to Scotland. I was 22 and it didn't really matter whether I moved around at the time but I have other commitments now and I'm 26. I want to be settling down, putting some roots down somewhere, and until I can get somebody to take that chance and say, 'Yes he's a great teacher give him the job', that's obviously not going to happen.
>
> (June 2007)

The guaranteed induction scheme 2005 to 2006

One of the first questions to be raised in the longitudinal study was how well the teachers would cope once the supports (both relational and structural) provided by the induction year were withdrawn. Generally, new teachers were positive about what were consequential changes. Ann, who gained a permanent appointment in her induction school, reflected nonetheless on the loss of the support that had been a feature of the official mentoring scheme, and the importance of establishing (and maintaining) those relationships with colleagues during the induction year that can engender the kind of informal support to which we have referred in Chapters 5 and 10:

> I still car share with the other probationer and I think now [...] that] I have lost my mentor this year which I miss very much [...] I think that's kind of been a bit of a mentoring time in the car coming back and forward. We still talk about things the way we did last year.
>
> (Ann, October 2005)

The experience of the previous year is seen as providing a solid foundation from which to move on. But for all the feelings of increased confidence, of having taken a step forward, the new teachers do not describe their momentum in terms of the entirely linear, but reflect instead on a process that is suggestive of the kind of rehearsals, or trial and error, that we explore more fully in Chapter 13:

> Thinking about what I was doing this time last year, [...] there are different ways that I can teach lessons now, and I am starting to put that into practice and see if it is successful or if it's not successful; so the teaching strategies are changing and becoming more of a bank rather than just 'I know this works, I will stick with it'. I am more confident with trying out things now.
>
> (Julie, October 2005)

> I'm more confident [...] you know you've not got that new feeling, you do feel kind of you've moved that one rung up the

ladder. You know you're not the bottom of the pile [...] I think I
do feel I'm re-learning in some ways, I mean it's totally different
because you've got that year's experience behind you. You are
thinking, 'okay I've done a year, I am a teacher', whereas last
year it was very much just starting out this is my first year. So
it's different in that way and I suppose ... you're learning from
your mistakes from last year.

(Linda, October 2005)

A feature that was prominent in the data of those teachers who
gained positions in their induction schools was a growing awareness
of their profile in the school. They spoke of the benefits of familiar-
ity, both their own knowledge of the school and also of being known
by the pupils, some of whom they had taught in the previous year.
On the question of classroom management during the induction
year itself, one new teacher (in the longitudinal sample) described
it as a 'matter of trying to establish yourself and once you have done
that, you know relationships; it is much easier with the first and
second years because they are new anyway'. This teacher went on
to suggest that it was harder to establish these relationships with
third or fourth year pupils because they in turn knew that she was
a beginner in the school and so she had yet to cement her identity
as a teacher. From the perspective of a permanent position in an
induction school however, the 'main differences' for Pat between
first and second year were:

Not the same nervousness, not intimidated by big groups of
people [in the staffroom, for example]. Almost as if as a new
teacher you make things happen because you jump on everything. I'm now a lot more relaxed and confident. Also I know
the pupils and they know me. Build up a reputation.

(Pat, October 2006)

By comparison, those new teachers moving to a different school
do face some disadvantages. If not quite 'starting out' again, they
must at least retrace their steps in a number of important areas.
Although the SFR assumes that new teachers in possession of the
requisite (cognitive) skills and knowledge can simply transfer to a
new school, it underestimates the task of developing relationships
with a new group of pupils and colleagues; of learning a new set of
school procedures and practices; of adapting even to the size, layout

and location of a new classroom or school. For Pat, the prospect of moving to another school invokes exhaustion:

> What do all these different bells mean? What times do the periods finish? [...] Where is the staffroom, where is the ladies' toilets? You know I cannot be bothered with it, I just don't feel as though I have got the energy right now to want to do that.
>
> (Pat, October 2006)

Moreover, as Linda suggests, new teachers must once again develop relationships with (and perhaps even prove themselves to) colleagues within their departments and school as a whole:

> I was pleased to move school because it was a completely fresh start and I thought staff wouldn't think of me as someone who had just been a probationer. When the new staff were introduced there was a bit of a muddle so I think some staff missed my name and I soon realized that some staff [...] still thought I was a probationer. Although I was fully qualified it was like finding my feet again but I was relearning in some ways and learning from my own mistakes from last year. I had to establish myself with classes and I kept thinking back to last year and asking myself what I could do to make things smoother.
>
> (Linda, March 2006)

Like those new teachers who remain in their induction school, those in Linda's position no longer have an official mentor; but unlike the example of natural mentoring from Ann above, they might not come to know their new colleagues quickly enough to identify someone who could otherwise act as an informal mentor during a possibly demanding transition. That Linda had to re-learn or learn from mistakes, and keep 'thinking back to last year' to smooth the process of establishing herself with classes, suggests that new teachers in a new school do not simply pick up where they left off at the end of the induction year.

The Early Professional Learning model: May to December 2006

The project's research-based model of early professional learning was derived from the close analysis of interviews with teachers in their first year (2004/05), with testing of the model and further enhancement taking place in two subsequent phases (secondary schools in 2005/06, and primary schools in 2006/07). The model could therefore be said to reveal much about the 'becoming' of new teachers. An advantage of the longitudinal study is that it provides the opportunity to explore the relevance of the EPL model to teachers' development beyond the induction year.

Structural

The model's structural dimension refers to the way in which the induction year is organized, including placement of new teachers within authorities and schools, and the support of new teachers by the means, for example, of a reduced timetable and an official mentor. Perhaps unsurprisingly then, by the end of the second and third years of teaching these issues no longer featured prominently in the data, apart from an occasional, and possibly nostalgic, reference to the security they provided, such as Lewis's recollection of 'the induction cocoon'. Yet Lewis does not 'feel [...] there was a huge difference between going from a point seven last year to a full timetable this year [...] possibly because I have been more familiar with some of the material [...] I have been teaching more but I have not had to do so much work in order to do that teaching' (May 2006). And although Julie felt 'very busy [...] at my maximum [...] it doesn't really feel that different from last year [...] so it is no problem' (October 2006).

Cognitive

During the induction year, the cognitive dimension revealed that new teachers tended to interpret their level of subject knowledge as being adequate to the demands of teaching. In years two and three, however, weaknesses in subject knowledge did challenge some new teachers as their responsibility for higher-grade classes increased:

> I think now, subjects aside, I feel a lot more established.
> (Geller, May 2006)

> I am also getting Advanced Higher [...] in terms of your teaching skills those classes aren't the greatest because you just teach them, but in terms of your subject knowledge they are better

because they push you and extend you and it is a bit of a worry next year going in to teach them.

(Ann, May 2006)

I'm so scared about the Higher [...] because you know you feel that it is that step up and you really have to have a lot more knowledge.

(Linda, May 2006)

For some, the combination of greater confidence and experience, as well as the opportunity to develop resources that could be reused, provided something of an answer to these concerns:

I think it does get slightly easier in that you build up resources so you're not trying to create all of that from scratch, you do have a bank of things that you can pull on so from a workload point of view I think that helps.

(Diane, November 2006)

Rachael   I think my confidence is definitely soaring high, in that I feel more ready to take risks, so if I do have a class and I am going into territory that I am not sure if I am up there material wise ...

Interviewer Yes, I wondered what you meant by risks, if it was subject matter or ...

Rachael   Yes it is more subject matter and when it comes to poetry I have this sinking feeling that I don't deliver it properly you know, one of the teachers in the department is absolutely fantastic and there are some times when I just wish I could say to her, 'Could you read this form for me and I'll tape it', because she brings it to life and I don't think that I do that yet. I don't know if it is because I don't have the confidence or if I just don't have those skills [...] But I am finding more and more confidence in that and tackling things like [Robert] Burns, and before I always relied on a tape which can be a bit soulless.

(Rachael, December 2006)

One of the things that you did during [...] probation is that you planned everything [...] you planned for this, you planned for that [...] and I think you are much more realistic now. In the sense that you have just got to go with the flow [...] I was terrified to do that before because I thought, 'Oh God, I haven't quite read over that yet [...] I am going to say the wrong thing' [...], and now I am not afraid to say to them, 'You know I cannot remember, but before you come back in the next time I will find out for you'. And the kids are fine about things like that, they know that you are not going to be the all-singing, all dancing oracle [...] I feel that I have got the confidence in my classroom to just let the kids do whatever it is they need to do in order to actually get to the core point [...] I just feel now much more settled, much more confident, much happier with what I do in the classroom to be able to let them do that.

(Pat, October 2006)

Ethical

It will be clear also from the concerns expressed above by Ann and Linda, that the ethical dimension (most often expressed in relation to the new teacher's responsibility for the progress and well-being of classes taught) continues to receive articulation. Rachael, for example, explained that it was 'upsetting when you see someone struggling in class', and described the difficulty for her at exam time of 'see[ing] these girls losing weight and their faces are all sunken in' (May 2006). For Pat, the determination to see her pupils succeed overrides even her concerns about relationships with colleagues:

I have kind of got to the point where we accept each other's irritations and just get on with our job and I really can't be bothered at the minute thinking about that because I am just too busy trying to get my kids through exams [...] that is the most important part of my job; I mean getting along with whoever I am working with is secondary towards getting these kids through their final exams cause it is more important that they get what they need, than I get what I need.

(Pat, October 2006)

Similarly, when Rachael's requests for a classroom of her own are ignored, it is the concern for her pupils that causes her the most upset: 'The senior management just turn the other way and so I have just got to the stage where it is like "get on with it" [...] but I think it is my pupils that I feel for [*crying*]'. (December 2006).

Relational

Pat's reluctance to do more than simply 'rub along with' a teacher who irritates her does not suggest that the importance of positive relationships with significant others has changed in the second and third years of teaching. Just as in the induction year, the relational dimension remains central to the experience. Pat's equanimity at the behaviour of a departmental colleague can be explained perhaps by the enlargement of the network of contacts that have become available to her, as the teachers by this time are much more involved in the wider life of the school:

> I feel that when I was a probationer it was really just my table in the staffroom I got to know and obviously the people in the department. But now I know so many [people] throughout the whole school.
>
> (Geller, May 2006)

> The staffroom was always one thing that I was a bit scared of as well, but you know it is like going to the staffroom now is no bother; there are people there who you can speak to and you can speak about school or you can speak about something totally different.
>
> (Linda, May 2006)

The teachers continued to talk about the confidence gained from knowing pupils and being known by them, which they felt made life easier both in the classroom and beyond it. Simple social contact in the corridor, or feeling confident enough to enforce school discipline beyond the classroom, was seen as evidence of having 'arrived', of belonging to the school:

> The majority of the children that you are seeing in your classrooms now either know you or know of you, rather than [you] being this completely unknown entity [...] You can walk through the corridors and there are maybe kids that you have never even taught before who will say to you, 'Alright Miss, how are you doing?' Because they know who you are [...] they now

sort of recognize you as a member of the school community and part of, you know, Fenchurch High School [...] And not a single one of the kids that I am teaching or have taught have got the vaguest idea that I was a probationer last year.

(Pat, October 2006)

The sense of belonging to a community emerged tentatively during interviews with new teachers in the later part of the first term of the induction year, as they became aware of the difference it made to be staying in school rather than going back to university at the end of a placement. By the end of the second and third years the teachers expressed this notion in more expansive terms:

I am very proud of this school and I regard it as my school, it's my school.

(Rachael, March 2006)

Well maybe the biggest thing is becoming part of the community, feeling part of the community. Before I didn't feel that I was in anything other than one department.

(Geller, May 2006)

For Lewis, in his third school in two-and-a-half years, the situation is somewhat different. He described his relationship with colleagues in the history department as being 'very good'; ironically, it is for this reason that he is not 'too disappointed' at the temporary nature of his post simply because many teachers in this otherwise 'close department' are on similar contracts and will shortly be 'replaced with more probationers'. But if friends are made, and bonds forged in adversity, then outwith the department he feels that 'people might recognize me as someone they have passed in the corridor a few times now, but whether they would know who I am or what I do here ...' (May 2006).

Material

For many new teachers the primary expression of the material dimension centred on whether or not they had a classroom of their own. As they moved beyond the induction year most were allocated one, which was seen as a source of both satisfaction and status:

In my probationer year it was kind of peripatetic so I was in lots of different classrooms over the course of the week and [...] that was an added kind of pressure, whereas now I am not 100 per cent in the one room all the time, but I pretty much have a base where I can settle myself in and [...] that is much better.

(Diane, November 2006)

When you share a room [...] I never really felt it was mine, could never do what I wanted and say, 'I will have this part of the wall for my [pupils'] work' [...] Even the seating arrangement – you can't change that when it is someone else's room. Now I have a place for everything, whereas last year I was living out of a box and having to carry it everywhere with me.

(Geller, May 2006)

But perhaps the importance of having a classroom of your own is most clearly, and dramatically, illustrated by Rachael, who, after two years of teaching, is still working in 11 different classrooms each week:

[*crying*] it is just that people take things for granted like a classroom and I would love a classroom because I don't feel my classes are getting 100 per cent of me because I am constantly aware that I can't lay out chairs the way I want, I can't put them into groups the way that I want, I can't do displays of their work and I can't take ownership of the room, you know? I just feel constantly like my colleagues have it so much better and it sounds crazy.

(Rachael, December 2006)

Shared resources proved to be an ethical and emotional tribulation for Rachael generally; however, teaching for a third year in her induction school, and 'know[ing] the way the department runs now', she could see the benefit of 'working in partnerships with other people in the department':

Before, if someone had a set of books, I wouldn't have said to them, 'well, you use them period three, but can I use them period five?' [...] I have learnt that you have got to stand your ground because it is not you, it is the pupils in your class [that must be considered] and so when it comes to resources and they are in short supply, then you have to be assertive and say, 'No, I am sorry, my class is using this resource at this time' [...] I just feel that I am doing my class a disservice if I don't [...] stand up for them to give them the same opportunities.

(Rachael, December 2006)

Emotional

Rachael's interview responses illustrate that the emotional dimension remains in evidence in the second and third years of teaching. Indeed, much of the language used by new teachers to describe their induction year – the 'roller coaster' effect – is still in evidence:

Interviewer   Everybody talked last year about being on the 'roller coaster ride' but that feeling is not restricted to new teachers.

Logan   That hasn't changed.

(Logan, June 2006)

Same as before have lots of good days, lots of bad days and lots of days in between.

(Geller, May 2006)

Every single day is a roller coaster because you just never know what you are going to get from them [the pupils].

(Pat, October 2006)

Some things are the same: highs and lows so it's still a roller coaster and still like that because every year there's a new set of pupils.

(Rachael, November 2006)

What seems to be different is that the teachers are no longer engulfed by such emotional swings, and see them instead as an inevitable part of teaching rather than as something peculiar to themselves, or their lack of experience. For example, whereas Rachael once experienced 'dread' at the issues raised by 'pushy parents', she now explains: 'I know how to deal with them, I know that I could show them all the evidence and if they decide to go over my head, then I have done what I could' (May 2006). And Linda too feels less worried, yes, definitely [...] less worried [...] When I go home at the end of the day I'm not thinking so much, 'oh my goodness, I've just had such horrific classes today'; you know you will think, 'I have had bad classes' [...] but they have been more manageable.

(November 2006)

Temporal

That new teachers are better able to cope with the 'roller coaster' phenomenon could be explained by the temporal dimension. During the induction year, time appeared to be experienced as elastic, and even unstable. Many new teachers reported stages of the year as passing unevenly, sometimes at breakneck speed, at other times lingering. Although, in the second and third years of teaching, the passage of days, months and terms continues to fluctuate, the cyclical nature of school life functions as a stabilizing influence:

Ann	I think [year two] has actually gone quicker than my probationary year [... but] because I have an idea of what each term feels like, you know, that is a big difference, [... I] feel more relaxed again and not so stressed out about how things are going.
Interviewer	So you are getting more used to the cycle of the year?
Ann	Yes very much the cycle of the year and getting used to my life being governed by the bell [...] just knowing that you [are] constantly checking your watch [...] I think that is why it makes it go so fast and you are always conscious of time and time is a huge battle isn't it?

(Ann, May 2006)

Recognizing an aspect of teaching as it comes round for a second or third time seems to be an important factor in building up confidence:

You have good lessons and bad lessons [...] having taught the course one year and then repeating it again was much better as well, because you make mistakes and you try to think [about] that the second time of teaching and that was where I felt much more confident.

(Ann, May 2006)

I think it's good as well being able to just reflect on last year and kind of think [...] this time last year where was I with this particular class in terms of either their work, or their ability, or their behaviour, or whatever; and it's good to be able to think back and think, well, there has been progress [...] and how can I keep going?

(Linda, November 2006)

But perhaps it is Logan who most succinctly captures the importance of time for informal learning during beginning teaching, something that is otherwise overlooked by the teleology of formal competence:

Interviewer   Do you still use the Standard as a point of reference in your teaching?

Logan   The specifications for getting full registration are a load of rubbish, they don't really teach you how to be a teacher.

Interviewer   What do you reckon does that – is it just time?

Logan   Time and experience. Working with other teachers who know what they are doing. Learning from other teachers.

(June 2006)

Conclusion: 2006 to 2007

At the end of the longitudinal study most of the new teachers continued to speak confidently of their second and third years of teaching:

I could see what things didn't work out in Forth [Academy] but then I have come here and I have [...] tried something else, so now I kind of know what works for this school and what the kids are [going to] take and what they won't take for this particular school.

(Linda, April 2007)

That the dimensions of the EPL model that emerged from induction data are still in play suggests perhaps that new teachers are given the opportunity to experience an authentic introduction to the teaching profession while still being afforded the support necessary to allow them to cope with what is an intense experience.

The teachers themselves are very positive about the induction year:

> We can work that year through and gauge on what you have done for that full year because you have taught a full curriculum without a problem. I think it is perfect, I think it is a great idea.
>
> (Pat, October 2006)

Even Lewis, whose experiences following the induction year were difficult, had no doubts about the value of the scheme:

> As it stands the scheme itself is fantastic. I was particularly well supported, and I don't think that was unique.
>
> (Lewis, July 2007)

The interviews from the induction year and beyond reveal that learning to be a teacher is a complex, multi-dimensional and highly interactive process. Those involved in the delivery of the induction scheme, the GTC, local authorities and schools themselves, should recognize this. The SFR may be important in monitoring the quality of new teachers, but it does not in itself contribute to their development. That role tends to be performed by those with whom new teachers work most closely, their colleagues and the pupils that they teach. Schools and authorities must ensure that those people whose influence will be important are equipped to undertake their assigned roles. It is then that new teachers will be allowed to develop in a supported environment before moving on to the challenges of full-time teaching.

References

Straka, G. (2004) 'Informal learning: genealogy, concepts, antagonisms and questions', occasional paper, Universitat Bremen.

Totterdell, M., Woodroffe, L., Bubb, S. and Hanrahan, K. (2004) 'The impact of NQT induction programmes on the enhancement of teacher expertise, professional development, job satisfaction or retention rates: a systematic review of research on induction', *Research Evidence in Education Library*, London: Institute of Education.

Chapter 12

The implications of early professional learning for schools and local authorities

Colin Smith

Introduction

There are implications from the Early Professional Learning project for research, theory and practice. This chapter focuses on the latter, with the aim of helping both schools and local authorities to look at their own practice in the light of these implications. The bulk of the chapter focuses on schools (inevitably since the research was carried out within them). The issue for local authorities here is to consider how best to support schools in working through these implications. A few implications specific to local authorities are considered at the end of the chapter.

However, for reasons that will hopefully be clear, there are no prescriptions to be given. Each school is a unique institution with its own combination of personnel and material and structural circumstances. The best that can be offered here are questions arising from our research, which schools and authorities in support can apply to their own situation. Schools and authorities are also bound by national policy and quality frameworks and have to balance this with their own circumstances. We will first turn to the concepts of performance-management discourse and practice-setting discourse (Spindler and Biott 2000) that we find useful in relation to this balancing act.

Performance-management and practice-setting discourses

Spindler and Biott begin from the premise that we are currently in an era dominated by performance management. Within this view, managers are seen largely as appraisers and staff developers.

This perception extends to those responsible for the induction of new teachers. Thus, formal procedures are put into place so that new teachers have their work observed, their progress reviewed and their development needs identified. There is also a language handed down for this process in documents such as the Standard for Full Registration in Scotland and Circular 5/99 in England, profile documents, and so on. So, the discourse around these procedures ('performance-management discourse') is cross-contextual to the degree to which it uses this imposed language.

However, Spindler and Biott were also struck by how schools would often mediate this discourse by embedding target setting in a broader range of support for new teachers that incorporated their own needs and a recognition of the particular school context. This involved a different discourse they call 'practice-setting discourse'. This discourse is concerned with helping new teachers to feel that they belong and can contribute to the school. It also concerns helping the new teachers to survive from day to day, to understand the particular ways the school does things and helping them to avoid difficulties. It is individual and particular to context.

Spindler and Biott point to how new teachers have to handle these competing discourses and imply that different schools may emphasize each in different ways and to different degrees. This is also our own experience. Indeed, it applies not only to schools but also to departments within them. For example, as we shall see, departments in the same school may vary in the degree to which they use performance-management discourse as a tool for controlling and/or developing new teachers. We have already seen in Chapters 1 and 7 that the performance-management discourse around the interim and final profiles seems of little relevance to the new teachers as they find it difficult to cross-reference it with their own experience. However, both Linda and her colleague, Rachael, seem to have been able to place the performance-management towards the background. Chapter 1 relates how they were aware that others were using the SFR but it was not a priority for them. They were more concerned with the direct feedback from observations and their own personal assessments of their progress.

In the discussion of the relational dimension, we have seen how empathy and support from more experienced colleagues mitigates any serious difficulties. However, if we want a clear indication of the importance of practice-setting discourse, we need go no further than the opening to Linda's story. Here she describes how a chance encounter with two boys, and the comments they made, enabled her to feel like part of the staff, with pupils seeing her as their teacher. We almost certainly cannot legislate so that pupils always provide new teachers with such a valuable piece of practice-setting experience. However, schools can think about how to enhance practice-setting discourse and how to minimize the experiences of many new teachers of performance-management discourse as being controlling, restrictive, irrelevant or inadequate to express their qualities and achievements.

Implications for schools and practice

We start from the assumption that neither head teachers nor their staff want to deliberately put obstacles in the way of their new teachers. Indeed, we have seen examples of actively trying to reduce them. However, it is always worth considering if more can be done and we have also seen examples where new teachers have experienced conditions as unwelcoming. Given the contextual nature of practice-setting discourse, we cannot prescribe particular steps or rules that schools should follow. In fact, that may become another form of performance-management. Instead we phrase our aim as a question, 'What in practice-setting discourse helps new teachers feel welcome and find their identity as teachers in a school?' Our answer will not be a set of prescriptions but a set of questions for you to apply to your own contexts in practice-setting discourse. The questions arise out of our research findings of what new teachers found positive and what they found negative. We also use the metaphor of 'navigation'. New teachers have to navigate the dimensions of early professional learning and practice-setting discourse aims to help them in this. We should emphasize that we are not expecting, or even wanting, to dispense with performance-management discourse altogether. Merely, as Spindler and Biott suggest, it is possible to empower, where this is needed, its embedding in the actual context of individual needs and school context through a more conscious use of practice-setting discourse. Get practice-setting discourse right and performance-management discourse seems to us more likely to take care of itself in supporting EPL.

Since the aim here is to focus on practical questions that schools and local authorities can ask, rather than to describe and explain EPL, it seems useful to simplify the model a little. We will, therefore, consider these practical implications under the idea of supporting new teachers in navigating the following:

1 The school building and environs (essentially the material dimension);
2 The school's systems and policies as they are embedded in the wider educational system (essentially the structural dimension);
3 The formal and informal social relations in the school (interactions within the relational dimension, as expressed through practice-setting discourse, performance-management discourse and everyday discourses);
4 The delivery of lessons (essentially the cognitive dimension as it applies to classroom practice).

The other dimensions, the emotional, ethical and temporal, run through these descriptions.

Navigation of the school buildings and environs

Many schools organized tours of the schools and their catchment areas, and new teachers generally welcomed this. However, not all schools did both:

> The first time I went to try and find the base I got lost, so ... I could have done with a wee tour round the school I have to say. They were very good insofar as they took us round the catchment area and showed us all the schemes and towns that most of the kids come from, which was good, it gave us a history of the area ... if only ... they [had] done the same for the building.
>
> (William)

Also, the building tour may have been some time before the new teachers joined the school, with the result that much of the layout was forgotten. If the tour was not repeated, then its effect was largely lost. Also, new teachers may remain uncertain about the school layout for a surprisingly long time. This may be worst for those who join the school at unusual times:

> This is now October and I have been here since February and I

still don't know where some departments are, but I have never been shown an actual tour of the school because when I came in February, it was rushed [and] I had to get into my classes. So, I just kind of vaguely know where departments are and it is quite confusing.

(Kat)

Certainly, time to get to know the place before being 'thrown into' actual teaching was welcomed:

Obviously it was nerve racking. I think any new job would be to be quite honest but it was helpful that it was an in-service day so it wasn't like trying to get to meet staff and classes at the same time. It was just a day finding my way round the school and around the department, working out where things were, just getting to know ... getting a feel for the job really.

(Lewis)

Clearly, Lewis was further on the road to feeling physically integrated into the school than William or Kat. Note also how he equates it with getting a feel for the job: it is practice-setting. However, for others the physical proximity of people they could call on for help seems a more immediate priority. Lizzie worked in an art department that was largely open-plan (a way of working she did not like for herself) but where she had been allocated one of two classrooms:

People are easily accessible when you need them and I've also got the benefit of having my own classroom ... . And they've obviously done a lot of work to make it that way, I think ... . In fact, since I've been here, I've probably strayed no further than the main corridor in my department but I'm hoping that will change ... . I think it's good to go out and see other areas, but at the moment I would say I'm quite blinkered because I'm focusing so much on what I'm doing.

(Lizzie)

However, not all new teachers find the support they need as easily.

Sometimes trying to find my way somewhere or you know like, if I need to speak to somebody for guidance it's like, 'How do I get there?'

(Gordon)

Others operate on a need-to-know basis.

I think in the first few weeks you are trying to get used to your own department rather than going too far afield. I know the PE [physical education] department, the lunch hall, reprographics, where SMT [senior management team] is and staff bases and, at the moment, that is all I need to know.

(Mark)

Lizzie, above, pointed to the importance of her own room. Having their own room is important in practice-setting discourse between the school and new teachers in at least two ways. First, as we saw in Chapter 6, it confers a certain status because it is 'your room'. It signals to the new teachers that they are valued – they are not expected to carry materials from one class to another. Teachers apologize if they interrupt you in your own room but if you are in their classroom they may sit down and work. Or you may not be allowed to move anything or only be granted limited access to resources while being restricted in what you are able to create or bring to the lesson. This may work against the new teachers in other ways as inappropriate or outdated resources undermined their classroom management and, consequently, lowered their confidence and self-esteem. Even the movement into the room at the beginning of the lesson can create problems:

It's a total nightmare because the teacher before you is still tidying up as your class is coming in.

(Ann)

Also, the new teacher may not have keys, so that their status in the eyes of the pupils is undermined as they wait to be let in by another teacher. Having one's own room is important in signalling to the pupils that the new teacher is a person with status within the school.

Second, partly through this confirmation of their status, it impacts on other aspects of learning to teach, such as the relational and cognitive dimensions. They can learn by organizing the room in their own ways, and have time to set up lessons. It makes relationships with the pupils so much easier to build. This set of extracts from one probationer summarizes most of this and the same sentiments can be found in many other of the probationers' comments:

> I love it, I absolutely love [having a room] I've got a Smartboard and stuff it's amazing. [...] I came in before just to sort it, put my pictures up and do everything that I wanted to do. And then I was here and [a maths teacher who is also a depute head] came in and I was like, 'Can I take that time, can I do this?' And he's like, 'Listen it's your room do what you want', I was just like standing there going oh! You know, very different experience to other people, it was brilliant. This is my room, the resources ... . I've got keys for all the resource cupboards; I can go in grab books, jotters everything ... . It's my own space, I've got everything organized [...] I know exactly [what is] in my cupboards, where everything is, I've got worksheets at a hand's notice. I don't have to, like, cart everything from classroom to classroom. I can set my Smartboard up for the day with all my lessons on it ... . With my room I dismiss them, you know I let them go out the room and [...] I'm here for the other ones coming in and I can put something on the board for them here to say hello. If I didn't [have] my own room I wouldn't be able to do all that and I think that makes a difference with the classes as well.
>
> (Moira)

As we saw in Chapter 6, Trixie was particularly unlucky in having to work in seven different rooms. For Fran, it was not just working in different rooms, but also never knowing until the lesson where she was going to be. Chapter 6 also related problems of primary teachers who found themselves in open-plan schools: noise, lack of places to display work and lack of storage space. In both primary and secondary, teachers without their own room may find it difficult to find a place to work during their 0.3 preparation and professional development time. Indeed, this may be a problem for primary teachers with their own room as the class still needs to be taught during this time.

As can be seen from these examples, the practice-setting

discourse between the school and the new teacher begins with some of the initial decisions made by the school. We can identify a number of questions that schools need to ask of themselves as they work to ensure that the material dimension is used to support practice-setting discourse in a positive way.

So, what are the issues that this section raises for head teachers? Naturally, the answers will be different for different schools with different layouts but the above suggests the following interrelated questions need to be dealt with when considering how to help new teachers to navigate the school.

- When to organize tours of the school and catchment area? Should there be a 'refresher' when the new teacher starts work for real?
- Are there particular circumstances (e.g. extra time for the new teacher due to a relatively unstructured in-service day or arriving at an unusual date in the school calendar) that will help or hinder the new teacher in learning to physically navigate the school?
- Does the location of the new teacher's teaching space enable all the support and resources they need to be physically close and accessible? If not, what is the minimum number of locations they need to know and how do we ensure that they can find them easily?
- Does the new teacher have his or her own room? If this is not possible due to lack of rooms or an open-plan format, how do we eliminate the problems this causes – conflicts of space and resources with other teachers, access to the room, noise, movement of resources and the negative messages it gives to both new teacher and pupil about status?
- How do we ensure adequate and appropriate resources to support their classroom management skills, confidence and self-esteem?

Clearly, as some of the above new teachers' comments indicate, answers to these questions also affect other aspects of integration into the school and finding one's identity within it. There are also other practical issues that need to be taken into account when asking how best to help new teachers settle in. These include immediate issuing of cards for entering the school or buying lunch, issuing of keys and passwords for access to the school or its relevant parts or computer systems, and the understanding that distance from the main staffroom inhibits networking. Schools seem often to be unaware of how all of the above questions and practical issues, if not dealt with adequately, can leave new teachers feeling as if they do not belong. They are features of practice-setting discourse that support other aspects of forming a teaching identity and we should not underestimate their importance. We have also seen indications that navigating the issues that arise from the schools' systems and policies impacts upon relationships. We turn next to this dimension.

Navigation of the school's systems and policies

New teachers talked generally of experiencing a steep learning curve here:

> The system is a big thing [...] There's so many things, there's so many, you know all the emails.
>
> (Eilidh)

This learning is often left to trial and error:

> I've learned just basic school policies and school ways of doing things, you know like lateness [...] things connected with form classes and stuff. Just all the kind of admin stuff has certainly been something that I've had to learn and get to grips with and find out, discipline procedures and all that. Which has basically been trial and error, find out for myself and check with faculty heads if that's right and ... constant asking of questions ... And just reading up stuff like the staff handbook.
>
> (Linda)

While trial and error may be intrinsic to learning how to teach, in the context of systems and policies, and on reading Linda's words, one feels that this type of trial-and-error process cannot be the most efficient way for her or the faculty heads. What would happen if the new teacher did not ask so many questions?

Problems may occur from giving information without sufficient explanation:

We have several different passwords for the computers and it wasn't really explained what they were for and there were certain things like the Phoenix system and you are new and you don't know.

(Garibaldi)

One cause of concern for the new teachers is that they experience a relationship between systems and how others evaluate their performance:

Particularly at first that your real anxieties are reporting to parents and dealing with disruption, those kinds of things, those things that are right there and now and, you know, you feel you are going to be judged on.

(Lynne)

There is an interaction here between practice-setting and performance-management discourses that the new teacher has to work through. Commenting on an in-service experience, Lynne goes on to emphasize the need for early information and reminders:

Lynne   [There was] a bit on disruption and there was a bit on reporting to parents and ... also a bit on child protection which was useful child protection information because it was about dealing with children that perhaps abuse, and not to touch the children, all those kind of ... common sense ...
Interviewer   Good reminders?
Lynne   Yes, particularly early on.

However, working through the relationship between the performance-management and practice-setting discourses can be difficult as the former may consist, in this context, of sketchy guidelines. New teachers may need detailed guidance on systems and policies, rather than be left to learn them as they go along, particularly when the pupils are experts:

The most issues that I have is actually with my register class, that was one issue that I don't think was well enough explained at the beginning ... . I have a very challenging third year class who know how to bend every rule in the book and so the simple guidelines that I was given, just don't apply ... a few of them are on special discipline and guidance strategies, so they have different rules and I mean, the house head is generally very good at popping in, but to be honest I need somebody everyday. I have always got a question because the class are, they know how to play the system ... . I feel that there wasn't enough information but it sounds silly to ask for it because it is such a simple part of the day, you just give them a tick if they are here ... but it is not, you know, there is a million other little things and forms that need to be filled in and, on the face of it, it is simple, but when [...] the kids know how to play it, you don't have a hope. So I could do with, to be honest, a good session on that.

(Vonnie)

As Vonnie is also pointing out, we should not assume that things that are simple for more experienced teachers are also simple for new teachers. Performance-management, through time, becomes one's common-sense way of working – as long as systems do not change too quickly, at least. From the point of view of the new teacher, however, there is clearly a place for on-the-spot support, a colleague to take a few minutes to show you what to do. We can think of this in terms of developing a practice-setting discourse that helps the new teacher to cope with the performance-management discourse particular to the school and its systems of operation.

So the issues to consider here are:

- How to minimize the amount of trial and error the new teacher has to use to navigate the school's systems and policies?
- How to ensure that new teachers feel comfortable asking questions, however trivial these may seem?
- How to get information on systems and policies to the new teachers early enough, including what may be useful reminders of what may seem common sense?
- How to support information with explanations, when necessary?
- How best to provide information to new teachers who are faced with additional challenges?

Perhaps, these questions can be summarized under one general question. What practice-setting discourse can we put in place to support new teachers in achieving the performance expectations imposed by our policies and systems of administration?

Navigating social relations in the school

One clear message is that the more quickly the authority and school act, the better:

> I was still on my third placement [as a student teacher] when I found out what school I was at. I thought they were really well organized with that, so whatever they are doing there they need to keep doing it.
>
> (Haddon)

And prompt action by the school can get social relations off to a good start.

> The PT from my department was phoning me, you know, minutes, practically minutes after I had opened the letter telling me I was coming here. So they were really on the ball.
>
> (William)

The importance of feeling welcome is summarized by Frankie as she discusses the factors that may help learning to be a professional:

> I think the relationship dimension is a big, important one. I think that's the most important because at the end of the day it doesn't matter what school you end up in, if the people are supportive and nice to you and welcome you with open arms … then it's going to be a good experience for you. But you end up with someone who is a mentor for example, who isn't supportive, it's going to be a nightmare.
>
> (Frankie)

New teachers value a form of practice-setting discourse that is welcoming and quickly introduces them to the school. However, the quality of that welcome can vary:

> I have worked in retail and I have had jobs where I was the first point of contact with people … but I just didn't feel welcomed by certain people in this school […] I had this form class and

the amount of people who have come into my class and spoken to the kids and gone back out again and I have had to say, 'Excuse me, Nicole, who was that man?'

(Katrina)

One reason for some of this apparent rudeness may be that even established teachers are a little shy of new faces:

There seems to be an issue a bit in schools where once people know you they will talk to you, but when you are new they don't.

(Aaron)

Perhaps practice-setting discourse requires encouraging. However, there may also be issues of status involved in Katrina's example that we will return to below.

We discussed above how the benefits of a school tour could be lost and a 'refresher' required. A similar issue arises here:

[A member of staff] took us round and introduced us to all the, like, senior management team, guidance staff, principal teachers of every department and that was before the holidays, so, I don't know, you are meeting so many new faces.

(Gordon)

[Another teacher] did that when I came back, she walked me down and she told me loads and loads of people and when we got to the end she said, 'Who can you remember?' and Brian the janitor was the only name that kind of stood out and that was the first person I had met.

(Beatrice)

One way round both staff reticence and 'the sea of faces' might be to organize occasions, perhaps over the first few months, when new teachers and different groups of staff can meet and get to know each other a little better. This would also encourage supportive practice-setting discourse.

Some schools, through the approachability of staff, seem to be able to open up informal pathways:

I find that with the heads and the deputies that they [...] pass

you [in the corridor and ask] 'How are you doing? How are
things going?' And I feel that although with some heads and
deputies you just say, 'Oh fine, yes ...' they are very approachable and you could say something along the lines of, 'Well, can
I speak to you about something?'

(Haddon)

As they did when talking about systems and policies, new teachers here emphasized how they appreciated the freedom to ask
what might seem to be trivial questions of staff at various levels.
Practice-setting and performance-management discourses interact
positively in these circumstances.

However, status was an issue for many new teachers. In the current Scottish induction scheme, with its extra support and reduced
timetable for new teachers, they are marked as something different.
One head of department seems to have anticipated this:

He said, 'This is the last time that I will refer to you as "probationers". In my department, you are just teachers, the same
as everybody else'. And he never has, he never says the word
'probationer'.

(Wendy)

In one simple piece of practice-setting discourse, this departmental
head backgrounded fears concerning status, and, along with that
performance-management discourse. Any discussions about how
the new teachers are doing will now be in that context of being
teachers, not probationers. However, for others their status of not
being permanent members of staff is to the fore. Did the visitors to
Katrina's form class think that she was not worth acknowledging?
In the following example, two new teachers (Gavin and Katie) in
the same department were victims of historical circumstances that
affected both their social relations and their delivery of lessons.

One thing that we constantly get reminded of is, 'Remember we
have got to take your classes over again next year', because they
had a bad experience of a probationer last year, 'so we want
you to teach them the way we want rather than you teaching
in your teaching styles'.

(Gavin)

This led to them feeling uncomfortable in the department, as will be described further in the next section. However, one other issue needs to be highlighted, one that head teachers may have little control over: the number of new teachers in schools or departments. New teachers talked frequently of the support they got from each other and in finding that they had similar kinds of problems. A single new teacher does not have that luxury. Some also talked of the support they got from the previous year's entrants or from others within their own age group. However, such informal support groups did not always form naturally and may need to be encouraged.

What are the questions for schools raised in this section?

- How to ensure that the authority acts quickly and positively in allocating new teachers to your school?
- How to ensure that an appropriate member of staff follows this up immediately by welcoming the new teachers and inviting them for a visit?
- How to ensure that certain staff members do not undermine (even unintentionally) the positive effects of the above by appearing unwelcoming or rude?
- How to organize existing and new staff coming together, getting to know each other, and overcoming shyness or reticence?
- How to ensure that key staff members, e.g. head teachers and other managers, come across as approachable so that informal contacts can lead to formal discussions where necessary?
- How to ensure that new teachers feel that their status as teachers is recognized while providing them with the support they may need?
- How to encourage informal support groups between new teachers, and/or new teachers and recent new teachers, and/ or age groups?
- If we have only one new teacher, how to compensate for the support not provided by other new teachers?
- How to make sure that new teachers are not victims of historical circumstances in particular departments that may limit their scope for development?

Navigating the delivery of lessons

Gavin and Katie came from college with merits for teaching and felt that they had learned something about a particular style of teaching, involving:

> an atmospheric classroom with discussion and things like that; but in here they want us to teach the kids to work in silence on their own, no discussion, we are scared when the PT walks in, just in case it is too noisy.
>
> (Gavin)

Both were keen to emphasize that they did not have a 'know-it-all' mentality.

> Even though you get a merit, you are still told the things that you can do better, there is a big difference between being told, 'here is what you are good at and here is what you need to do better', than just being told you need to do everything better.
>
> (Katie)

A new teacher from another department in the same school suggests that this was a departmental rather than a whole school approach to new teachers:

> Well, I found that Cruella and I have both got classes that were taught by a teacher who will remain nameless and I have been told that man will never be allowed back in this school and you know what it is like teaching his classes, they are really hard work, but I have never had anything but total encouragement. I never had, 'Oh we had so and so teaching them and you had better not make those mistakes'. I have had nothing like that.
>
> (Jezebel)

Other new teachers seem to have a degree of freedom and, sometimes at least, learn their own lessons about how to handle particular classes:

> Instead of standing there, well, talking the way that I probably should as a teacher, I will be more slangy with them because that is what they understand and I will be, not their friend, but

I will be more friendly with them than what I probably should be … I call one of the boys, I say, 'Come on Shauny Shaun', and it is like, 'Nobody calls me that, just you'. You know, he appreciates that, but I would never do that with any other class but that is what they need … I started thinking … I need to respond to you the way that you need me to … and that has worked.

(Kerry)

Although it appears to be a balanced judgement that is working in this case, situations such as this might need careful monitoring to avoid some new teachers stepping beyond professional relationships. Against this, new teachers may bring skills that should be encouraged. Gavin and Katie were neither given the chance to find how to develop their own skills and conceptions of teaching, or to share them with their colleagues. Practice-setting discourse can be limiting for both new and established teachers if it does not find the balance between innovation and maintaining the status quo. Gavin and Katie also tell how their head of department used performance-management discourse to control them. Unlike other probationers, they were not allowed to choose the classes for their formal observations or the focus points. The head of department referred to them as 'crits' and came in with her own checklist.

Probationers often felt that they had adequate subject knowledge. However, one pattern that was noticeable in some new teachers was an initial concern with how to establish discipline and relationships with both pupils and colleagues. Once these were established, a concern with subject knowledge and how to convey it followed and some did not feel entirely confident. Degree knowledge might not be the same as that taught in schools, or it might be some time since it was acquired:

With history there are so many different eras that you can study and it is a long time since I studied at university, so I am constantly having to make sure that I am topping up my subject knowledge and a lot of it is still quite new to me.

(Kate)

Developing this subject knowledge, and how to deliver it in the school context did not appear to be formalized in any of the schools in the EPL sample. However, some heads of department seemed approachable and helpful when asked:

> I am having a wee thick moment here and I don't understand how to go about teaching or [there is] something I am supposed to be teaching that I don't understand [...] he sits down and goes through it with me ... and I go away quite happy ... and then he will come back and he will say, 'How did you teach that?' [...] then he tells me how to focus my points.
>
> (Cruella)

Perhaps this apparently skilled combination by the head of department of performance-management and practice-setting is something that schools should seek to support.

We have already seen in the context of navigating the school two other major themes concerning the delivery of lessons. Firstly, the value to new teachers of having their own room that they could organize as they wished. Apart from suiting their own teaching styles, this helped tremendously in establishing authority, as it signalled to pupils that they were 'real teachers'. We saw, where this was not possible, that new teachers talked of the difficulties in moving rooms period by period, carrying resources, ensuring any required technology was in place and sometimes just gaining access to the room. This often added unnecessarily to discipline problems and/or difficulties in delivering their lessons as planned. Secondly, some schools or departments did not seem to be efficient in pointing out the available resources or allowing new teachers advance access to them. Again, there were many comments on how this constrained the quality of lessons they delivered. So the questions asked earlier could equally have been asked in this section. It should also be noted that new teachers often felt that they had made significant contributions to available resources by updating or extending them, but that this was not always appreciated.

Beginning with the last question from the previous section (which seems to belong equally in both), what are the considerations to be added?

- How to make sure that new teachers are not victims of historical circumstances in particular departments that may limit their scope for development?

- How to ensure the school achieves the balance between allowing new teachers to use their own (perhaps new or unique) skills and personalities to relate to the pupils while not stepping beyond professional relationships?
- How to support, when required, new teachers in developing both their subject knowledge and pedagogical knowledge? How do we balance practice-setting discourse and performance-management discourse to achieve this?
- How to support the development of a practice-setting discourse that allows ideas and knowledge to transfer in both directions between new and more experienced teachers?

Implications for local authorities

Again there are no prescriptions that can be offered but only some questions. The most obvious question for local authorities is, 'How to support our schools as they explore the questions identified above?' Other questions follow from this.

- Should we as a local authority make it a matter of policy that schools should explore these questions and identify their responses in terms of policies and procedures that they will put in place?
- Although schools are unique in many senses, should there be opportunities for them to share their responses and practice across the authority?
- Are there additional resources (time, materials) the authority can supply to support the schools in both identifying and implementing their answers?
- Is there action we can take as an authority to ensure that school systems and structures, while adapting to the individual circumstances of the school, are more 'friendly' and accessible to new teachers?

One clear area for review by local authorities is that of how well they work with schools in, firstly, informing the new teacher which school they will be going to and, secondly, how quickly they ensure contact by an appropriate member of the school's staff and the new teacher. New teachers praised those authorities and schools that were perceived to do this well.

Another clear area local authorities might like to review is the in-service support they give to new teachers. Among the positives the new teachers identified were:

- reminders of good practice (common sense) when dealing with pupils, reporting, child protection, and so on;
- timely delivery of courses at appropriate times of the year, for example, a session giving advice on how to fill in application forms and tips for interviews was welcomed by many as they moved into that phase of their probation when they were beginning to look for a permanent post;
- a chance to share experiences with other new teachers;
- opportunities to learn about, and perhaps practice, new teaching strategies.

Among the negatives were:

- repetition of what they had already done in detail during teacher training;
- lack of an opportunity to share experiences with other new teachers;
- stage-inappropriate sessions – e.g. secondary teachers finding themselves at a course most appropriate to primary teachers and vice versa;
- sessions that did not match the teaching philosophy being espoused, for example, sessions consisting entirely of lengthy lectures while advocating that this is not a good way to deliver content.

Also, although this is not necessarily directly the responsibility of local authorities, there was a great deal of anger on the part of some new teachers that there was a shortage of jobs available as follow-up to successful completion of their probation. This was particularly acute among those who had been 'lured away' from other careers. It is worth considering the negative effect this will have on their teaching and relationships with the pupils during the latter stages of their probation, and if there are ways to help them through the psychological impact of this situation.

Reference

Spindler, J. and Biott, C. (2000) 'Target setting in the induction of newly qualified teachers: emerging colleagueship in a context of performance management', *Educational Research*, 42:275–85.

Chapter 13

The invention of teachers

How beginning teachers learn

Ian Stronach

Introduction

> I thought PGCE was a steep learning curve, but God, this is vertical.

> It wasn't my style and I didn't know what my style was, so there was all that, what am I going to be like?

This chapter develops a theory of early professional learning based on a study of Scottish and English beginning teachers. It draws on data from 2004 and 2005, involving 25 teachers in Scotland and 20 in England. The Scottish sample were interviewed up to 11 times in their first year by teacher-researchers from the same school as the beginning teachers. The account builds on work on the nature of professionalism (Stronach *et al.* 2002), as well as on earlier work on initial teacher experiences and competences (Stronach *et al.* 1994; McNally *et al.* 1997). We earlier argued that professionalism was a fraught 'juggling' between various 'economies of performance' (exam results, league tables, prescribed curriculum and pedagogy, set pace of learning) and 'ecologies of practice' (such as vocational commitments, sense of identity, institutional ethos). These tensions mobilized a shifting, plural and contradictory sense of the professional self as an 'uncertain being' and focused on the performative nature of professional acts. Since the research was based on experienced teacher and nurse identities, we had little to say about the 'becoming' rather than the 'being' of professional identities, and our hope in this chapter is that we can cast further light on professional identity by looking at how it is created in the first two years of occupational experience.

Induction 'versus' initiation: an uneven contest

> Apprenticeship always gives rise to images of death, on the edges of the space it creates and with the help of the heterogeneity it engenders.
>
> (Deleuze 1994: 26)

There is a common failing in narratives of early professional learning. Even qualitative accounts tend to construct and work from the fantasy of the *average experience* (e.g. Bullough and Young 2002). The teacher is transformed by respectable procedures of generalization, idealization and normalization into what anthropology has long called the *collective individual* (Stronach *et al.* 2002). We want to resist that process and hold on to the *singularities* of the experience, the fragmentations of the self, the sheer contingencies of time, place and event (although this is not to argue that we deploy a strict anthropological notion of 'initiation' – its neoliminal status and imbrication with induction need to be noted). Those acts of singularization are dominant in the data:

> I don't think I'm applying anything apart from my personality; you have to be a bit of a lot of things. You have to be an entertainer, you have to be a monitor, you have to be a nanny, you have to be an ogre.

And, of course, you also have to be the person who knows which of these personae to adopt in which circumstances. Split selves have 'vertical' as well as 'horizontal' dimensions; it may be significant that one of the failing teachers, who subsequently left the job, said, 'I just want to be me, teaching', and found it difficult to adopt any other persona. The rather singular recipe knowledge of induction fragments into plural and highly contingent working repertoires that themselves receive more or less judicious selection, adaptation, development and appraisal. If the first question that beginning teachers ask themselves is 'What works?', the first answer is that 'It depends':

> Because sometimes it just doesn't work like that, it depends on the class completely if it is going to work or if it is going to go completely out of the window. It depends on the personalities

in the class which is totally something I have realized [...] I was used to working especially for crits and things, like tick that one off, you've done that.

If they are going from one class to the next, then they are leaving one class reasonably calm but if they are messing about by the time they get to the next class, they are hyper.

Beginning teachers quickly find out that the common objects of teaching – pupils, classes, timetable slots, lessons, etc. – are extremely labile. Induction seeks to define them in tractable, if singular, sorts of way. The experiences of initiation mobilize and disseminate them – professional work is about doing the difference, not doing the same:

I thought all kids are the same and they're not, [they're] all totally different. What will work for one child will certainly not work for another and I've learned that through making mistakes.

Nor do those singular accommodations and transitions proceed in a linear manner. A recurrent theme is the unpredictability and reversibility of experiences – whether disciplinary, relational, emotional, pedagogical or curricular:

I think it's up and down, that's day to day, not even week to week. I'll have good days and bad days as well.

There are days when you come home and feel, oh I don't want to go in tomorrow, and when you've had a bad day and you're expecting the same the next, and then the next day is just fine.

It's only Wednesday, so far so good [...] it could all be changing next week. What are you looking forward to? Nothing. I hate it, that's it.

I've learned that no two lessons are the same [...] that no two classes are the same and not to expect them to be the same though you are preparing the same work, and it never works out the same [...] I think that keeps it fresh and alive for you.

A theory that applies to one person may completely fail to others. You have to have many strings to your bow as a teacher.

This unpredictability and singularization sometimes develop into a critique of the generic and idealized features of induction, heightening the sense of a chasm between preparation and the demands and responsibilities of 'real' performance. And that notion of the 'real' itself turns out to be multi-dimensional, involving items as different as teaching load, type of class allocated to the teacher, sense of responsibility for assessment results, the enduring nature of the commitment and the nature of personal engagement, as well as the development of relationships with and within classes.

There is an emotional corollary to such engagements. We might say that for beginning teachers the job can go all the way up ('The kids are great. I love my job'; 'I love it, I really do'), and all the way down ('worst experience of my life'; 'terrifying'; 'could have strangled them'). There are tears and breakdowns in the data, just as there are highs. Teaching, for many, is an emotional job in its early phases:

> I mean, how many times have I been in tears in my room saying, 'I'm leaving' and they're saying, 'No, you're not.' 'I am.' I've just been crying the first half term, it's just dead hard and I'm just so tired.
>
> (female, withdrew from teaching)

> There was one point when I went to the [induction] teacher and I broke down because this certain class was being really awkward and awful to me.
>
> (male, now recently qualified)

Initiation, then, could be crisis-ridden, epiphanic, unpredictable and reversible as well. As this teacher reports, looking back at the half-term holiday's unpleasant legacy:

> I thought, 'Oh God, can I do this again?' Just like the first day and I never expected that. Yes, I think that was the reason for part of the nerves because I realized I hadn't done any preparation during the hols and I was cocky, thinking ten weeks now, I'm a teacher now. I'm a teacher now, I don't need to do this – so on Monday I was right back to earth.

There was no once-and-for-all about these initiations. In their neoliminality they were incomplete, plural and reversible, an uncertain 'gift' that might be snatched back at any time. Doubts about career choice and/or teaching ability were frequent:

> There are moments of thinking that I am in the right profession, I'm really enjoying it here, I think I am in the right profession, I am not sure, because [...] then other times you think, 'Oh God I am so crap'.

> Sometimes I just think, 'Oh, I am just being rubbish' but then you realize that you have only been here a month and I thought that I had been here an awful lot longer than that.

> But there was one time when I was, like, 'Is this for me?'

Such primary emotional labour was full of swings in mood and self-evaluation, reflecting also the unusually solitary performances that constitute teachers' work as opposed to other professions where the work team offers more of an ongoing apprenticeship, more immediate feedback on what is possible and desirable, and of course, where the clients do not come in unruly bundles of 20 or 30. The more closely we were able to track the teachers, the more aware we were of a 'roller coaster' effect:

> You know, I will be absolutely honest, I have really a few times thought, 'Have I done the right thing here, is this for me?' And there was one day when I could really feel myself getting so stressed and I was thinking, 'This is actually going to kill me'. [And yet] on my good days, I think, 'No, they will be eating out of my hand by the end of the year'.

A final feature of the 'initiation' concerns performance. Beginning teachers do not just perform 'roles' for which they have been 'educated' and then subsequently 'trained', they also and more importantly perform *rehearsals* of, and *write plays* for, the teaching self that they hope to be. Doing and becoming are in peculiar dialectic. Sometimes that performance is deliberately deferred ('Mr Strict-till-Christmas'); sometimes it is denied if the pupils will not recognize the performance in the way the teacher hopes or intends (a teacher in his second year was determined to leave his very challenging school because he wanted to 'let my true teaching come out'); but on all occasions it implies the performance of a person-to-come, who represents certain values, beliefs or relationships. It was for that reason that this chapter began with a new teacher's quintessential question: 'What am I going to be like?' That is the defining uncertainty for beginning teachers in almost all of our sample[1]: 'Well, obviously you are tense because you know that something is about to happen but you, you know, it is an unknown, it is a complete unknown'; 'I feel out of control as I don't know what to expect from day to day'.

Thus far, we have treated induction and initiation as experientially separate, and that has an immediate plausibility since preparation precedes performance in the training sequence. We now want to look at the ways in which these two moments of early professional learning both come apart and come together. The latter phenomenon can be seen in the data in relation to successful transitions whereby the serial experiences of initiation and induction coalesce in the construction of notions such as 'reputation', 'name', or the emergence of 'Sir' or 'Miss'. How does that kind of transition learning take place?

Experimentation

We have argued that surface phenomena, like shifting notions of time or strange elisions of memory, indicate a rupture between the rationalities of induction and the exigencies of initiation. Both induction and initiation are forms of 'test', but their results are radically different and beginning teachers have to learn to insinuate themselves via the results of these 'tests' into the gaps between the reach of the former and the grasp of the latter. These early performances are therefore hybrid events: they are performances that act as rehearsals for future professional selves; they absolutely exceed the possibilities of induction, and they frequently fail to live up to some of the demands of initiation while at the same time exhibiting positive aspects drawn from both. There is no shortage of paradox and contradiction in becoming a teacher. The gap between induction and initiation is also both the threat to, and the promise of, an emergent professionalism. In this sort of conceptualization, we argue, professional identity and motivation are generated in a neglected improvisation between the two. Beginning teachers learn to 'sign themselves' into a 'name' or 'reputation' across these gaps. To put it another way, they come to 'make their mark' both with pupils and peers. It is to these forms of early 'signature' that we now turn.

To an extent that may be surprising, early professional learning was a matter of what was usually called in the data 'trial and error': 'loads of trial and error and when things don't work it's just the most [...] downhearting thing.'

> I don't think that being a teacher is a case of taking a theory and applying it.

> Quite a steep learning curve for me and a lot of it has been making pure mistakes and making massive mistakes and learning from that, recognizing it. You've got to recognize it, and evaluate.

Interestingly this last teacher then goes on to say, 'I've not had time for reflection and that's the biggest thing'. The paradox between 'evaluating' and not 'reflecting' can be explained by the immediate, tactical nature of evaluation of performances, as opposed to longer-term, more strategic reflection. The following quotations mark that distinction and its proportion in the data:

> I've learned more this year than in my PGCE year, much more, through making mistakes and dealing with it myself. (tactical)

> I thought to myself, is it the way I've dealt with it, or the way I've come at it, or, I don't know, or is it the case of they don't want to work. I don't know, but it's something I'm going to have to look at. Is it my teaching style? But it's just with that one class. (tactical)

> So I am having to write myself notes to maybe prepare it, so I've got it for use in the future, so I suppose it's a positive thing in a way that I'm learning from having taught it once, thinking, right, it would have been better having X, Y or Z, so I'll maybe try and prepare that for the next time. (tactical)

> There is a slight fear at the back of my head [...] I really want to have it clear in my head, you know, what are my key principles,

what are the reasons for this and what from university did I agree with [...] or change my views on. (strategic)

The most common report was 'learning from your mistakes'. That learning was often emotionally charged, negotiating the 'switch' from discipline to relationship, or from knowledge of the class to the individuals in it. Failure and/or success could attend these efforts:

> I think there is no substitute for learning on the job, OK, the kids may be the guinea pigs but at least they have your energy and enthusiasm.

> One of the third year boys who is constantly in trouble and talking to him and taking the time to understand how he felt and his emotions, and he actually broke down in tears and after that he's always been most helpful and I think it was because he knew he could trust me.

Early professional learning is inevitably antagonistic to 'theory' but it was clear from the data that even practice lessons during ITE were sometimes experienced as a kind of 'theory', being regarded as idealistic, abstract and formulaic – in contrast to the rush and imminence of 'real' teaching to 'real' kids for whom you had a 'real' responsibility: 'in the PGCE year, it's often laid out for you, lesson plans, what a good lesson is, and you'd have to copy what you'd seen in other lessons.' The key motivators for teachers in this phase of early professional learning were responsibility, care, reward, relationship, improvement and identity. We deal with each briefly (with the exception of relationship, which we discuss fully in Chapter 5), by way of illustration before arguing that these are key elements in the 'signature' of the beginning teacher. We then turn to an examination of the *nature* of professional learning in terms of experimenting, evaluating, concluding and reforming.

Responsibility

Responsibility is an unrehearsable aspect of professional perform-ance. In ITE, student teachers felt that they 'borrowed someone else's class'. They were not their 'own'. 'My class', 'my classroom', 'my teaching' were either weak or non-existent categories. As a result, 'my style' remained an enigma or a piece of training rhetoric. Now they were 'forced to take responsibility' and to realize that 'it is me, I'm the one'. They had to produce results:

> You're [grade] D? Oh, I'm sorry about that. I know you needed an A but there was nothing I could do about that at the time, but now I know how I can sort it.

Such responsibility was not simply or even mainly a matter of 'results' – a crude acknowledgement of the 'economy of performance' to which they had suddenly and fully become responsible. The 'ecological' features were expressed in trivial events that were not at all trivial to the beginning teacher's sense of responsibility, as in the example of Linda in Chapter 1:

> I had two boys approach me saying we won't be in Philosophies on Thursday because of football practice and we had a little bit of conversation and that really didn't happen in placement school because they would go to their RE teacher even though I was taking their class. That's definitely been a huge thing.

If a key question to ask of early professional learning is 'What is practice that theory is not?', then the answer has much to do with 'responsibility' and its articulation with other key elements, such as care.

Care

The 'love' of teaching is familiar in the data and in the literature (Nias 1996; Stronach and MacLure 1997). It was a feature of our data, and also received more ambivalent yet still positive expression:

> [I] want to be with them even though they drive me crackers.

> Although it's hard, I love teaching.

> He just comes up, shows me his work all of the time. 'Am I doing it right?' I'm like, 'Yeah that's fantastic', so it's that, it's that kind of personal … human side of it that is exactly what I came in here for.

It was also something that could develop from early experiences, rather than an *a priori* vocational commitment:

> You can see the differences that you can make in some, and you get disappointed when they do something bad when you are not expecting it from them, obviously shows that you care about what they are doing [...] I feel more passionate about it than I did, say, coming in.

Reward

'Reward' is an intrinsic category of 'return'. It was also prominent in the data, and as the above quotation shows, overlaps with investments of care in the emotional economy of beginning teachers. Most often, the reward reflected the emerging visibility of learning:

> You see the lights going on.

> I guess I *have* taught them something.

> You see them looking at you as if to say, 'What are you trying to tell me here?' So it's just been stepping back a little bit and coming at it from a different angle. You see the eureka sign on their face and it's quite satisfying and I'm thoroughly enjoying it.

The reward could be a simple matter of recognition – in the corridor, in the supermarket, by 'your' kids, or even others who recognized that you were a teacher at 'their' school. Or it could reflect a straightforward enthusiasm, either way:

> 'But we like you Sir, why can't we have you all the time?'

> [The pupils have] been saying 'It's great fun', which is nice to hear as they are going away from the class, or asking, 'Are we doing this tomorrow?' [...] It's quite rewarding when you see them really going for it rather than just going through the motions.

> I'm using the word 'work' but I don't see myself coming into work in the morning, I see myself as going out, doing something I'm enjoying.

Sometimes, the reward was more compensatory than absolute:

> I will go home some nights and I will have a glass of wine and a good cry and say, you know, I don't want to go back tomorrow. But you will go in and you will have some minor achievement of, you know, little Johnny in 2Y11 sat beautifully quiet and did two pages of work and you just think that makes it worthwhile. And then you are as high as a kite for the rest of the day.

It is important to note the rather characteristic disproportion in that account, whereby 'two pages of work' can make the respondent 'high as a kite'. It doesn't take much to make beginning teachers soar, or crash.

Cost

As we have already seen, the emotional costs are high for beginning teachers. The costs sometimes seemed to outweigh the benefits at first, and teachers noted the long hours, the extraordinary efforts they had to make, and hoped that it would get easier in succeeding years. Setting limits, time-management and reassurance strategies were evident:

> Don't beat yourself up when things go wrong.

> I took home about 90 jotters and sat till midnight marking them. I thought, 'Oh no, this is awful, this can't be right'. But if you time-manage, it's OK.

Taking things less personally was a recurring report. A 'thick skin' was necessary: 'they're just seeing how far they can go and how you're going to react, it's nothing actually to do with you personally.' Costs were often indicated in terms of finding a 'balance' or 'happy medium' between competing demands of the job and life. One of the most difficult was emotional: balancing commitment with the kind of strategic disengagement necessary to not taking things personally.

Improving

The final cluster from the data concerns a switch that most beginning teachers were able to make, from a predominant concern for discipline and classroom ethos to a concern focused more on curriculum, pedagogy and relationship, producing a kind of initial and provisional teacher identity, one that was established partly as a 'gift' of the pupils; 'having an identity with students'. The crafting of identity was, of course, aided by informal and formal mentoring, and by induction CPD in the first year. But it is very much the case that teachers invented themselves, in the mutually expedient trafficking between these different sorts of concern. Identity was the precipitate of these processes, the 'teacher' as product rather than agent of its construction. The beginning teacher comes last, not first, in initiation learning. And yet can be announced as a pre-existing 'real' me:

> No, I think initially I went in there thinking I had to be hard because the lady that had them before was hard, and then I realized that it wasn't actually me. I'm tough, I'm firm but fair, but I'm not as harsh as perhaps she was and I realize it didn't necessarily *suit me*, it didn't necessarily do me any favours to try and be *something that I wasn't* so I just went in and decided I was just going to *be me* with that form, that's the way I won them round. (our emphases)

Again, the trial-and-error processes of self-invention can be seen in the trail of 'if … then' logics that the beginning teacher begins to develop. As we will later demonstrate, the teacher very quickly moves from 'tip' prescription (do this and that will happen) through a period of more complicated experimentation with class relations until a stable resolution is secured. The process of invention is obscured in such teacher accounts because the self they invent is immediately renamed 'myself', and the process of trial and error is presented as a recovery rather than a discovery. In this sense the 'baptism of fire' is a naming that un-names the previous selves as selves of mere rehearsal rather than the creature of authentic performance.

Processes of invention

Thus far, we have mooted a positive *and* a negative gap between induction and initiation. In that gap, for better or worse, beginning teachers set about the task of inventing the teacher selves they will have. We stressed the trial-and-error nature of those experiments, and their necessarily singular nature. We argued that the data suggested that there are key areas wherein teacher identity was forged. In moving through these recursively a kind of preliminary signature was established, the originating of a 'name', 'reputation', and identity within the self, the class and the school. Occasionally, such a signature was easily achieved; around four weeks into teaching, one teacher contrasted the initial 'pressure cooker' feelings with his current equanimity: 'I can understand how I felt like that, in hindsight I can say it wasn't absolutely necessary to be that worried [...] now it feels as if I am the boss and I have got the handle on the class.'

More often the experience was of a kind of liminal vortex of challenging events, and provisional gains and losses. But even then some sort of signature emerged, something that deciphered the year-old teacher as a new 'sort' of person. It is striking how affectively dominated this kind of initiation learning is. The early-teacher self is forged in a largely emotional economy, where being responsible, caring and feeling rewarded (or not) dominate the construction and destruction of preliminary teacher identities. This is so because initiation learning invariably exceeds prior induction learning just as the experience of initiation dominates induction. But becoming a teacher is not at all a question of feeling (affect) rather than thinking (cognition). Indeed we will argue that one of the things that we most need to understand is the *thinking of feeling* that teachers undertake, especially in that phase of experimentation.

The purpose of this last section is to analyse the precise nature of the kind of trial-and-error thinking that makes up so much of the initial learning of teachers. Our approach here has to be illustrative and in-depth rather than comprehensive. The examples are chosen because they seem to us to best convey the kinds of thinking that new teachers more generally were carrying out. We start with the 'thinking of feeling' experiences of Catherine, in her first placement[2]:

> And there is one kid that actually I cannot stand him, I hate him, I think the reason I [do] not like him [is], he has been

re-integrated into the system, and he constantly says – 'Can't understand what you saying' – and I know that's because he knows he upsets me and I take it personally what he says, and I can't help it because on one front you are trying to get professional and you are saying 'Come on and we read the section, do you need any help?'. I think I have taken a step back and thought about how I am with him, he has no idea that I hate him because I am so with him and he is a complete bastard and I really don't like him, because I do take what he says personally and I think he is out of order and I think what he says to me he should get into more trouble for, and he doesn't. He says you're a T-W-A-T in your face and you just think 'Get lost'.

Catherine's emotional work is intense. There are seven vivid markers of her dislike of the pupil ('cannot stand'; 'hate'; 'not like', followed by 'hate'; 'complete bastard'; 'really don't like'; 'get lost') and three implicit criticisms of the school ('they let him back in after exclusion'; 'they respond weakly to his behaviour'; he is 'out of order'). Elsewhere in the interview she describes him as 'horrible, a horrible boy'. But there is no simple polarity here. She also stands back from that mutual antagonism – 'on one front you are trying to be professional', hiding her dislike and trying even to transcend it: 'I am so with him.' She is accorded a regimic self – 'Are you new, miss?' – and as such tries to cultivate a calm front, never shouting or confronting because 'they hate losing face in front of their mates so much'. Then again, she stands back from all of that in order to less emotionally review the gamut of her emotional responses: 'I have taken a step back and thought about how I am with him.' So a number of selves proliferate and police each other in this attempt to behave professionally.

The amount of emotional 'churning' is obvious; less obvious is the way in which 'professional' identity requires both a draining out and a filtering in of emotion work – and it can take much more demanding 'emotion work' to construct the 'unemotional', 'calm self'. Meanwhile, there is also a personal self that the 'kid' knows he has got at ('he knows he upsets me and I take it personally'). That personal self is also revealed by the odd disproportion between her response to being called a 'T-W-A-T' and the seemingly much less insulting 'Can't understand what you saying'. Her accent is 'southern', though deliberately neutralized through university at Liverpool and work in a care home there – she takes the swearing, the shouting, the sexism, and does her best to suppress all of that and find a more positive relation, but the accent thing gets to her. Why? Perhaps because she posits herself in opposition to the superficialities of background and accent, as fundamentally someone who cares, who has a 'strong social conscience':

> They [other trainee teachers] say to me, 'God, you are awful' [swearing about the kids]. Why am I being awful? They *are* [her emphasis] being bastards. And they [other trainees] are just sailing along with it all [...] And this is what I think, but I am passionate about it and this comes out in the way that I am ... and if it upsets me or whatever that is just because I care about them and want them to do well, and sometimes how bloody stupid they can be. Whereas I think if you've got no passion and they don't bother you – you are just 'Whateva', I won't let it get to me – why are you doing the job you're doing, because you just don't care.

The 'kid's' offence, in our reading? He is not allowing her to *care*. Hers? She knows it already, and the data has many references to the need to develop the same limiting mechanism – *not* 'taking it personally'.

Finally, we should underline the emotional intensity of these early 'professional' encounters and their impact on notions of self: 'It's weird how quick you feel you've transformed.' In particular, inventing an entirely fictive 'calm self' to respond to provocation is neither an easy nor a minor accomplishment:

Catherine   And I say, 'Get out' and he says 'I am not f-u-c-k-i-n-g going anywhere', and it is the way they speak. Like it takes all of my strength not to just scream in his face – God this is awful – because I just want to spit in his face, because I just think you are such a bastard.
Interviewer So what do you do then?
Catherine   I just very calmly say, 'Get out'.

Of course, such events are at one end of the range of situations in which beginning teachers and trainees find themselves. But the intense emotion work is common across the data. The emotional making of a teacher, their 'thinking of feeling', is not a simple or even an entirely rational matter.

The case of Rob illustrates the complexity of this emotion work from a different angle. Rob is completing his first year of teaching when interviewed and observed, with the author being present as a 'classroom assistant' in a very challenging urban school. At first, there did not seem to be emotional problems. He said he was 'laid-back', 'thick-skinned'. Then his response modulated towards a different acknowledgement:

Interviewer	What's the worst thing that any kid has said to you this year?
Rob	That's a really good question. I've not really taken anything on board. They've said it and I've just brushed it off [...] In the first part most of year eight were referring to the size of my head, just little things like that, but in the first couple of weeks I got really agitated about it. I thought they're just lads they just picked on me and they had a nickname for me which was 'Stakehead' and other lads said 'Eddie', like Eddie Murphy, and also referring to the size of my head [...] there's only one lad has carried it on, everyone else has just forgotten about it and just got on with it because if Sir's not reacting to it, it's null and void.

Denial and confession alternate in this account, most intensely in the rather Freudian juxtaposition and reduction – 'size of my head/ little thing like that'. It turned out that he had 'broken down' earlier in the year and gone to see the induction tutor for newly qualified teachers. And classroom observation did not confirm the sort of pupil 'forgetting' that he had claimed in the interview: the notes record a rowdy lesson whose crescendo Rob tried to quell with:

Rob (shouting above the hubbub)	I'm absolutely amazed that someone's talking while I'm talking.
Pupil	He's not happy.
Pupil on other side of class *(shouting back)*	If you'd a head like that you'd not be happy. (laughter)

The 'little things' that 'just lads' might say turn out to be ongoing, confrontational and very hard to handle. Even in small group conversation with Rob, pupils interspersed normal interaction with asides, delivered in a soft, quick undertone: 'Yeah, but you got a big head though'. It's a kind of edgy, one-way banter, and I feel that it's only a matter of time before I am included – Eddie joined by Nosey?'

If we think about Rob's story in relation to emotion work, of course we see a beginning teacher being tormented by some of his class. The painful nature of that is obvious. We also see him reluctant to do two things. First, he is ambivalent and partial about acknowledging his trials to the researcher. Second, and more important, we would argue his reluctance to fully acknowledge his problems is a form of self-protection, an emotionally necessary stage of partial self-deception. That script is necessary to his survival, as something that he believes will be in place even if his claims that it is already in place are unconvincing. Emotionally, he needs to say these things *until they come true*. More broadly, he is waiting for 'himself' to arrive. It may be touch and go.

We turn now from the 'thinking of feeling' and how that cashes out in terms of early professional learning, to a consideration of the 'thinking of thinking' – those *kinds* of thinking through which beginning teachers 'experiment' themselves into being and becoming. Again, our strategy is to offer in-depth illustrative accounts, because we are not concerned here with what new teachers in general think and do so much as the specific sorts of reasoning they deploy in order to learn.

As we have already mentioned, the teachers generally moved quickly from recipe knowledge (the standard injunctions about lesson planning, tips, etc.) to more elaborate forms of reasoning grounded in their accumulating experience. Typical 'recipes':

> You don't realize the significance of it, that's right, because even though you might let only small things go by, but they see that as 'oh'. You give them an inch and they take a mile turns out to be very true in this school.

> If someone starts talking I'll try and get them to be quiet straight away rather than letting it boil up so there's a few people talking.

If that is level one, then level two is less directly behavioural and prescriptive, and more indirect, complex and strategic. In the following illustration, the teacher does not make an example out of the individual, so much as perform an exemplary enactment of her own disciplinary self:

> Sometimes the way you deal with a certain incident doesn't actually affect the pupil you are dealing with so much, because some of them are so difficult, and might come from a certain background that doing whatever you do isn't going to do anything to them, but it's the impact it has on other pupils that's probably as important, because they see you dealing with that issue.

The notion of levels is problematic. In particular we would resist putting simple cumulative values on these levels. Teachers need a mix of different kinds of reasoning. Our point, however, is to illustrate the range of reasoning and to argue that CPD or mentoring interventions need to be able both to match and to engender those levels of complexity. If the notion of levels can suffice, however, as a kind of shorthand, the following extract might be regarded as level three:

> I am quite jokey and I will have a wee laugh, you know, and I feel that is myself and that is what works for me and I think my pupils all like it [...] Myself, when I came in, I was [very strict]; if I am going to keep going like this [being very strict] nobody is actually going to do it, it's only going to be through fear, because I'm going to yell at them. Or they're not going to do it because they don't like you, because they find that well, 'You are treating us like we are so far beneath you', and I have seen it happen a few times, and I just think that is not what I want to be, I am just going to be myself. And it took me a while to realize that and think, 'Well, I do know my stuff, why are you doubting yourself?' [...] I am actually a proper teacher.

The extract begins and ends with the 'real me' version of the teacher, and takes us through an array of 'if ... then' arguments; there are a whole series of conditional statements. If that strict, then: pupils won't work for me; fear-based discipline; yelling; not like me (present self); not respecting pupils; not a me I'd like (future self). Our point is not to recommend such strategies, or to privilege such accounts. It is to note the argued complexity of the reasoning, the multiplicity of consequences considered, and the appeal both to local evidence and experience, as the teacher reasons the transition from an initial disciplinary relation to one based on relationship qualities (e.g. respect, humour, confidence, identity, authenticity). Perhaps significantly, unlike Rob's data, there are more 'then' statements than there are 'if' conditionals. She may or may not have become a 'proper' teacher, but she did have a 'proper' story.

What struck us most was how quickly many teachers arrived at this sort of extended, situated, provisional, contingent and propositional reasoning, and in contrast, how simplistic and 'unreasonable' training rubrics could seem. Our concluding example comes from a teacher at the end of her first term (November 2004). Again, we offer it as an example of the 'thinking of thinking' that reflects beginning teachers inventing the selves they wish to claim as the 'real me' teacher:

> I found that if you've got usually some of the more lower ability SEN [special educational needs] issue pupils, they cause a problem which makes the attitude of the others different, so they'll be more surly while they're around the class [...] so you're trying to settle down the lower ability ones quicker, and that keeps the others more occupied because they're getting more interested, but because we do a lot of practical lessons the lower ability tend to do that anyway so once they realize that I trust them and they can start trusting me, and, if I do tell them off, if I've got to discipline them, I've found that if I take them out of the classroom, if that's possible, more than if you sort of punish them or whatever in the middle of their friends, they do tend to respond better.
>
> (Wendy)

There are six 'if' statements in that account. There are nine consequential statements ('because', 'so', or implicit). All of these are contained in one sentence, and again we see the enormously rapid growth in complexity and range of early professional learning. These complex algorithms constitute real professional knowledge, they are highly diagnostic in nature, and while far from impervious to outside influence, they do seem to dominate the inventing, experimenting and finding out that beginning teachers usually undertake.

Beginning teachers sometimes felt that abstract training in broad constructs such as 'inclusion' or 'national priorities' were premature:

'they [PGCE tutors] never say, "During the first four weeks in school you had better know this, and do this."' How to fill in a register, lodge marks or attendance in the computer, and so on, are on the one hand trivial but they do mark 'face' issues for the teacher in successfully performing the role in front of pupils who are sometimes eager in the 'trying it on' stage to see such performances fail. This is not to recommend a 'trivial' curriculum, but we do suggest that teachers in training lack access to accounts of what the 'real' experience may be like, and that such anticipatory accounts would help reduce unknown aspects of initiation, as well as increasing the possibility for reflective learning. In this chapter we have made no attempt to portray the variable qualities of induction, but we stress that induction can be and was in many cases a positive if relatively slight influence on subsequent performance. Our intention, instead, has been to portray early professional learning as best characterized not by stages, or linear developments (although these are not excluded) but by recursive, disruptive rehearsals that are best understood within philosophies of difference, and which occur in what we claim to be an *unavoidable* gap between the reach of induction and the grasp of initiation:

> One is static, the other dynamic. One is repetition in the effect, the other in the cause. One is extensive, the other intensive. One is ordinary, the other distinctive and singular [...] One is developed and explicated, the other enveloped and in need of interpretation. One is revolving, the other evolving. One involves equality, commensurability and symmetry, the other is grounded in inequality, incommensurability and dissymmetry [...] One is inanimate, the other carries the secret of our deaths and our lives, of our enchantments and our liberations, the demonic and the divine [...] One concerns accuracy, the other has authenticity as its criterion.
>
> (Deleuze 1994: 27)

References

Bullough, R. V. and Young, J. (2002) 'Learning to teach as an intern: the emotions and the self', *Teacher Development*, 6:417–32.
Deleuze, G. (1994) *Difference and Repetition*, trans. Paul Patton, London: The Athlone Press.
McNally, J., Cope, P., Inglis, W. and Stronach, I. (1997) 'The student teacher

in school: conditions for development', *Teaching and Teacher Education*, 13:485–98.

Nias, J. (1996) 'Thinking about feeling: the emotions in teaching', *Cambridge Journal of Education*, 26:293–306.

Stronach, I. and MacLure, M. (1997) *Educational Research Undone: The Postmodern Embrace*, Buckingham: Open University Press.

Stronach, I., Cope, P., Inglis, B. and McNally, J. (1994) 'The SOED "competence" guidelines for initial teacher training: issues of control, performance and relevance', *Scottish Educational Review*, 26:118–33.

Stronach, I., Corbin, B., McNamara, O., Stark, S. and Warne, T. (2002) 'Towards an uncertain politics of professionalism: teacher and nurse identities in flux', *Journal of Educational Policy*, 17:109–38.

Notes

1   We say 'almost' advisedly. There *were* new teachers who said, in effect, what's the fuss, it's a job. Or who described themselves as 'just plodding along fine'. There were others who had seemingly effortless introductions to teaching, feeling settled by mid-September of the first year: 'Now it feels as if I am the boss and I have got the handle on the class.' Nevertheless, most of our sample would recognize much of the above picture.

2   This was a 'hot' interview in the sense that it took place during the placement. It was an emotional event for the interviewee in that she found it 'therapeutic' and even 'inspirational' to unload her feelings at coping or trying to cope with difficult classes in a 'challenging' school in Manchester. This took place during a 90-minute unstructured interview. She later said of that interview, 'nobody ever really asks you that [referring to her confrontation with the 'kid'] and you'd never really say to someone, "Well, I think it's something personal, it's something that really upsets me", because you don't want to look an idiot'. At a subsequent 'cold' interview, some months later, she summed up the difference between the two interviews: the first had been 'therapeutic' but the second was 'insightful now, because I'm not in a stressful situation'. It should be added by way of relevant context that Catherine was rated a very good student teacher by her tutor, and by teachers at the school. She was subsequently approached by the school to see if she wanted to work there.

Index

Entries in **bold** denote references to tables.

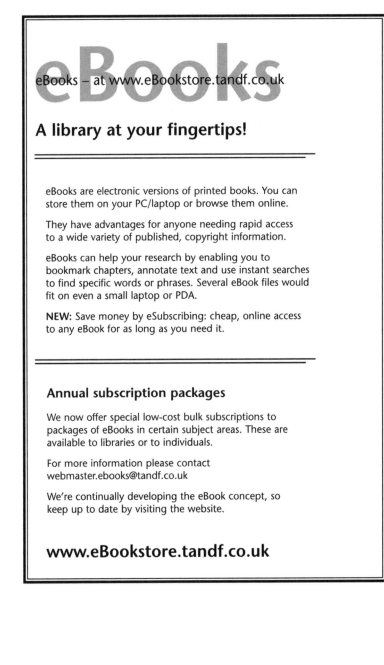